Routledge Revision: Questions &

Commercial Law
2011–2012

Routledge Q&A series

Each Routledge Q&A contains approximately 50 questions on topics commonly found on exam papers, with answer plans and comprehensive suggested answers. Each book also offers valuable advice as to how to approach and tackle exam questions and how to focus your revision effectively. New **Aim Higher** and **Common Pitfalls** boxes will also help you to identify how to go that little bit further in order to get the very best marks and highlight areas of confusion. And now there are further opportunities to hone and perfect your exam technique online.

New editions publishing in 2011:

Civil Liberties & Human Rights	Equity & Trusts
Commercial Law	European Union Law
Company Law	Evidence
Constitutional & Administrative Law	Family Law
Contract Law	Jurisprudence
Criminal Law	Land Law
Employment Law	Medical Law
English Legal System	Torts

For a full listing, visit **http://www.routledge.com/textbooks/revision**

Routledge Revision: Questions & Answers

Commercial Law

2011–2012

Jo Reddy, LLB, LLM
Barrister

AND

Howard Johnson, LLB (BIRM)
Senior Lecturer and Deputy Head of Bangor Law School

Routledge
Taylor & Francis Group

LONDON AND NEW YORK

Sixth edition published 2011
by Routledge
2 Park Square, Milton Park, Abingdon, Oxon, OX14 4RN

Simultaneously published in the USA and Canada
by Routledge
270 Madison Avenue, New York, NY 10016

Routledge is an imprint of the Taylor & Francis Group, an informa business

© 1994, 2000, 2003 Paul Dobson and Jo Reddy
© 2007, 2009 Routledge
© 2011 Jo Reddy and Howard Johnson

Previous editions published by Cavendish Publishing Limited

First edition   1994
Second edition   2000
Third edition   2003

Previous editions published by Routledge-Cavendish

Fourth edition   2007
Fifth edition   2009

Typeset in TheSans by RefineCatch Limited, Bungay, Suffolk
Printed and bound in Great Britain by TJ International Ltd, Padstow, Cornwall

British Library Cataloguing in Publication Data
A catalogue record for this book is available from the British Library

Library of Congress Cataloging-in-Publication Data
Reddy, Jothi
    Commercial law / Jo Reddy and Howard Johnson. — 6th ed.
        p. cm. — (Routledge questions & answers series)
    Commercial law, 2009–2010. 5th ed. 2009.
    Includes bibliographical references and index.
    ISBN 978–0–415–59324–3 (alk. paper)
        1. Commercial law—England—Examinations, questions, etc. I. Johnson, Howard (Howard Allun),
1948– II. Reddy, Jothi. Commercial law, 2009–2010. III. Title.
KD1554.R43 2011
346.4207076—dc22   2010033660

ISBN13: 978–0–415–59324–3 (pbk)
ISBN13: 978–0–203–83286–8 (ebk)

Contents

Table of Cases

Table of Legislation

STATUTES

STATUTORY INSTRUMENTS

EU AND FOREIGN LEGISLATION

Guide to the Companion Website

http://www.routledge.com/textbooks/revision

Visit the Routledge Q&A website to discover even more study tips and advice on getting those top marks.

On the Routledge revision website you'll find the following resources designed to enhance your revision on all areas of undergraduate law.

The Good, The Fair, & The Ugly

Good essays are the gateway to top marks. New to this edition, this interactive tutorial provides sample essays together with voice-over commentary and tips for successful exam essays, written by our Q&A authors themselves.

Multiple Choice Questions

Knowledge is the foundation of every good essay. Focusing on key examination themes, these MCQs have been written to test your knowledge and understanding of each subject in the book.

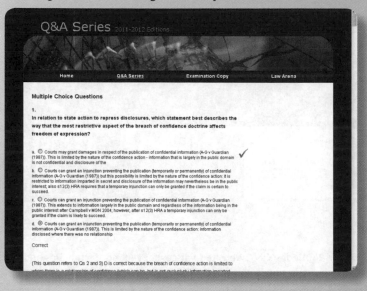

Bonus Q&As

Having studied our exam advice, put your revision into practice and test your essay writing skills with our additional online questions and answers.

Don't forget to check out even more revision guides and exam tools from Routledge!

Lawcards

Lawcards are your complete, pocket-sized guides to key examinable areas of undergraduate law.

Routledge Student Statutes

Comprehensive selections; clear, easy-to-use layout; alphabetical, chronological, and thematic indexes; and a competitive price make *Routledge Student Statutes* the statute book of choice for the serious law student.

Introduction

This book is intended to be of help to students studying commercial law who feel that they have acquired a body of knowledge, but do not feel confident about using it effectively in exams. This book sets out to demonstrate how to apply the knowledge to the question and how to structure the answer. Students, especially first-year students, often find the technique of answering problem questions particularly hard to grasp, so this book contains a large number of answers to such questions. This technique is rarely taught in law schools and the student who comes from studying science or maths A-levels may find it particularly tricky. Equally, a student who has studied English literature may find it difficult to adapt to the impersonal, logical, concise style that problem answers demand. A student who has done largely project work will often find a three-hour unseen paper written examination very daunting. It is hoped that this book will be particularly useful at exam time, but may also prove useful throughout the year. The book provides examples of the kind of questions that are usually asked in end-of-year examinations, along with suggested solutions. Each chapter deals with one of the main topics covered in commercial law courses and contains typical questions on that area. The aim is not to include questions covering every aspect of a course, but to pick out the areas that tend to be examined because they are particularly contentious or topical. Many courses contain a certain amount of material that is not examined, although it is important as providing background knowledge. It cannot be emphasised enough that it will help students to have an awareness of the general context of the subject and what issues are currently topical or controversial. Examiners are always impressed if an answer alludes to a current issue to illustrate an argument, particularly if it is not one the lecturer has raised.

PROBLEM AND ESSAY QUESTIONS

Some areas tend to be examined only by essays, some mainly – although not invariably – by problems, and some by either. The questions chosen reflect this mix, and the introductions at the beginning of each chapter discuss the type of question usually asked. It is important not to choose a topic and then assume that it will appear on the exam paper in a particular form unless it is in an area where, for example, a problem question is never set. If it might appear as an essay or a problem, revision should be geared to either possibility: a very thorough knowledge of the area should be acquired, but also an awareness of critical opinion in relation to it. In most cases, unless there has been a change of personnel or revision of the syllabus past exam papers should always be looked at carefully. Reading the rubric and understanding it is absolutely essential. Students should not assume that all questions will be confined to a single area of the subject – commonly in commercial law there may well be an issue about exemption clauses or damages alongside for example an issue about the application and scope of the implied terms in **sections 12–15 of the Sale of Goods Act 1979**.

LENGTH OF ANSWERS

The answers in this book are about the length of an essay that a good student would expect to write in an exam. Some are somewhat longer and these will also provide useful guidance for students writing assessed essays, which typically are between 2,000 and 3,000 words. In relation to exam questions, there are a number of reasons for including lengthy answers: some students can write long answers – about 1,800 words – under exam conditions; some students who cannot nevertheless write two very good and lengthy essays and two reasonable but shorter ones. Such students tend to do very well, although it must be emphasised that it is always better to aim to spread the time evenly between all four essays. Therefore, some answers indicate what might be done if very thorough coverage of a topic were to be undertaken.

THE FOOTNOTES

Some of the questions also provide footnotes exploring some areas of the answer in more depth, which should be of value to the student who wants to do more than cover the main points. Some answers provide a number of footnotes; it would not be expected that any one student would be able to make all of the points they contain, but they demonstrate that it is possible to choose to explore, say, two interesting areas in more depth in an answer once the main points have been covered. It cannot be emphasised enough that the main points have to be covered before interesting, but less obvious, issues can be explored.

EXPRESSING A POINT OF VIEW

Students sometimes ask, especially in an area such as, say, the imposition of bank charges for unauthorised overdrafts, which can be quite topical and politically controversial, whether they should argue for any particular point of view in an essay. It will be noticed that the essays in this book tend to do this. In general, the good student does argue for one side but he or she always uses sound arguments to support his or her view. Further, a good student does not ignore the opposing arguments: they are considered and, if possible, their weaknesses are exposed. Of course, it would not be appropriate to do this in a problem question or in some essay questions but, where an invitation to do so is held out, it is a good idea to accept it rather than sit on the fence. Individual expression is not something to be avoided but should be based on reasoned and rational arguments.

EXAM PAPERS

Commercial law exam papers vary in relation to the number of substantive topics included in the syllabus, e.g. some will deal with agency but others not; however, normally they will include one question on each of the main areas of the syllabus. For example, a typical paper might include problem questions on the implied terms, (**ss 12–15 Sale of Goods Act 1979**), passing of property and risk (**ss 16–20 Sale of Goods Act 1979**), the nemo dat rule and its exceptions (**ss 21–25 Sale of Goods Act 1979, s 2 Factors Act 1889, Pt III Hire-Purchase Act 1964**), if dealt with retention of title (Romalpa Clauses), and some aspect of remedies. As said subsidiary issues such as the validity of an exclusion clause in a business-to-business contract will probably appear. If agency has been dealt with then questions on the authority of an agent and the scope and application of the Commercial Agents Directive are favourites. Some courses will deal with consumer credit law, others will not or will treat it as part of a separate consumer law module, so do not be surprised to find in the book answers to questions on areas you will not have dealt with in the module offered by your law school. Therefore, the questions have to be fairly wide-ranging in order to cover a reasonable amount of ground on each topic. Some answers in this book therefore have to cover some of the same material, especially where it is particularly central to the topic in question, e.g. the scope and application of the implied term as to satisfactory quality in **s 14(2) Sale of Goods Act 1979**.

COMMON PITFALLS AND EXTRA MARKS

A new innovation in this edition is that at the end of some questions we have included a list of common pitfalls and also indications of what might gain extra marks or credit when you are looking to achieve either a first class or good upper second examination mark. It is hoped this will help focus your mind on things to avoid but also things that you can develop and expand on in an answer.

SUGGESTIONS FOR EXAM TECHNIQUE

Below are some suggestions that might improve exam technique; some failings are pointed out that are very commonly found on exam scripts. A pre-question plan is a very useful idea particularly in a problem question – as many marks are lost by bad technique as are lost by lack of knowledge. A very good example of this is a question of tracking a series of transactions to determine whether the buyer at the end of a line of sub-sales has obtained a good title, involving the nemo dat rule and its exceptions – it is all too easy to miss a transaction or party out if a proper structure plan is not prepared indicating the main points and cases to discuss:

(1) When tackling a problem question, do not write out the facts in the answer. Quite a number of students write out chunks of the facts as they answer the question – perhaps to help themselves to pick out the important issues. It is better to avoid this and merely to refer to the significant facts.

(2) Use an impersonal style in both problem and essay answers. In an essay, you should rarely need to use the word 'I' and, in our view, it should not be used at all in a problem answer. (Of course, examiners may differ in their views on this point.) Instead, you could say 'it is therefore submitted that' or 'it is arguable that'; avoid saying 'I believe that' or 'I feel that'.

(3) In answers to problem questions, try to explain at the beginning of each section of your answer what point you are trying to establish. You might say, for example: 'In order to show that liability under s1 will arise, three tests must be satisfied.' You should then consider all three, come to a conclusion on each, and then come to a final conclusion as to whether or not liability will arise. If you are really unsure whether or not it will arise (which will often be the case – there is not much point in asking a question to which there is one very clear and obvious answer), then consider what you have written in relation to the three tests. Perhaps one of them is clearly satisfied, one is probably satisfied and the other (arising under, for example, **s 1(8)**) probably is not. You might then say: 'As the facts give little support to an argument that **s 1(8)** is satisfied, it is concluded that liability is unlikely to be established.'

(4) You do not get double the marks for saying the same thing twice; you waste time and may not complete the paper. Say what you have to say and move on to the next question – if you are a little unsure about whether you wish to say more, leave some space and come back to the question. Try to avoid tacking on bits to a question at the end of the paper; these can obviously be overlooked. Equally avoid contradicting yourself – it is surprising the number of students who change their mind in the course of an answer and do not correct an earlier statement, so initially say 'A obviously has a good claim' but then on the next page 'It is clear A cannot succeed'!

(5) Remember essays and exam papers are also an exercise in writing the English language – try to avoid overlong, complex sentences. Use paragraphs and break up the work. Have a structure – in simple terms, a beginning, middle and end. Avoid overly pretentious language; wherever possible, use simple English. Avoid

what can be called the 'stream of consciousness approach', just pouring out material in a more or less continuous fashion with few or no paragraph breaks and very long sentences. If an examiner can read and follow your answer easily, it may well be reflected in a better mark.

(6) Particularly in essays a good strong conclusion is helpful – you need not come down on one side or the other but you want to leave the examiner in no doubt that you are aware of the issues involved. Again, in essays proposals for changes or reform will usually gain extra marks. Do not leave things in the air – if the question has asked you to critically evaluate, you want to show you have done so and not be simply descriptive or just let the essay tail off into nowhere.

(7) Answer the question set and not the one you would have liked to be set, e.g. if the question asks you to discuss the issues of 'satisfactory quality' in **s 14(2) Sale of Goods Act 1979** and you have learned a lot about 'sales by description' in **s 13 Sale of Goods Act 1979** but this has not come up elsewhere on the paper. You waste time and will probably fail the question if you spend a lot of time talking about **s 13** and little or no time discussing **s 14(2)**, however happy you feel that you have shown the examiner that you are fully on top of **s 13**!

(8) A statement of the obvious but often overlooked: use a good writing implement – if you have very small writing, using a pale blue biro with a thin nib does not help!

General Questions

INTRODUCTION

This chapter contains four questions which are not confined to one particular part of the syllabus but are broader. Such questions are often included in examinations in order to test your knowledge of recent developments in the subject or simply to give you an opportunity, which most questions in law papers do not, to demonstrate a wider knowledge of the syllabus. The first question poses an important general question: 'What is commercial law?' Question 2 is of a general type often found in examinations, inviting the student to take an overview of commercial law and its function in the business world. The third question requires a good knowledge of the whole area of sale of goods and related law. Question 4 is centred around the **UN Convention on Contracts for the International Sale of Goods (the Vienna Convention 1980)** which now plays, and will play, a very important role in regulating contracts for the international sale of goods.

QUESTION 1

What is commercial law?

Answer Plan

This is a challenging question and one to which there can be no definitive answer. This is because commercial law means different things to different people. You may wish to consider some often quoted definitions. Goode: 'the totality of law's response to needs and practices of mercantile community'. Bradgate: 'the law relating to commercial activity, especially transactions concerned with the supply of goods and services and financing thereof'. But neither absolutely defines commercial law.

The problem we face is that England does not have a self-contained body of principles and rules specific to commercial transactions. English commercial law has been developed by common law, and its principles are all over the place in case reports. It is almost impossible to rely on law reports alone. We depend on academic textbooks, practitioner texts and journals but such materials do not form a commercial code. Authors do not create law; they merely explain it. Students need to set their own boundaries in answering this question and the challenge is to engage in the discussion rather than striving to a conclusion as to its definition.

ANSWER

It is almost anything. The boundaries of commercial law are not easily defined. That is because the UK does not have a code. It does not have a self-contained integrated body of principles and rules specific to commercial transactions (unlike American Uniform Commercial Code). It certainly goes beyond regulation of relationships between merchants and traders. Although no single definition is possible, there are several approaches to answering 'What is commercial law?'

(1) COMMERCIAL LAW TEXTBOOKS

The simplest (and possibly the least instructive) approach is to take the lead from commercial law textbooks. The content of commercial law textbooks determines or reinforces ideas about what commercial law is. The obvious problem with defining commercial law in this way is that we do not know *why* some topics are included while others are not dealt with or are categorised as being only 'ancillary' to commercial law. A textbook definition of commercial does not create law; it merely explains it. With a few exceptions, commercial textbooks do not attempt to present a definitional framework for (and theories of) commercial law. Commercial textbooks contain various topics with the unifying theme of trade and commerce. This suggests that there is a connection between commercial law and business activity. But the reason for the selection of topics lies on the authors' own perceptions (however informed) of commercial practice. Nevertheless it would help to know what guides these choices.

The various topics however reveal an enduring theme. In all aspects of commercial law, the focus is on transactions. Some commercial law (for example, sale of goods) regulates transactions directly. Other areas (for example, banking and insurance law) concern mechanisms necessarily ancillary to such transactions. Others (for example, product liability) stem from the consequences of transactions even where the party seeking the help of the law is not a direct party in the transaction.

One conclusion which can be drawn from this textbook approach to defining commercial law is that authors are unsure of where topics should be placed. Most commercial law courses are a sort of 'miscellaneous section', that is, topics are bundled together because they do not fit conveniently into courses of their own. Furthermore, the textbook approach gives rise to boundary problems. Authors draw boundaries in different ways. For example, Professor Goode limits boundaries of commercial law to law that governs commercial *transactions* (for example, contract law, sale of goods), so he excludes law governing commercial *institutions* (for example, company law and partnership law). The difficulty with this is that the boundary between transactions and institutions is not clearly drawn and is ultimately unhelpful. It is arguable that aspects of the **Companies Act 2006** are no more than an application of general agency principles, and so fall within the scope of transactional law (qualifying as commercial law). It is equally arguable that the **Companies Act** is crucial to the structure and functioning of companies (and so classified as institutional law).

The content of commercial law textbooks determines or perhaps reinforces ideas about what commercial law is. Textbooks also represent authors' perceptions of commercial law as it is practised, that is, commercial law is what commercial lawyers do. This leads to the second approach to answering the question.

(2) COMMERCIAL LAWYERS

Commercial law is what commercial lawyers do. But what does 'commercial lawyer' mean? It does not really tell us very much, other than a commercial lawyer can be distinguished from, for example, a family lawyer or an international lawyer. Even these distinctions are debatable. As textbook-based definitions show, commercial law has many specialisations. A banking lawyer, for instance, has little in common with an intellectual property lawyer.

The work of a commercial lawyer may involve any aspect of law as it relates to business clients, and the role of lawyer is to facilitate business clients' commercial transactions with third parties. A commercial lawyer may be asked to advise a client on both non-contentious and contentious work. Non-contentious work involves advising clients on drafting of contracts, whereas contentious work involves consequences of breach of contract.

From this perspective, commercial law has distinctive and interrelated characteristics. Generally, however, commercial law is pragmatic in its approach. Commercial law is about getting things done; it is about problem-solving. Commercial law has been developed in response to the needs of commerce. Without trading, there would be no commercial law. As Professor Goode says, 'commercial law represents the totality of the law's response to mercantile disputes.' The fundamental purpose of commercial law is the facilitation of commercial activity. Commercial law tends to take a non-interventionist approach. Commercial law intervenes only if contract terms are so restrictive or oppressive that they offend public interest. A contemporary argument is whether commercial law should promote fairness and good faith. Each characteristic is present in different degrees, and each is debatable. The definitional problem may be due to shifting commercial practices, and to shifting legal responses to those practices.

Furthermore, the Civil Procedure Rules provide that the Commercial Court has jurisdiction in 'any case arising out of trade and commerce in general'. This includes (but is not limited to) any case relating to a business document or contract; the export/import of goods; the carriage of goods by land, sea, or air; insurance; banking and financial services; and business agency. The remit of the court therefore also represents a succinct statement of the type of disputes which might be regarded as commercial.[1] The scope and extent of what commercial lawyers do is vast.

(3) HISTORICAL ORIGINS OF COMMERCIAL LAW

Another approach to defining contemporary commercial law is by examining its historical origins. The existence of a body of law controlling mercantile life has been recognised since medieval times when special courts existed for the purpose of dealing with trade disputes. It was developed out of medieval law merchant (*lex mercatoria*), which governed practices and disputes between merchants and traders before incorporation by the common law, a process which began in the seventeeth century and culminated in a series of codifications (for example the **Sale of Goods Act 1893**, the **Factors Act 1889**).

One conclusion to be drawn from this is that modern commercial law is, and always has been, a body of rules relating to trading and business relationships. This would explain topics such as negotiable instruments and contracts of carriage. Of course, modern business transactions are different from those in the nineteenth century. Modern commercial law has added new topics. But even taking recent additions into account, the overall picture remains unchanged: commercial law is driven by, and is responsive to, the needs of commerce.

On closer inspection, however, this definitional approach is more complex than a simple historical evolution suggests. For one thing, some modern legal historians discount the idea that *lex mercatoria* was 'borrowed' by common law. Whether or not *lex mercatoria* was borrowed or was merely influential, it is interesting to note that some features of *lex mercatoria* suggest that contemporary developments in commercial law may in fact be revisiting ideas and practices that characterised law merchant.

....

1   There are two further courts to consider. First, the county court administers a high volume of commercial law. It has unlimited jurisdiction in claims in contract and tort. Claims worth less than £15,000 must be commenced in the county court. Secondly, the commercial court is a specially constituted companies court which provides for speedy resolution of commercial disputes.

The origins of law merchant lie in the customary rules and practices developed by merchants and applied by mercantile courts. These transcended local custom or law. Law merchant is characterised by transnational application, adaptability and relative freedom from the technical rules of evidence and procedure. *Lex mercatoria* was more a law of values and principles than a law of structures and rules. One significant principle was the commitment to good faith as an overriding requirement in the making of agreements.

These characteristics of *lex mercatoria* are important in answering 'What is commercial law?' One view is that mercantile law was made by lawyers, not for lawyers but for laymen, that is, codification gives businessmen legal certainty and helps avoid litigation. The opposing view is that it was the lawyers who wanted legal certainty and mercantile law worked more to help lawyers, not to assist commercial interests. It is therefore arguable that commercial law codes were commercial law *for* commercial lawyers.

The history of commercial law suggests a need for caution in explaining the relationship between commercial law and commercial practice. It is arguable that the history of regulation of commercial activity reveals shifts and overlaps between self-regulation by merchants themselves (that is, *lex mercatoria*) and external regulation by lawyers, courts and government agencies. What we do know is that commercial law is constantly in a state of change.

CONCLUSION

These different approaches show different issues buried in the question. How do we go about defining commercial law? If we take the textbook approach, then commercial law is predominantly doctrinal (or 'black-letter') in its methodology and orientation. If we take the commercial practice approach, then commercial law is essentially pragmatic – it is the law of 'getting things done'. If we take the historical approach, then modern commercial law is beginning to resemble medieval law merchant.

It may be that 'commercial law' no longer has any relevance, at least not for practitioners. It is interesting to note that major law firms (if one looks at their websites) do not use the term 'commercial law' to describe the services offered; instead, they refer to specialisations, for example banking and finance, or intellectual property law. Perhaps the question 'what is commercial law?' is primarily a problem for academics. Even so, there is value in taking a step back. There are benefits to be gained for commercial law academics and practitioners in asking 'what is commercial law?' The answer is less important than what can be learnt by engaging in debate.

QUESTION 2

'The strength of English commercial law has been its concern to provide solutions to practical problems facing commercial parties.'

▶ **Discuss.**

> ### Answer Plan
>
> This question is not an opportunity to discuss commercial law in a general way. A good answer requires you to identify what the needs of the commercial community are and then identify how the courts and legislature have responded to those needs. You need to illustrate these points by drawing from a range of areas of commercial law.

ANSWER

In order to answer the question, it is necessary to identify what problems commercial parties face and how English commercial law helps them by providing solutions. If commercial law is about commercial activity, then the fundamental purpose of commercial law is the facilitation of commercial activity.

(1) CERTAINTY AND PREDICTABILITY

The commercial community values legal certainty above all. Business people want to know that courts will be reliable and will consistently interpret transactions in a particular way. This allows for planning and anticipation of liability. Many transactions (many of high value) are undertaken on the basis that courts will continue to follow rules laid down in preceding cases. Business people do not want the law to be based on a random application of local custom and idiosyncrasies of individuals. Of course, this is not guaranteed because judges' thinking will change over time but, on the whole, courts have consistently promoted certainty of outcome over those of fairness and justice. This is what business people want.

As Lord Mansfield said, it is more important that a rule is certain than what the rule is.[2] An example is the postal rule.[3] It does not matter if acceptance is deemed to take place at the time of posting or receipt. Parties to a contract merely need to know.

---

2   *Vallejo v Wheeler* (1774): 'In all mercantile transactions the great object should be certainty; and therefore, it is of more consequence that a rule should be certain, than whether the rule is established one way or the other. Because speculators in trade then know what ground to go upon.'

3   *Adams v Lindsell* (1818).

If the law is clear and certain, the outcome of a dispute may be predicted and parties may resolve it without having to litigate. If litigation is necessary, at least disputes can be dealt with quickly. This is especially important in a price fluctuation market.

The use of documentary credits is an example of courts' approach to ensure certainty. Documentary credit is a bank's assurance of payment against presentation of specified documents. It is the most common method of payment in international sales. Although the Uniform Customs and Practice for Documentary Credits[4] only applies if it is expressly incorporated into a contract; because of its wide acceptance amongst international bankers, courts are likely to view the UCP as impliedly incorporated as established usage. There are two general principles involved with documentary credits. First, the doctrine of strict compliance dictates that a banker must comply exactly with its client's (the buyer) instructions as to payment. Even if the value of some documents required by the buyer is questionable, 'it is not for the bank to reason why'.[5] Even a minor discrepancy will disentitle the banker to reimbursement from its client. A clear example is the case of *Equitable Trust v Dawson* (1927) where the buyer's instructions was payment against a certificate signed by experts, whereas the banker paid against documents signed by one expert. The House of Lords held that the banker had acted against his instructions and was thus not entitled to reimbursement.[6]

Secondly, the principle of autonomy of credit dictates that a bank is not concerned with any dispute that the buyer might have with the seller. As Lord Denning said in *Power Curber v National Bank of Kuwait* (1981), a letter of credit ranks as cash and must be honoured. Courts have consistently defended the autonomy principle on grounds that an irrevocable letter of credit is the 'life-blood of international commerce'. It thus must be honoured and be free from interference by the courts, otherwise trust in international commerce would be damaged. The commercial value of the documentary credit system lies in the fact that payment under a letter of credit is virtually guaranteed (subject to the strict compliance principle). Certainty of payment is of paramount importance to the business community, thus irrevocable credits are treated like cash by courts.

....

4   The current, seventh, edition, is often known as UCP 600.
5   Devlin J in *Midland Bank v Seymour* (1955).
6   *Lord Sumner*: 'There is no room for documents which are almost the same, or which will do just as well.'

(2) PARTY AUTONOMY

Business people should be free to make their contracts and they are entitled to receive what they bargained for. The aim of commercial law is to enforce the intention of the parties, not frustrate that intention by a rigid set of rules.[7]

Courts take a non-interventionist approach, justified on the basis that it promotes certainty. Courts should only intervene if the contract terms are so restrictive or oppressive that it offends public interest. Whenever there is a contest between contract law and equity in a commercial dispute, contract law wins hands down. This is one reason why so many foreigners select English law to govern their contracts and English courts to decide the case. Business people know where they stand with English law and English judges.[8]

(3) RECOGNITION OF COMMERCIAL PRACTICES

Courts have always recognised and given legal effect to customs and practices of the business community. The most common way is by implying a term into the contract, for example where the parties are in the same trade and there is a particular custom of that trade. By judicial recognition, commercial practice has become part of the common law.[9] An example is the agency doctrine of the undisclosed principle. In this situation the existence of an agency is not disclosed to the third party, who therefore thinks he is contracting only with the agent in his own right and is unaware that the agent is acting for another. Nevertheless, the general rule is that the principal can intervene and enforce contract with the third party. This is an exception to doctrine of privity under the common law.[10] It is important to bear in mind that the initial contract is between the agent and the third party. The undisclosed principal intervenes in an existing contract. The justification for the doctrine of the undisclosed principal has been the subject of much discussion by academic writers. It is generally accepted that although it runs against the fundamental principles of privity of contract (that is, there must be agreement between the parties), the doctrine is

---

7   Lord Goff of Chieveley in an article analysing the objectives of judges when interpreting commercial contracts in *Commercial Contracts and the Commercial Court* (1984) LMCLQ 382: 'We are there to help businessmen, not to hinder them; we are there to give effect to their transactions, not to frustrate them; we are there to oil the wheels of commerce, not to put a spanner in the works, or even grit in the oil.'

8   Around 65% of disputes heard before the Commercial Court involve only foreign parties, that is, parties have expressly chosen England as the jurisdiction for dispute resolution.

9   For example, the bill of lading is recognised as a document of title to goods at common law.

10   This is not an exception under the Contracts (Rights of Third Parties) Act 1999, because the undisclosed principal is not identified nor identifiable at the time of the contract, so the Act does not apply.

justified on grounds of commercial convenience. Generally, in commercial law, courts assume that buyers and sellers are willing to buy/sell to anyone. Contracts are not personal and business people are not concerned about the identity of the other contracting party.[11] There is no reason for the undisclosed principal rule other than that courts recognise that this is what business people do. It is purely a matter of recognising commercial practice.

(4) FLEXIBILITY

Commercial people keep finding new ways of doing business. The internet is a good example. The internet environment is constantly changing and the law must respond. Business people need the law to adapt to accommodate these changes. The English courts have been flexible. Legislation has also been flexible; whenever reform is proposed, extensive consultation takes place with the business community before a Law Commission report is produced. For example, amendments to the **Sale of Goods Act 1979** include **s 20A**.[12] Business buyers had complained that they had paid for goods but where the seller became insolvent before delivery, their claim against the receiver failed on grounds that the buyer has no property in unascertained goods. Commercial people wanted this change. **Section 20A** essentially gives a buyer who has paid for goods before delivery some measure of protection if the seller becomes insolvent. The buyer acquires property in an undivided share and he becomes an owner in common of the bulk pro rata.

However, flexibility is often at the expense of certainty. For example, **s 15A** says that if a buyer is not dealing as a consumer and the breach of description or quality of the goods is so slight that it would be unreasonable for the buyer to reject the goods, such a breach may be treated as a breach of warranty unless it is reasonable for the business buyer to reject. Although this allows for some flexibility, its application is uncertain.

(5) RESOLUTION

No matter how certain and predictable the law is, there will always be disputes. What commercial people need is a quick, inexpensive and efficient way to deal with problems. This need has been met in several ways. For example, commercial courts are special courts. These are separate courts of the Queen's Bench Division. They do nothing but hear commercial disputes. The procedure is flexible with relatively little formality. Courts themselves have been willing to develop new remedies, for example,

---

11 Lord Lindley in *Keighley, Maxsted v Durant* (1901): '. . . in the great mass of contracts it is a matter of indifference to either party whether there is an undisclosed P or not.'
12 Inserted as an amendment by the 1995 Act.

the development of the *search and seize order*, allowing seizure of evidence which might otherwise be destroyed.[13]

(6) FAIRNESS AND GOOD FAITH

A contemporary argument is that the law should promote fairness and good faith (especially if commercial law is to include consumer transactions). But English law has developed without a general duty of good faith. Examples include *The Mihalis Angelos* (1971), where a party can exercise the right to terminate a contract for breach even though the breach causes him no loss. This is so even if the sole motive for termination is market price fluctuation.[14]

Many countries have a general duty of good faith. In England, the idea of good faith is the subjective standard of honesty, rather than an objective one of fair dealing. Partly because of harmonisation of commercial law in the European Union, there is a growing reference to an objective standard of good faith. For example, under the **Unfair Terms in Consumer Contracts Regulations 1999**, the test is no longer *you* are being unfair, merely *it* looks unfair.[15]

SUMMARY

The main challenge for commercial law is to strike the right balance between these competing principles to provide solutions to problems faced by commercial parties. Where the balance should lie depends on the circumstances of the case. For example, if the parties involved are multinational corporations in the shipping trade, certainty might take precedence, whereas if there is a significant imbalance between the parties (especially if one party is a consumer), some certainty may be sacrificed in favour of fairness or flexibility.

Tensions are unavoidable. Business people want the law to be predictable in its application. But this is not always possible. More predictability means more detailed rules. At the same time, business people want flexibility, to allow them to develop new ways of doing business. This is very well, but how does commercial law deal with these competing principles? Essentially, it is a balancing act. Commercial law rules need to be sufficiently predictable to generate confidence so business people can depend on it. At same time, the law must be responsive and flexible enough to

....

13   Other ways developed to deal with disputes include arbitration and alternative dispute resolution (such as mediation).

14   Another example is *White & Carter v Macgregor* (1962) where a party can perform his obligations against the other party's wishes and remain entitled to claim the full value of the contract price.

15   *Director General of Fair Trading v First National Bank* (2001).

allow the development of new markets. On the whole, English commercial law does provide solutions to practical problems facing commercial parties.

QUESTION 3

'Despite developments in recent times, the law of sale of goods is still permeated with the following key concepts: freedom of contract, privity of contract and *caveat emptor*.'

▶ **Discuss the extent to which this is true.**

Answer Plan

This question is a generalised one of a type often treated by students as one to tackle as a desperate last resort. Being generalised, it requires a good overall knowledge of the subject. In this particular question, three different concepts are expressly referred to and therefore it is required that each be addressed. There is every reason to take a straightforward approach and deal with one concept at a time.

ANSWER

FREEDOM OF CONTRACT

The law of sale of goods was originally developed by judges in deciding cases. In the first **Sale of Goods Act** of **1893**, Parliament set out to incorporate this common law into statute form and the **1893 Act**, in its **Preamble**, described itself as an Act to codify the law. Most of the provisions of the **1893 Act** are now contained, often word for word, in the current **1979 Act**. There is no doubt that the freedom of contract philosophy underpinned much of the common law development, this philosophy being that the parties were free to decide for themselves what contract to make and what terms to incorporate into it. The law set out to provide for what would be the position if the parties had not themselves determined what it should be. Thus, throughout the **1893 Act**, one finds provisions such as 'unless otherwise agreed' and also a general provision (now to be found in an amended form in **s 55** of the **1979 Act**) that where any right or liability would arise by implication of law, it can be negatived (excluded or varied) by express agreement between the parties. This was the embodiment of the freedom of contract principle. The amendment now found in **s 55** relates to the rules on exclusion clauses. Since the original **Act** of **1893**, it had become clear that the freedom of contract principle could be abused by a party who was in a very strong bargaining position and who could insist on (often quite harsh) terms being in the contract. This was particularly true of standard form contracts made between a business and an ordinary private consumer and was not confined to contracts of sale of goods. It occurred in hire purchase contracts and contracts such as those to buy railway tickets or to park one's car in a car park. The abuse often took the form of an insistence on the incorporation of clauses excluding liability towards the consumer. After initial legislative attempts to control these exclusion clauses in particular contracts (for example, hire purchase agreements), Parliament enacted general legislation on exclusion clauses in the **Unfair Contract Terms Act 1977**. This Act has introduced a very clear restriction on the freedom of contract principle in the following ways. First, it deals with the terms as to title, description, quality and sample implied by **ss 12–15** of the **Sale of Goods Act** (and by other Acts in relation to other contracts involving the passing of property or the hire of goods). It distinguishes between consumer deals and non-consumer deals and, broadly speaking, it makes it impossible for a seller to exclude or restrict liability for breach of the implied terms as to title and, where the buyer is a consumer, makes it impossible for a seller to exclude or restrict the other implied terms just referred to. Where the buyer is not a consumer, a clause purporting to exclude or restrict liability for these latter terms is subject to a test of reasonableness, which is also the position with any other exclusion clause using standard terms.

The **Unfair Contract Terms Act** deals only with exclusion clauses. With that important exception, the freedom of contract principle remains largely intact. Thus, for example, whether an express term is a condition or a warranty is a matter the parties are free to determine. A term as to the time of delivery will normally be construed by the courts as a condition, but it is still open to the parties expressly to state otherwise. Similarly, the rules in **ss 17–20** of the **Sale of Goods Act** on the passing of property and risk apply only where the parties have not expressed a contrary intention.

A further significant inroad into the principle has derived from the **1993 European Directive on Unfair Contract Terms**. This was implemented in Britain by the **Unfair Terms in Consumer Contracts Regulations 1994**, which have since been replaced by the **1999 Regulations** of the same name. These apply with certain exceptions to any term (in a consumer contract) which, contrary to a requirement of good faith, causes a significant imbalance in the parties' rights and obligations to the detriment of the consumer. It is not just exclusion clauses which can be declared 'unfair' and thus of no effect; provided it is not a core term (for example, in a sale of goods contract, a term which states the price), almost any term is subject to this possibility. An important feature of this piece of legislation is that it gives the Office of Fair Trading and other approved enforcers such as Local Trading Standards Authorities[16] the duty to consider complaints about unfair terms and the power to bring court proceedings seeking an

----

16   Part 8, Enterprise Act 2002.

order or injunction to prevent a trader from using unfair terms (see, for example, *Director General of Fair Trading v First National Bank* (2001)). These Regulations apply, of course, only to contracts between a business and a consumer – the typical example where there is a substantial imbalance of bargaining power between the parties.

In 2002, the Law Commission published a Consultation Paper in which it proposed that the two pieces of legislation referred to above (the **Unfair Contract Terms Act 1977** and the **Unfair Terms in Consumer Contracts Regulations 1999**) be: (a) combined; and (b) rewritten to make the language more accessible and user-friendly. In February 2005, the Law Commission submitted its final recommendations together with a draft Bill.[17] The Bill proposes that the 1999 Regulations be extended to apply not only to business-to-consumer contracts but also to business-to-business contracts. That would mean that in a business-to-business contract, it would not only be exclusion or limitation of liability clauses which would be challengeable under the legislation. Any standard term (other than a core term) in a business-to-business contract would be open to challenge as being unfair/unreasonable. Arguably, this is necessary since, even in business-to-business contracts, there is no guarantee that there is a level playing field. There can, in such a contract, be a great disparity between the bargaining power of the two parties. The proposal would involve a further inroad into the freedom of contract principle, but this may be necessary in order to redress an imbalance in bargaining power.

To sum up: the freedom of contract principle is, and is likely to remain, largely intact except for those instances where legislation proves necessary in order to protect a weaker party (often a private consumer) from the abuse of power that that principle would otherwise allow to the stronger party.

PRIVITY OF CONTRACT

This is still a central element of sale of goods law. Thus, the implied terms which create strict liability generally apply only as between seller and buyer. This has two effects. First, a buyer (let us call him Harry) who has bought, say, a defective car which is not of satisfactory quality can in general sue only his seller for breach of the implied term as to satisfactory quality. Although his seller can then sue the person from whom he bought the car, Harry cannot take the shortcut of himself suing someone further up the distribution chain. This could leave Harry without a remedy in the situation where his seller has become bankrupt. There is, however, one important inroad into this principle of privity of contract which could assist Harry if he has used

17   No implementation date has yet been set. The full text of the Bill can be found at: www.lawcom.gov.uk/docs/lc292bill.pdf.

credit to purchase the car. This can be found in **s 75** of the **Consumer Credit Act 1974** which would allow a buyer to bring the claim for the seller's breach of contract (or misrepresentation) against the creditor. This is a section which can apply where the creditor is someone different from the seller, where the credit agreement was a regulated debtor–creditor–supplier agreement within the meaning of the **Consumer Credit Act** and where the cash price of the item exceeded £100 and did not exceed £30,000. In this age of e-commerce, it is worth noting that if Harry bought his car on the Internet with his credit card, he could still rely on **s 75** even though the contract of sale was with a non-UK supplier (*Office of Fair Trading v Lloyds TSB plc* (2005)).[18]

The second effect of the doctrine of privity is that only a party to the contract can sue on it. So, if Harry and his wife are both injured because the car is not of satisfactory quality, his wife will not (unless she was a joint purchaser) be able to seek a remedy by relying upon the implied (or express) terms in Harry's contract. There is now an important exception to this second effect of the doctrine. Thus, a third party can now enforce a contract where the third party is able to rely on the **Contracts (Rights of Third Parties) Act 1999**. This enables a third party to enforce a term of a contract if either: (a) the contract expressly provides that he may; or (b) the term purports to confer a benefit upon the third party. To be able to enjoy this right, the third party must be expressly identified in the contract by name or as a member of a class or as answering a particular description. This statute is too recent to have generated much case law, but its effect is clearly very limited and does not extend to anyone who is neither expressly given a right in the contract nor purported to be given a benefit by the contract.[19] Harry's wife is unlikely to be able to rely upon it unless, perhaps, the contract expressly referred to the fact that Harry was buying it as a present for his wife. Even that may not be sufficient, for it is arguable that even then the contract does not purport itself to confer a benefit on Harry's wife, but rather to put Harry in a position where he can confer a benefit upon her by making a gift to her.

There is now, however, a different way – that is, outside the law of contract – where a buyer (or indeed a consumer who, like Harry's wife, was not a buyer) may be able to have a remedy against someone for damage caused by defective goods. This is by relying on **Pt I** of the **Consumer Protection Act 1987**. This introduces a regime of strict liability into the law of tort to enable a claim to be brought against the manufacturer (or importer into the European Union). This is not so much an inroad into the doctrine of privity of contract as the provision of a way round it. The consumer brings the claim outside contract altogether. This is not, however, a complete solution to the problems presented to consumers by the doctrine, because although the **1987 Act** allows an

---

18   See Question 25.
19   *Avraamides v Colwill* (2006)

action for damage caused by the defective product, it does not allow a claim to be brought in respect of damage to that product or in respect of the fact that the product is worth less than it should be; to put it another way, the **1987 Act** does not provide for a claim in respect of loss of bargain. A buyer of a defective product which has caused no damage is left with only the possibility of a claim against the seller or (if the purchase was financed by the relevant kind of consumer credit agreement) against the creditor under **s 75** of the **Consumer Credit Act** (*Office of Fair Trading v Lloyds TSB plc* (2005)). The only way round that restriction at present is if someone else, for example the manufacturer, has given a guarantee which could then be relied upon. Any doubts about the enforceability of such guarantees (for example, on grounds of lack of privity of contract) have now been removed since the **Sale and Supply of Goods to Consumers Regulations 2002** came into force on 31 March 2003. These regulations implement the **1999 European Directive on Consumer Guarantees**. They also, in **reg 15**, make the seller liable to the consumer in respect of a guarantee given by the manufacturer (or any other third party, such as an importer or distributor).

CAVEAT EMPTOR

The notion 'buyer beware' is to some extent tied up with the two concepts already discussed. The freedom of contract principle means that the buyer can, if he can make the seller agree, have all sorts of protections and guarantees built in as express terms of the contract. Of course, the reality is that this seldom happens and that therefore the buyer receives only such legal protection as is automatically built into the contract. This amounts to the following: the ability to rely upon any misrepresentation which was one of the causes that induced him to make the contract; the ability to rely upon any express term of the contract (for example, as to the date of delivery); the ability to rely upon the terms implied into the contract by **ss 12–15**. The latter include the terms as to satisfactory quality and fitness for purpose, which constitute the buyer's principal legal protection as to the quality of the goods he is buying, and which are implied only where the seller is selling in the course of a business. Thus, the notion 'buyer beware' is particularly strong where the buyer buys from his neighbour, or at the church fete, or as a result of replying to a small advertisement in the newspaper, or in some other way from someone who is not selling in the course of a business.

The buyer's ability to rely upon any misrepresentation, express term or implied term of the contract is backed up by the provisions in the **Unfair Contract Terms Act** and the **Unfair Terms in Consumer Contracts Regulations**, discussed above. As we saw, the consumer as buyer is guaranteed the benefit of the implied terms and, so far as liability for misrepresentation or breach of an express term is concerned, any exclusion clause will need to satisfy the requirement of reasonableness. Thus, so far as the consumer buyer is concerned, there is quite a degree of protection. It is fair, however, to say that the buyer does need to 'beware' in some sense. He really needs to ask questions and also to let the seller know for what purpose(s) he wants the goods. This is because the seller is liable for any misrepresentation, but this does not extend to making him liable for not making a statement and, turning to **s 14(3)** of the **Sale of Goods Act**, there can be no liability for the goods not being reasonably fit for a particular purpose if the buyer has not made known to the seller what that purpose was.[20]

It also should be pointed out that the consumer's legal protection is no longer confined to the contractual liability of the seller. As we have seen, there can be strict liability under the **Consumer Protection Act 1987** for damage caused by defective goods – although, as observed, there is no liability under that provision for loss of bargain.

In conclusion, the notion *caveat emptor* still applies so that the wise buyer still asks questions, makes tests and makes known why he wants the goods. The notion is less strong in the case of a consumer as buyer. The privity of contract doctrine has been relaxed for consumers (or made circumventable) in certain circumstances (see **s 75** of the **Consumer Credit Act** and the provisions of the **Consumer Protection Act**). Also, the **Contracts (Rights of Third Parties) Act 1999** has created an exception for the third party upon whom the contract purports to confer a benefit. The principle of freedom of contract is still intact, but is subject to some exceptions (see the **Unfair Contract Terms Act 1977** and the **Unfair Terms in Consumer Contracts Regulations 1999**). The common theme is that these three notions, each derived from a body of commercial law developed largely to regulate the position between merchants, have had to be qualified to some extent in order to achieve justice for consumers. It is worth noting that both domestic and EU consumer protection measures can be enforced on behalf of the collective interest of consumers, reluctant to pursue individual litigation by the Office of Fair Trading and other UK and EU-qualified enforcers under **Pt 8** of the **Enterprise Act 2002** – this injunctive procedure, though not providing compensation for individuals but only restricting future conduct, further strengthens the position of modern consumers.

QUESTION 4

Is the **Vienna Convention on Contracts for the International Sale of Goods (CISG)** better suited to international contracts than existing English sales law?

▷ Critically evaluate this question.

---

20   Unless of course the description of the goods points to one purpose only, eg a hot water bottle: *Preist v Last* (1903).

Answer Plan

This question gives you an opportunity to compare the main provisions in the **CISG** against existing English contract law, with particular emphasis on matters relating to commercial contracts. The amount of detail required will be restricted to the time available, so do not get carried away!

Adoption of the **CISG** would provide important benefits to UK exporters and importers of goods. Parties negotiating international sales contracts often find the 'choice of law' issue to be among the most contentious. Each party is familiar with its own domestic sales law, and prefers that its local rules apply to the transaction. A widely acceptable and accepted uniform and generally understood set of rules avoids all of those problems. The **CISG** attempts to eliminate obstacles to cross-border contracts by putting into place internationally accepted substantive rules on which contracting parties, courts and arbitrators may rely.

ANSWER

The **Vienna Convention on Contracts for the International Sale of Goods (CISG)** now accounts for two-thirds of all world trade international sales law[21] and, in practice, supersedes the sales law of many of the countries with which the UK trades. Adopting the **CISG** gives parties the advantage of a widely accepted and increasingly understood text. The **CISG** does not seek to deprive parties of the freedom of contract; its provisions merely act as a gap filler governing the parties' rights and obligations where their contract is silent on these issues. There are considerable differences between the contract laws of individual countries, and a common core has to be found. An attempt is made by **CISG** to eliminate obstacles to cross-border contracts.

---

21   As at 7 July 2010, the following 76 countries subscribe to the CISG:

Albania, Argentina, Armenia, Australia, Austria, Belarus, Belgium, Bosnia and Herzegovina, Bulgaria, Burundi, Canada, Chile, China, Colombia, Croatia, Cuba, Cyprus, the Czech Republic, Denmark, Dominican Republic, Ecuador, Egypt, El Salvador, Estonia, Finland, France, Gabon, Georgia, Germany, Greece, Guinea, Honduras, Hungary, Iceland, Iraq, Israel, Italy, Japan, Republic of Korea, Kyrgyzstan, Latvia, Lebanon, Lesotho, Liberia, Lithuania, Luxembourg, Macedonia, Mauritania, Mexico, Moldova, Mongolia, Montenegro, The Netherlands, New Zealand, Norway, Paraguay, Peru, Poland, Romania, Russian Federation, Saint Vincent and Grenadines, Serbia, Singapore, Slovakia, Slovenia, Spain, Sweden, Switzerland, Syria, Turkey, Uganda, Ukraine, United States of America, Uruguay, Uzbekistan and Zambia.

The **CISG** recognises the basic principle of contractual freedom in the international sale of goods. **Article 6** enables parties to exclude the application of the **CISG** and parties have the right to pick and choose those parts of the **CISG** by which they agree to be bound. The **CISG** depends in important ways on standards such as reasonableness and good faith, which are familiar ideas and concepts to English lawyers. Another important feature of the **CISG** is its very limited use of technical legal terms and concepts. It has the characteristics of simplicity, practicality and clarity. It is free of legal shorthand, free of complicated legal theory and easy for business people to understand.

APPLICATION

The **CISG** only applies to international commercial sale of goods. Each of the following elements constitutes an important limitation on the scope of the **CISG**'s applicability. First, the sale must be international in character, that is, it involves parties whose places of business are in different States. Secondly, the **CISG** covers the sale of goods and does not automatically apply to service contracts. Finally, the **CISG** only applies to commercial transactions, that is, sales between merchants of goods. Amongst other limitations, it does not cover consumer sales, auction sales, sales of negotiable instruments or securities, nor does it cover sales of ships or aircraft.

FORMATION OF CONTRACTS

The **CISG** does not subject the contract of sale to any requirement as to form. There are, however, aspects of the **CISG** relating to irrevocable offers and counter-offers which are novel – novel, that is, to English lawyers.

Under English law, the offeror's right to withdraw an offer is not restricted where the offeree has not given consideration, even if the offer is expressed to be irrevocable (*Payne v Cave* (1789)). Under **Art 16** of the **CISG**, an offer can be made expressly irrevocable because a time for acceptance is fixed; this is contrary to *Routledge v Grant* (1828). An offer is also irrevocable if it was reasonable for the offeree to rely on the offer as irrevocable and the offeree has acted in reliance on it.

The rationale behind **Art 16** is that commercial interests are enhanced by the greater certainty of dealing that arises from irrevocability. It is interesting to note that the law of major trading countries, including the USA and much of Europe, is consistent in this respect with the **CISG**.

Under English law, an acceptance which is not the mirror image of an offer does not give rise to a contract – it is regarded as a counter-offer, not an acceptance (*Hyde v Wrench* (1840)). Under **Art 19** of the **CISG**, a reply to an offer which purports to be an acceptance but contains additional or different terms which do not materially alter the terms of the offer constitutes an acceptance rather than a counter-offer. This is subject to the absence of a timely objection by the offeror. **Article 19** is designed to maintain the contract if the differences between the offer and 'acceptance' are immaterial. Such a provision would do away with the problem in English law of 'battle of the forms'.

Furthermore, under the **CISG**, an acceptance of an offer becomes effective at the moment the indication of assent reaches the offeror; to that extent, the postal acceptance rule would be abolished.

The **CISG** thus facilitates serious dealing, removes the differences arising from different forms of communication and takes account of new technology. Although none of the changes should present any difficulty, care should be taken in respect of irrevocable offers.

The **CISG** is concerned with neither the validity of the contract nor the rights of third parties. Possible issues left to be determined by national legal systems are thus many: contractual capacity, mistake, penalty and liquidated damages clauses, illegal and unconscionable contracts, for instance, which may make a contract or a contract term void or voidable.

CONCEPT OF FUNDAMENTAL BREACH

The **CISG** imposes a much stricter standard for rejection and cancellation (referred to as 'avoidance'). Under the **CISG**, a buyer cannot reject defective goods unless there has been a fundamental breach. 'Fundamental breach' under the **CISG**[22] is quite distinct from the concept under English law. English law permits a buyer to reject the goods or the tender of documents if they fail to comply with conditions of the contract (subject to qualifications, such as **s 15A** of the **Sale of Goods Act 1979**). By contrast, the **CISG** restricts a buyer's right to avoid the contract in circumstances where the buyer would be substantially deprived of what he is entitled to expect under the contract.

(a) *Partial/excessive delivery* **Articles 51–52** of the **CISG** regulate partial and excessive performance and these differ in detail from existing English law. For example, under the **CISG**, a shortfall in the quantity delivered justifies the buyer's

---

22   A breach is fundamental, according to **Art 25** of the **CISG**:

  '. . . if it results in such detriment to the other party as substantially to deprive him of what he is entitled to under the contract, unless the party in breach did not foresee and a reasonable person of the same kind in the same circumstances would not have foreseen such a result.'

avoidance of the contract only if the failure amounts to a fundamental breach and, in the case of excess performance, only the excess can be rejected. By contrast, **s 30** of the **Sale of Goods Act 1979** allows the buyer to reject the whole delivery, unless the shortfall (or excess) in the quantity of goods delivered to the non-consumer buyer is so slight that it would be unreasonable for him to do so.

(b) *Anticipatory breach* Under the English doctrine of anticipatory breach, the innocent party is entitled to avoid the contract by reason of the other party's repudiatory breach. Under **Art 72** of the **CISG**, the right to avoid for anticipatory breach arises only if 'it is clear that one of the parties will commit a fundamental breach' (**Art 72**).

DELIVERY OF CONFORMING GOODS

Under the **CISG**, the seller must deliver the goods, hand over any documents relating to them and transfer the property in the goods as required by the contract. These duties are unlikely to cause difficulty for English lawyers.

The basic obligation of conformity of the goods is that the seller must deliver goods which are of the quantity, quality and description required by the contract (including packaging). Conformity is spelled out in terms of fitness for ordinary purpose and for any particular purpose known to the seller, unless the buyer did not reasonably rely on the seller's skill and judgement. Again, these duties are unlikely to cause difficulty for English lawyers, but the wording of the obligations differs from the **Sale of Goods Act 1979** – for instance, there is no reference to conditions and warranties – but the substance appears not to differ in any significant way.

The rules relating to the consequence of non-conformity are, however, new. The **CISG** buyer loses the right to rely on a lack of conformity of the goods unless notice is given within a reasonable time after discovery of the defect or within two years of the actual delivery of the goods (whichever is the earlier).

REMEDIES

Remedies are critical in the effective operation of law in an area such as this. It is not surprising that the **CISG** gives them a great deal of emphasis, introducing a range of remedies not to be found in English law.

(a) *Seller's right to cure* The **CISG** emphasises saving the contract by enabling the seller to cure the breach. The **CISG** permits a seller to remedy a tender of defective documents (**Art 34**) and non-conforming goods (**Art 37**) up to the time fixed for delivery, as long as the exercise of these rights does not cause the buyer unreasonable inconvenience or unreasonable expense. **Article 48** gives a seller the right to remedy 'any failure to perform' if he can do so without unreasonable delay and without causing the buyer unreasonable inconvenience. This right to remedy applies to a breach by failure to deliver on time. The procedure to be followed is that the seller must give notice to the buyer suggesting a new deadline for delivery. If the buyer does not answer within a reasonable time, the seller has the right to perform and the buyer has the obligation to accept performance within the new deadline. Since the seller's notice to the buyer is assumed under the **CISG** to include a request that the buyer consent or refuse his consent, this means that a buyer who does not respond to a notice that the seller will deliver late will be in breach if the buyer refuses to accept delivery.

(b) *Price reduction* Under **Art 50**, if the seller delivers goods which do not conform to the contract, whether or not the price has already been paid, in addition to recovering damages, the buyer may unilaterally reduce the price in the same proportion as the value that the goods actually delivered bears to the value that conforming goods would have had at that time. If the goods are delivered late, but they do conform to the contract, **Art 50** does not apply. The right to reduce the price is a substantial right and there are situations in which **Art 50** can provide better relief than a damages claim (for example, in the case of a falling market). This is good news for the buyer but bad for the seller (the seller may, of course, revise the limitation of liability clause in the contract to reduce the effect of **Art 50**).

(c) *Damages* The basic right to damages under **Art 74** of the **CISG**[23] is stated in terms of foreseeability and appears to conform with the basic rule of damages in *Hadley v Baxendale* (1854). There is under the **CISG** an obligation on a party relying on breach to mitigate the loss.

(d) *Specific performance* **Articles 46** and **62** of the **CISG** permit both the buyer and seller to require performance of the other party's obligations under the contract. However, this is subject to the qualification that a court need not grant an order for specific performance unless it would do so under its own law in non-**CISG** cases involving similar contracts of sale. English courts have invariably been reluctant to grant specific performance where damages are an adequate remedy (*Harnett v Yielding* (1805)).

---

23   Article 74:

'Damages for breach of contract by one party consist of a sum equal to the loss, including the loss of profit, suffered by the other party as a consequence of the breach. Such damages may not exceed the loss which the party in breach foresaw or ought to have foreseen at the time of the conclusion of the contract, in the light of the facts and matters which he then knew or ought to have known, as a possible consequence of the breach of contract.'

PASSING OF RISK

Although the **CISG** deals with passage of risk of loss or damage, it does not contain provisions governing what we call transfer of 'title' or 'property'. Of course, the **Sale of Goods Act 1979** contains detailed provisions specifying when title passes. Although the **CISG** does not regulate the transfer of property, it does provide a clear basis on which relevant arrangements, including insurance, can be made. Under the **CISG**, risk in general passes on the handing over of the goods to the carrier (**Art 67**) or to the buyer if he is taking direct delivery (**Art 69**).

FRUSTRATION

The **CISG**[24] deals with the issue of the excusing of a non-performing party because of impossibility in a similar way to the doctrine of frustration in English law. However, **Art 79** operates only to prevent an action in damages. It does not bring the contract to an end, which is unlike the English law position (*Hirji Mulji v Cheong Yue Steamship Co* (1926)). However, if a failure to perform is a fundamental breach, the other party may declare the contract rescinded for breach.

CONCLUSION

Because the **CISG** is still so new, the ramifications of its provisions are uncertain. However, with so many nations having become parties to it, and with so many alternative sources and markets available to purchasers of manufactured goods or producers of raw materials, British exporters and importers are no longer in a position to have their way with respect to choice of law and forum selection. The attitudes and lack of a widely accepted alternative that made the 'laws of England' the common contractual choice of law in international commercial transactions are gone, or are changing. A seller or buyer who refuses to deal on the **CISG** terms may find himself losing business opportunities to competitors who will.

> ### Aim Higher ★
>
> One crucial issue is, of course, the failure of the UK to adopt the Vienna Convention. A good answer would express a view whether the UK is justified in its refusal to adopt the Convention.

---

24   Article 79 states the basic rule:

   'A party is not liable for a failure to perform any of his obligations if he proves that the failure was due to an impediment beyond his control and that he could not reasonably be expected to have taken the impediment into account at the time of the conclusion of the contract or to have avoided or overcome it or its consequences.'

2

Description and Quality

INTRODUCTION

The questions in this chapter relate to the statutory implied terms as to description, quality and fitness for purpose, to exclusion clauses and also to product liability. In some courses, the law of trade descriptions is dealt with in questions which also raise contractual issues (for example, under **s 13** of the **Sale of Goods Act 1979**). This has not been done in this book because a number of sale of goods courses do not include trade descriptions in their syllabuses.

QUESTION 5 ---

Olive is a physiotherapist who works from home. She sees a poster in the window of Conman Ltd, a furniture shop: 'Massage tables £300. Suitable as an occasional bed or table for the discerning masseuse. Self assembly.' On the notice is a photograph of a pink table. The table is much cheaper than equivalent tables sold in nearby shops. Olive points to the poster and tells Shelly, the sales assistant, 'I will buy a massage table.' She then adds, 'I will also need a side chair.' This is selected from a photograph of a range of chairs sold by Conman. It is agreed that the items will be delivered to Olive's home on 1 February.

On 1 February, the table and chair are delivered in sealed cardboard boxes, but Olive had to leave that day to visit her mother who had fallen ill. She returns on 15 February, but she is too upset to assemble the furniture until 1 March. It is only then that she discovers the table is green. She had particularly wanted pink because that is the colour of the decoration in the room she uses for her clients. In addition, one of the table's safety screws is missing, the table is not long enough to take anyone taller than five foot lying down, and the table is too high for the chair she bought from Conman.

▶ Discuss Olive's possible remedies.

Answer Plan

This question involves a lot of points being included. It is testing your ability to spot each of the issues raised, as well as your ability to deal with them. So, a good answer must acknowledge each of the points raised, and must not concentrate on some of the issues to the exclusion of others. The main points that need to be discussed are as follows:

- ❖ description: s 13 of the **Sale of Goods Act 1979**;
- ❖ satisfactory quality: s 14(2);
- ❖ fitness for purpose: s 14(3);
- ❖ misrepresentation;
- ❖ when a buyer loses the right to reject goods;
- ❖ remedies.

ANSWER

Olive wants to know what remedies she might have against Conman Ltd. She agreed to buy a table and chair from the shop and has found that the table is defective because (i) it is the wrong colour, (ii) one of the safety screws is missing, (iii) it is not long enough, and (iv) it is too high for the chair she bought.

WRONG COLOUR

The shop poster included a photograph of a pink table. This was the colour Olive had assumed her table would be when delivered. In fact, the table she received was green in colour. If Olive had specifically agreed with Conman that she was buying a pink table, it seems clear that if a green one was supplied, then Conman would be in breach of an express term of the contract, as well as being in breach of s 13 of the **Sale of Goods Act 1979**. What appears to have happened here is that nothing was said in relation to colour, but that Conman's poster included a photograph of a pink table. The question is whether this was sufficient to imply into the contract that the table was to be pink.

If it does amount to an express term of the contract, the fact that the table as delivered was green would amount to a breach, and Olive's remedy depends on whether this breach substantially deprives Olive of what she might have expected under the contract. It is likely that the court will consider this breach a slight one, not entitling Olive to terminate the contract, but that Olive may be entitled to damages if she suffers any loss (*Hong Kong Fir Shipping v Kawasaki Kisen Kaisha* (1962)).

Whether a photograph of a pink table forms part of 'description' for **s 13** of the **Sale of Goods Act 1979** purposes is debatable. If Olive has specifically agreed the colour, the delivery of a green table would certainly amount to a breach of **s 13**. If 'pink' forms part of the description of the goods for **s 13** purposes, it is immaterial that Olive suffers no loss (*Re Moore and Landauer* (1921)). This is because **s 13** is a condition implied into her sales contract. Although Olive is a physiotherapist and she buys the table and chair in order for her to work from home, she does not buy the goods for the purposes of reprocessing and resale in the course of her business. Thus, following *R and B Customs Brokers v United Dominion Trust* (1988) and the more recent *Feldaroll Foundry v Hermes Leasing* (2004), Olive is a consumer for the **Sale of Goods Act** purposes, and the court's discretion under **s 15A** of that Act does not apply. As long as Olive relied on Conman Ltd's description of 'pink' table, Olive will be able to claim breach of **s 13**, entitling her to reject the table.

However, in the circumstances, it is a little unlikely that the courts will view 'pink' table as forming part of the description of the goods. We are told, however, that a further problem with the table is that one of the screws is missing. This is very serious indeed.

SAFETY SCREW MISSING

Conman Ltd sells in the course of business (*Stevenson v Rogers* (1999)), thus further conditions under the **Sale of Goods Act** are implied into the sales contract, namely **s 14(2)** and **s 14(3)**. As discussed earlier, Olive will be treated as a consumer under the Act. Even if the court holds that the contract with Conman Ltd is not a consumer transaction, the fact that a safety screw is missing is a serious breach and the court is unlikely to exercise its **s 15A** discretion to disallow a business buyer from rejecting defective goods.

Under **s 14(2)**, the table is required to be of satisfactory quality. The test is what a reasonable person would regard as satisfactory, bearing in mind the price, description and other relevant circumstances. Although we are told that the table is much cheaper than equivalent tables sold in nearby shops, this is not sufficient to imply that the defect in the table, the missing safety screw, was brought to Olive's attention. Furthermore, although Olive paid a fairly low price and therefore cannot expect too high a standard in goods (*Brown v Craiks* (1970)), the fact that one safety screw is missing cannot be regarded as anything but unsatisfactory (*Rogers v Parish* (1987)). Aspects of the quality of goods include the purposes for which goods of that kind are commonly bought, freedom from minor defects and safety. A reasonable person would not regard a table with one safety screw missing as anything but defective. Thus, it appears that Conman is in breach of the implied condition as to satisfactory quality.

Since the description 'massage table' points to its use (*Preist v Last* (1903)), **s 14(3)** implies a condition that the goods supplied by Conman must be fit for that purpose. It is reasonable in the circumstances for Olive to rely on Conman's skill and judgement to supply a table fit for use as a massage table (*Teheran Europe v Belton (ST)* (1968)). Since one safety screw is missing, this amounts to a breach of **s 14(3)**.

Olive's remedies for breach of **s 14(2)** and **14(3)** will be discussed later under Remedies.

TABLE NOT LONG ENOUGH TO TAKE ANYONE TALLER THAN FIVE FOOT LYING DOWN

Conman's poster advertised the table as 'suitable as an occasional bed or table for the discerning masseuse'. Not every statement about the quality or fitness of the goods can be treated as part of description. For **s 13** to apply, words must constitute an essential part of the description of the goods. The key to **s 13** is identification, that is, the words must constitute a substantial ingredient of the identity of the goods sold. Conman's statement is unlikely to constitute words forming part of the description of the goods. In *Ashington Piggeries v Christopher Hill* (1972), herring meal, which had been contaminated with a substance rendering it not suitable for feeding to mink, was sold to the buyer for use as mink food. The House of Lords held that there was no breach of **s 13**, because the goods had been properly described as herring meal. This is because not all descriptive words form part of the terms of the contract. So, the fact that the table was not suitable for use as a massage table because it was not long enough to take anyone taller than five foot lying down is unlikely to amount to a **s 13** breach.

However, the advertisement might amount to a misrepresentation of material fact (*Smith v Land and House Properties* (1884)) which Conman intended buyers to rely on and which Olive did rely on. Conman cannot argue that no reasonable buyer would have relied on their notice. If Olive did rely on it, this will be sufficient (*Museprime Properties v Adhill* (1990)). As long as one of the reasons Olive bought the table was because of Conman's statement that it was suitable for use as a massage table, this will found an action for misrepresentation (*Edgington v Fitzmaurice* (1885)). Olive's action against Conman would be for negligent misrepresentation and, by virtue of **s 2(1)** of the **Misrepresentation Act 1967**, Olive is entitled to claim damages as if the misrepresentation was made fraudulently, unless Conman can prove that they had reasonable grounds to believe and continued to believe up to the time of the sales contract with Olive that the statement was true. It does not seem likely that Conman will be able to discharge this heavy burden of proof (*Howard Marine v Ogden* (1978)), thus entitling Olive to damages in the tort of deceit (*Royscot Trust v Rogerson* (1991)). Whether or not Olive may rescind her contract with Conman will be discussed later under Remedies.

TABLE TOO HIGH FOR THE CHAIR SHE BOUGHT

Whether Olive has a remedy against Conman because the table was too high for the chair she bought from them depends on whether Olive's statement to the sales assistant Shelly ('I will also need a chair') amounts to impliedly making it known to Conman the purpose for which Olive needed the chair, that is, to be used with the table which she is buying from Conman. If Olive has impliedly made it known, then it would be reasonable to rely on Conman to supply her with a chair suitable for that purpose. Since the chair is not suitable for the table, Conman may be in breach of **s 14(3)**.

REMEDIES

As discussed above, Conman may be in breach of **ss 14(2)** and **14(3)**. Since these are conditions of the contract, this means that Olive is entitled to reject the goods and claim damages. However, the right to reject goods is lost if Olive keeps the goods beyond a reasonable time in which to examine them (**s 35**). We are told that the goods were delivered to Olive on 1 February in sealed boxes. By virtue of **s 34**, a buyer must be given a reasonable opportunity to examine the goods to ensure they conform with the contract. Olive does not examine the goods because she left almost immediately to visit her mother until 15 February. The approach taken by the **Sale of Goods Act** is that as long as the buyer has a reasonable opportunity to examine, then **s 34** is satisfied. Olive is not under an obligation to inspect the goods. **Section 34** merely requires that a buyer is given an opportunity to do so if she wishes. It is unlikely the courts will interpret **s 34** subjectively to extend the period of time Olive has to examine the goods due to her absence to visit her mother. By **s 35**, if the buyer retains the goods and does not complain about them beyond a reasonable length of time, she is deemed to have accepted the goods. We are told that Olive only discovers the defects in the goods on 1 March. This is some four weeks after delivery. Whether or not this is beyond a reasonable time in which to examine is a question of fact. Although *Bernstein v Pamson Motors* (1987) has been criticised, the court indicated that three weeks may be beyond a reasonable time to examine a car. The goods here are a table and chair, not such complex goods, and Olive has had them for four weeks. It is likely that Olive will be deemed to have accepted the goods.

Thus, if Olive has lost her right to reject the table and chair because she is deemed to have accepted them under **s 35**, she will nevertheless be entitled to damages as long as her loss satisfies the remoteness rule (*Hadley v Baxendale* (1854)). It is unlikely Olive will be entitled to non-pecuniary loss to cover for her disappointment (*Addis v Gramophone* (1909)), although the court may award damages if Olive suffers loss of reputation and goodwill if she was unable to provide her physiotherapy service to her clients due to incomplete equipment (*Gibbons v Westminster Bank* (1939); *Anglo-Continental Holidays v Typaldos* (1967)). This will depend on whether Conman knew at the time the contract was made with Olive that Olive required the table and chair for her work at home (*Victoria Laundry v Newman* (1949)).

Furthermore, since Olive is a consumer, she has additional remedies under **s 48A**. She may demand that Conman repair the table at their cost; failing that, Conman could replace the table, or agree to reduce the purchase price, or if none of these is possible, Olive will retain her right to rescind the contract. **Section 48A(3)** raises a presumption that if the goods are defective within six months of delivery, the goods were defective at the time of delivery, although the presumption depends on the nature of the goods. The table and chair are not complex goods, as discussed, and they were delivered some four weeks ago. It may be that Olive can no longer claim her **s 48A** rights.

As far as Olive's claim in misrepresentation is concerned, her primary remedy is rescission. This equitable remedy is lost if the misrepresentee has affirmed the contract (*Long v Lloyd* (1958)), or due to a lapse of time (*Leaf v International Galleries* (1950)). What is clear is that the innocent party loses her right to reject goods for breach of contract more quickly than she loses her right to rescind the contract for misrepresentation. So, although Olive may have accepted the goods for **Sale of Goods Act** purposes, Olive may nevertheless retain her right to rescind the contract for misrepresentation.

> ## Common Pitfalls ✖
>
> Students need to discuss the application of the law. Clearly, **s 13** of the **Sale of Goods Act** applies, but often students just point out that there was a breach of **s 13** without explaining what the section means, how it is applied and why it might have been breached. It is never sufficient to avoid these issues by saying that 'it is up to the court to decide'.

QUESTION 6

Bimmer Ltd is a British manufacturer of Bimmer electrical switches. It supplies them to, among others, Fayad Cie, an Egyptian company which makes Fayad microwaves in Cairo. These microwaves are imported into Britain by Borat plc and supplied to the retail market through a distribution system. A year ago, Louise bought a Fayad microwave for £250 from Harry's electrical shop in London. Yesterday, the Bimmer switch in the microwave smouldered and set fire to the microwave. Louise was badly burnt in putting out the fire, but managed to limit the damage so that, apart from her burns, the only damage done was that the microwave was a write-off and Louise's kitchen carpet (worth £250) was burnt and has had to be replaced.

Advise Louise, bearing in mind that Harry's shop has stopped trading since Harry became bankrupt last week.

How, if at all, would it affect your advice if the Bimmer switch which caused the fire was a replacement one supplied and fitted three months ago by Harry's electrical shop after Louise had complained about the microwave not switching on at a sufficiently low temperature?

Answer Plan

This question demands a discussion of product liability. A claim by Louise under the **Sale of Goods Act 1979** is clearly ruled out by the statement that Harry has become bankrupt, but this must be stated in your answer. That leaves the answer to deal with two possible grounds of liability, at common law for negligence and for product liability under the **Consumer Protection Act 1987**. Some, maybe many, commercial law (or consumer law) courses are taken by students after they have taken basic subjects such as tort. It is therefore not always easy to know how much basic tort law, such as negligence, to include in an answer. In a question such as this, as a priority, make sure that you deal fully with the issues raised under the statute and that you do cover in some way the negligence issues. It is a matter to some extent of your own judgement as to how much space you can afford to give the negligence issues.

Most commercial law courses will not specifically include coverage of conflict of laws issues; thus, in this answer, those problems in relation to Fayad Cie are no more than hinted at.

ANSWER

The claim which Louise may very well have for breach of express or implied terms in her sale of goods contract with Harry is clearly not going to yield much, if anything, for her, since Harry is bankrupt. Nor can Louise bring that claim against the manufacturer or importer or anyone else earlier in the distribution chain, as there is no privity of contract between her and any of them. Thus, any claim against one of the other parties will have to be a claim in negligence under the principle in *Donoghue v Stevenson* (1932) or a product liability claim under **Pt I** of the **Consumer Protection Act 1987**.

NEGLIGENCE

Louise has a claim in negligence against anyone in respect of whom she can establish three things: (1) that that person owed her a duty of care; (2) that that person (or one of his employees in the course of his employment) failed to take reasonable care; and (3) that that failure to take care caused her damage which was of a foreseeable type occurring in a generally foreseeable sort of way. Given that the source of the damage was an apparently defective electrical switch, it is unlikely that those three elements could be shown except in relation to Bimmer Ltd which manufactured it, or possibly Fayad Cie which incorporated it into one of its machines. The principal difficulty in the case of Bimmer Ltd would be proving a failure to take reasonable care, since clearly Bimmer Ltd owed a duty to the ultimate consumer to take care in the design (or in its adoption) and manufacture of the switch. Whether reliance on the doctrine of *res ipsa loquitur* would help Louise prove negligence would depend very much on what evidence of care and systems is put forward by Bimmer Ltd. So far as Fayad Cie is concerned, there is no doubt in English law that a duty of care in the manufacture of machines was owed to the ultimate consumer, and little doubt that this extends to taking reasonable care to ensure that only safe components are used. The difficulties with a claim in negligence against Fayad Cie are: (1) getting an English court to take jurisdiction; (2) proving that the duty just outlined was broken, that is, that Fayad Cie failed to take reasonable care; and (3) the fact that, even if the claim were successful, damages would be recoverable only for Louise's burns and the damage to the carpet. Damages would not be recoverable in respect of the loss of the microwave itself, just as damages would not have been recoverable by Mrs Donoghue for the value of the ginger beer, this loss being an unrecoverable economic loss (*Murphy v Brentwood* (1990)). Thus, so far as negligence is concerned, Louise's best bet is a claim against Bimmer Ltd, in which case, Louise will face the difficulty of proving a failure to take reasonable care. In the event of such a claim succeeding against Bimmer Ltd, it is debatable whether the damages would include compensation for the loss of the microwave. On the one hand, that is damage caused 'by' and not 'to' the item (the switch) manufactured and put into circulation by Bimmer Ltd. On the other, the switch was clearly designed to be incorporated into and subsequently supplied as a component of another item.

PRODUCT LIABILITY

Louise's best claim may well be one in respect of a defective product under **Pt I** of the **Consumer Protection Act 1987**. She has, it seems, been the victim of two defective products, a switch and a microwave. They almost certainly were defective, that is, not as safe as persons generally are entitled to expect (**s 3**). Liability is strict and therefore negligence does not need to be proved. Nothing given in the problem suggests that any of the defences in **s 4** will apply, unless perhaps the damage was entirely attributable to something in the microwave design, as opposed to something in the switch. In that case, there would be no liability under **Pt I** in respect of the switch, but only in respect of the microwave (**s 4(1)(f)**).

In the problem, there is no one who is an 'own brander'. So, the persons potentially liable (see **s 2**) are the manufacturers, that is, Bimmer Ltd and Fayad Cie, and the importer into the European Community, Borat plc. The problem does not precisely state that Borat plc imported the microwaves direct into Britain from Egypt. If, in fact, someone else imported them from Egypt into another country of the European Community, for example France, and Borat plc only imported the goods from France into Britain, then Borat plc would not be liable. Instead, liability could be fixed on whoever imported them into France. It will now, however, be assumed that Borat plc did import them from Egypt directly into Britain.

Bimmer Ltd as producer can be held liable in respect of the defective switch, and Fayad Cie as producer can be held liable in respect of the defective microwave. Borat plc as the importer can be held liable in respect of both. Given the possible difficulties of proceeding against a foreign company, with maybe no presence in Britain or even in the European Community, it may make sense therefore for Louise to contemplate claims only against Bimmer Ltd and Borat plc. These claims would certainly include a claim in respect of Louise's personal injuries, that is, her burns. So far as property damage is concerned, no claim can succeed unless the property damage claimable amounts to more than £275 (**s 5(4)**). This means that Louise's claim can succeed only if she is able to claim for both the loss of the microwave (£250) and the damage to the carpet (£250). If she is able to claim both, then she is entitled to recover the whole of the £500, that is, including the first £275. There is nothing (apart from the need to exceed £275 in total property claims) to rule out her claiming for the carpet, which is clearly property for private, as opposed to business, use. However, Louise cannot claim for the damage to the microwave. So far as the claim (against Borat plc) in respect of the defective microwave is concerned, the damage to the microwave is unrecoverable (**s 5(2)**). It can be observed that, although **Pt I** of the **Consumer Protection Act** talks about liability for defective products, it defines 'defective' in terms of safety and thus, in truth, creates liability for *dangerous* products. It creates a liability for damage caused by them, but not for damage caused to themselves. The position is exactly the same when one considers the claim against Bimmer Ltd (and also Borat plc) in respect of the defective switch. Any argument that the damage caused by the defective product (here, the switch) to other things includes the damage to the microwave is ruled out completely by **s 5(2)**. This subsection prevents recovery of damage for loss or damage to any product (here, the microwave) which has been supplied with the defective product (here, the switch) comprised within it. Thus, the damage to the microwave is not recoverable and thus it follows that the damage to the carpet is also ruled out because it does not exceed £275 in value.

In conclusion, therefore, it appears that in respect of her burns, Louise has a good claim under **Pt I** of the **Consumer Protection Act 1987** against Bimmer Ltd and Borat plc. The claim against Borat plc may be a little more secure in that, even if Bimmer Ltd were able to show (under **s 4(1)(f)**) that the defect was not in the switch but in the unsuitability of the microwave for the particular switch, Borat plc would be still be liable as the importer into the European Community of the defective microwave. It seems, however, that any claim in respect of the carpet would have to be brought in negligence.

CONTRIBUTORY NEGLIGENCE

It is possible, if unlikely, that in trying to put out the fire, Louise was herself negligent. It is unlikely since instinctive reactions in the heat (literally perhaps) of the moment are not normally regarded as amounting to contributory negligence (*Jones v Boyce* (1816)). If she were contributorily negligent, then her damages for her burns, whether under the common law of negligence or under the **Consumer Protection Act** (see **s 6(4)**) would be reduced proportionately. It does not follow, however, that any damages (that is, assuming they are recoverable) for the damage to the carpet or microwave would also be reduced, since although it is very likely that any negligence of Louise in choosing to fight the fire may have been one of the causes of her being burnt, it is unlikely that that negligence caused the damage to the microwave and the carpet. Indeed, her fighting the fire, far from being a cause of property damage, almost certainly prevented more occurring.

THE RIDER

There are two possibilities. The first is that the switch was defective. The second is that the microwave was defective, a defect wholly attributable to its design, making it unsuitable for a switch which presumably was listed as one of its replacement parts. If the second possibility is the reality, then Bimmer Ltd will not be liable, but the advice given above as to the liability of Borat plc for product liability will remain unaltered. It seems more likely that the first possibility is the reality. In that case, Bimmer Ltd will remain liable for product liability, but Borat plc will not be liable at all, since presumably Borat plc did not import into the European Community the replacement switch which Louise fitted and which caused the damage. Furthermore, Bimmer Ltd's liability can now include liability for the loss of the microwave, since Louise's microwave was not supplied to her with that switch comprised within it. This means that Bimmer Ltd's liability under the 1987 Act will include liability for the microwave and the carpet, the two together amounting to property damage exceeding £275.

QUESTION 7

Feldarolla plc recently bought two used cars, each six months old, for its executives to drive. Anthony, managing director of Feldarolla plc, first saw the two cars at Dodger's Garage a month ago, when he noticed that one, a Catalan, had an engine oil leak and the other, a Toyotan, had a water leak in the boot. He did not, however, look in the boot of the Catalan. Dodger assured him: 'They are good little buses; you can rely upon them.' After test-driving both cars, Anthony, on behalf of Feldarolla plc, signed two contracts of purchase, one for each car. Anthony left the Catalan with Dodger to have the oil leak repaired and drove away in the Toyotan. Two weeks later, he returned the Toyotan for its boot leak to be repaired and collected the Catalan. The next day, he discovered firstly, that the Catalan had a water leak in its boot; secondly, that the engine oil leak had not been repaired and was irreparable (meaning that a new engine was necessary); and, thirdly, that soon after delivery to its first buyer, the Toyotan had been in an accident and subsequently treated by its owner's insurance company as a 'write-off'. Upon learning these facts, Anthony informed Dodger's Garage that he was rejecting the cars and demanded the return of the purchase price to Feldarolla plc.

▶ Advise Feldarolla plc.

Answer Plan

This question follows a certain style of setting questions, which involves a lot of points being included. The question is testing your ability to spot each of the issues raised as well as your ability to deal with them. Thus, a good answer must acknowledge each of the points raised and must not concentrate on some of the issues to the exclusion of the others.

The issues raised in this question are:

❖ liability for breach of the conditions as to satisfactory quality and fitness for purpose;
❖ liability (for an express term and/or misrepresentation) arising out of the statement about the cars being 'good little buses', etc;
❖ the remedies available to the buyer and, in particular, whether there has been acceptance of the goods so as to preclude rejection.

A sensible order of treatment is:

❖ implied conditions in s 14;
❖ express term/misrepresentation;
❖ remedies.

ANSWER

This question raises issues of liability for express and implied terms of the contract, for misrepresentation, and the extent of any remedies available to Feldarolla plc. There may be liability in respect of the implied conditions as to satisfactory quality and fitness for purpose, liability for breach of an express term that the cars were 'good little buses', and liability for misrepresentation arising out of the same assertion by

Dodger. These possible liabilities will be considered, as will the remedies that may be available to Feldarolla plc. It is to be observed that a separate contract was signed in relation to each car and, therefore, presumably the parties intended two distinct contracts. This answer will proceed upon that assumption. Feldarolla plc was not a 'consumer' as defined in the **Sale and Supply of Goods to Consumers Regulations**, which implement the **European Directive on Consumer Guarantees**. Thus, the new rights as to repair and replacement do not fall to be discussed in this answer.

SATISFACTORY QUALITY

Because Dodger clearly sells in the course of business, terms regarding satisfactory quality and fitness for purpose are implied as conditions into the contracts of sale negotiated with Feldarolla plc. However, one condition, in **s 14(2)** of the **Sale of Goods Act 1979**, is not implied as regards any defect specifically drawn to the buyer's attention before the contract was made or, given that Anthony made a pre-purchase examination of the cars, as regards any defect which 'that' examination ought to have revealed. The engine oil leak in the Catalan and water leak in the boot of the Toyotan both appear to be defects falling into one or both of these categories, most clearly the latter category, since we are told that Anthony noticed them. Assuming the water leak in the Toyotan can be repaired, it seems clear that in respect of that leak, no reliance can be placed by Feldarolla plc upon **s 14(2)**.

The engine oil leak of the Catalan has turned out, however, to be irreparable without a complete engine replacement. This suggests that the true nature and/or extent of the defect was not something which was either drawn to Anthony's attention or which ought to have been revealed by his pre-contract examination of the car. Neil LJ in *R and B Customs Brokers v United Dominions Trust* (1988) indicated, *obiter*, that a defect of which the buyer is aware but which he reasonably (and mistakenly) believes will be rectified at no cost to himself is not excluded from the effect of **s 14(2)**. It seems therefore that Feldarolla plc can rely upon the condition in **s 14(2)** as regards the engine oil leak in the Catalan. The condition as to satisfactory quality might also apply to the water leak in the boot of the Catalan and to the fact that the Toyotan had been an insurance 'write-off'. The first of these *might* be a defect which Anthony's pre-purchase inspection *ought* to have revealed. It seems clear that that inspection did not in fact reveal it because Anthony did not in the course of that inspection look into the boot of the Catalan. In *Thornett and Fehr v Beers* (1919), it was held that a buyer who had, before the purchase, inspected the outside of some barrels but not the inside was precluded from relying on the condition as to satisfactory quality as regards defects which would have been revealed if he had inspected the inside. It is submitted, however, that a minor change to the wording of **s 14(2)** effected in 1973 (to the then **Sale of Goods Act 1893**), namely, the change from 'such examination' to 'that examination' has reversed the effect of the 1919 case. Thus, Feldarolla plc is precluded from relying on those defects that ought to have been revealed by the examination which Anthony actually made, but is not prejudiced by him having made a less extensive examination than he might have made. Put another way, the leak in the Catalan's boot was not a defect which ought to have been revealed by the examination which Anthony actually made.

So, do the engine oil leak and boot leak in the Catalan make the car of unsatisfactory quality, and does the fact that the Toyotan was an insurance 'write-off' make the Toyotan of unsatisfactory quality? **Section 14(2A)** requires us to ask in each case whether the car reached a standard that the ordinary person would regard as satisfactory, taking account of any description given to the goods, the price and any other relevant circumstances. Undoubtedly, one of the relevant circumstances is the fact that, in each case, the car was not new but was six months old. **Section 14(2B)** lists a number of aspects of the quality of the goods, including their 'fitness for all the purposes for which goods of the kind in question are commonly supplied'. Thus, the purposes for which a car is bought include not merely the purpose of driving it from place to place, but of doing so with the appropriate degree of comfort, ease of handling and pride in its outward and interior appearance (*Rogers v Parish* (1987)). This general approach applies also to second-hand cars and the question is whether, in this case, the defects were sufficiently serious to render even these second-hand cars of less than satisfactory quality. A second-hand car which, unknown to the buyer at the time of the contract, had been an insurance 'write-off' has been held for that reason not to have reached the necessary standard (*Shine v General Guarantee Corp* (1988)). The two leaks in the Catalan are less easy to decide upon. On the one hand, one is to expect minor defects in a second-hand car (*Bartlett v Sydney Marcus* (1965)). On the other hand, it could be said that the oil leak which requires a new engine for it to be remedied is actually a major defect. As regards the newly discovered water leak in the Catalan, much will depend upon its extent and the ease with which it can be repaired. Therefore, it is submitted that in the case of both cars, Feldarolla plc has a valid claim under s 14(2), but whether that extends to the boot leak in the case of the Catalan will depend upon the seriousness of the latter.

FITNESS FOR PURPOSE

Feldarolla plc's claim in respect of the defects discussed above might equally be made under s 14(3). Anthony told Dodger of a particular purpose for which Feldarolla plc wanted the cars, namely, the purpose of being driven by the company's executives. The defects already being relied upon under s 14(2) render the cars not reasonably fit for that purpose. Feldarolla plc may have no claim under s 14(3) in respect of defects of which it was aware (for example, the Toyotan's leaky boot) if Feldarolla plc placed no reliance upon Dodger's skill and judgement in respect of them. It will still have a claim in relation to the other defect (*Cammell Laird v Manganese Bronze and Brass* (1934)).

'GOOD LITTLE BUSES'

Dodger's assertion that the cars were 'good little buses' arguably implied that the cars were in good condition (*Andrews v Hopkinson* (1957)). This may have amounted to:

(1)   an express term, either a condition or a warranty, of the contract; and
(2)   a misrepresentation.

Assuming it was an express term of the contract, it is submitted that that express term was broken in the case of the Catalan by virtue of its engine oil leak necessitating a new engine. Whether the same can be said of water leaks in the boot is more problematic. Much will depend upon the seriousness of those leaks and the ease with which they can be repaired.

A claim for misrepresentation can succeed only if Anthony relied upon Dodger's statement. Did his pre-purchase examination of the cars indicate a lack of such reliance? Presumably not, because the statement appears to have been made *after* those examinations. Did Anthony's subsequently going for test drives indicate that he was not relying on Dodger's statement? It seems not, since Dodger's statement referred to the cars' reliability (that is, presumably, over a period of time) and one or two test drives could not disclose the truth or otherwise of that. It is not necessary for Feldarolla plc to have relied exclusively upon Dodger's statement.

An untrue statement of fact by Dodger which was one of the reasons Feldarolla plc was induced into buying will give Feldarolla plc a right to rescind the contract. If, however, Feldarolla plc wishes to claim damages for a misrepresentation, it may do so, either as an alternative to rescission (when the issue of whether to award damages is at the discretion of the judge – **s 2(2)** of the **Misrepresentation Act 1967**) or as an independent claim for damages under **s 2(1)**. In the latter case, Dodger will have a defence if he can show, on a balance of probabilities, that at the time of the contract he had reasonable grounds to believe, and did believe, the statement to be true (**s 2(1)** of the **Misrepresentation Act 1967**).[1]

REMEDIES

Remedies for misrepresentation have just been discussed. For any breach of contract, there is a right to claim damages. Feldarolla plc has also purported to reject the cars and required the return of the price for each. Assuming that there was breach of the implied term in either **s 14(2)** or **s 14(3)**, Feldarolla plc undoubtedly had a right of

---

1   This burden is a very heavy one to discharge (*Howard Marine v Ogden* (1978)) **and it is unlikely that Dodger will manage to prove such a defence.**

rejection, since both of those terms are implied *conditions*. The same is not necessarily true of the express term encompassed by the words 'They are good little buses; you can rely upon them'. Assuming that this amounted to an express term of the contract, it would have to be decided whether the parties intended it to be a condition, that is, a term any breach of which would give Feldarolla plc the right to reject the goods and regard the contract as repudiated. The tendency of the courts is not to regard as a condition any express term (other than one as to the time of delivery), unless the parties have very clearly indicated it (*Cehave v Bremer, The Hansa Nord* (1976)). Thus, the test of whether Feldarolla plc had any right of rejection/repudiation for breach of the express term depends upon whether the breach was sufficient to deprive Feldarolla plc of substantially the whole of the benefit of the contract (*Hong Kong Fir v Kawasaki Kisen* (1962)). It is submitted that neither the boot leak in the case of one car nor the boot leak and the engine oil leak in the case of the other was sufficiently serious.

Assuming that Feldarolla plc was, because of the breach of the conditions in **s 14**, within its rights in rejecting the cars and demanding the return of the price, it will nevertheless have lost that right if, by the time it rejected the cars, it had already 'accepted' them within the meaning of **s 35**. Feldarolla plc rejected the Toyotan just over two weeks after taking delivery. After a similar period of time, the buyer in *Bernstein v Pamson Motors* (1987) was held to have accepted the car. Even under the law as it then stood, that decision was controversial. Since then, however, **s 35** has been amended so that, in determining what is a reasonable length of time, it is relevant to ask whether the buyer has had a reasonable opportunity to examine the goods for the purpose of ascertaining whether they comply with the contract. It is thus arguable that Feldarolla plc had not, in just over two weeks, had the Toyotan long enough to have examined it for that purpose. If it had not, then it was entitled to act as it did in rejecting it. Similarly, Feldarolla plc arguably had not had the car long enough that it could be said to have affirmed the contract – and thus was entitled to rescind the contract (and reject the car) for misrepresentation.[2]

Whatever may be a reasonable period of time for the buyer to examine the goods to see if they conform to the contract, there may be added to that period of time a further reasonable period. This may, for example, be a period during which the buyer investigates any apparent non-compliance (*Clegg v Andersson* (2003)) or a period during which the seller repairs the goods under an arrangement with the buyer (**s 35(5)**). So, Feldarolla plc clearly had not lost its right to reject the Catalan. Indeed, Feldarolla had taken delivery of the Catalan only one day before rejecting it.

....

2   In *Feldarol Foundry v Hermes Leasing* (2004), the Court of Appeal held that a period of five to six weeks in relation to a defective car was not beyond a reasonable time in which to examine it, and thus the contract had not yet been affirmed.

Consequently, Feldarolla plc is entitled to the return of the Catalan's purchase price. It might also claim damages, although these are unlikely to be substantial in the case of the Catalan. In the case of the Toyotan, if Feldarolla plc is held to have lost its right to reject the car, the damages would be more substantial. Assuming that the breach in relation to the Toyotan was due to the fact that it had been an insurance 'write-off', the amount of damages would be the difference between the market value the car would have had it not got that particular history and the lower value it currently has.

QUESTION 8

George is a well-known dealer in antique vases. On 1 March, he went into China Emporium and asked the shop assistant if they had anything special. He was shown a vase described by the shop assistant as a 'Xing' vase and, after examining it behind a glass case, George agreed to buy it for £3,500 and took the vase with him. George was very pleased with the purchase because he had a customer who would pay handsomely for such a vase.

On 12 March, George left the vase with his customer to see if he would be interested in buying it for £4,000. The vase was returned two days later because it emerged that it was not genuine and that it was worth less than £250. A week later, during a dinner party, George discovered that water leaked from the vase which he was using to display a bunch of flowers.

George contacted China Emporium immediately, demanding his money back, and was told that it was not the shop's policy to make refunds in any circumstances.

▶ Advise George.

Answer Plan

The central issue in advising George is whether he is better off arguing that the pre-contractual statement that the vase was a 'Xing' vase had become part of the contract or suing for misrepresentation. The main points that need to be considered are as follows:

- ❖ China Emporium's policy about not refunding money (was this part of the contract anyway?);
- ❖ description: s 13 of the **Sale of Goods Act 1979**;
- ❖ satisfactory quality: s 14(2);
- ❖ fitness for purpose: s 14(3);

- ❖ misrepresentation, common law and the **Misrepresentation Act 1967**;
- ❖ when a buyer loses the right to reject goods (acceptance/affirmation);
- ❖ remedies.

ANSWER

George has bought a vase which he now wishes to return and has been told that he is not entitled to a refund of the purchase price. It is clear that any attempt to restrict or limit liability is subject to the strict requirements of incorporation. China Emporium's policy of refusing refunds in any circumstances cannot be effective to prevent George from pursuing the matter against them if a term to that effect has not been incorporated into their contract. We are not told what the express terms and conditions were under the contract, or whether reasonable notice of the policy had been given before or at the time of the contract. Indeed, if there was such a notice displayed, perhaps in the shop, then such a term will be incorporated within their contract even if George did not read it. Assuming that there was no such notice, China Emporium is not entitled to rely on a policy which has not been disclosed to George, and the question of whether or not the policy is reasonable is not in issue. If there were such a notice, it would probably be ineffective by virtue of the **Unfair Contract Terms Act 1977**

It is clear that George was not dealing as a consumer. Thus, the amendments to the law made by the **Sale and Supply of Goods to Consumers Regulations 2002** do not apply. Whether George has the right to return the vase will depend on finding a breach of a term of the contract or an actionable misrepresentation. There are four possible grounds here:

- ❖ description;
- ❖ satisfactory quality;
- ❖ fitness for purpose;
- ❖ misrepresentation.

DESCRIPTION

The relevant description in this case is that it was a 'Xing' vase. **Section 13** of the **Sale of Goods Act 1979** states that where goods are sold by reference to a description, it is an implied term that the goods should correspond with the description. In considering whether the sale is one by description, the court will have regard to *Harlingdon and Leinster v Christopher Hull Fine Art Ltd* (1990), that is, whether the seller in making the description has held himself out as having special knowledge and whether the buyer has relied on that description. In that case, a painting was sold described by art dealers, who were not experts in German art, as one by the German painter Gabriele Münter. The buyer, who did not make further inquiries but was an expert in German art, bought the painting for £6,000. It later transpired that the painting was a fake, worth less than £100, and the buyer rejected the painting on the ground that it did not comply with its description. The Court of Appeal held that the sale was not one by description since the description was not influential in the sale.

Applying the *Harlingdon* case to the question, although we are told that George is a well-known dealer in antique vases, we are not told whether China Emporium, with its name, was a known expert in this type of vase. Only if it was within the reasonable contemplation of the parties that George would rely upon the description 'Xing' could there be a sale by description. If China Emporium was, unlike the art dealers in *Harlingdon*, knowledgeable in 'Xing' vases, or held itself out to be, George would be entitled to reject the vase and claim damages.

We are told that George examined the vase before agreeing to buy it. A sale of goods is not, however, prevented from being a sale by description solely because the buyer himself selects the goods (**s 13(3)** and *Beale v Taylor* (1967)).

SATISFACTORY QUALITY

China Emporium clearly sells in the course of business so the implied term in **s 14(2)** applies. The goods will not be of satisfactory quality if they do not meet the standard a reasonable person would regard as satisfactory, taking account of the price, any description and all other relevant circumstances (**s 14(2A)**). One relevant aspect of their quality is their fitness for all the purposes for which goods of the kind in question are commonly supplied. The issue which needs to be looked at here is whether the vase was fit for the purposes for which it might commonly be supplied. George paid £3,500 for the vase. It is reasonable to assume that most people paying this high price for a vase will be buying it as an investment or for its resale value. Thus, the vase should be of satisfactory quality as an investment, but what of the fact that the vase is only worth £250? The Court of Appeal considered this point in the *Harlingdon* case, and Nourse LJ's view was that the purpose or purposes for which goods of this kind are commonly bought are the 'aesthetic appreciation of the owner or anyone else he permits to enjoy the experience'. Thus, even if there was a defect in the quality of the vase, it was not one which made it 'unsaleable'. The question of whether goods are reasonably fit for resale cannot depend on whether they can or cannot be resold without making a loss. The test is an objective one, not dependent on the purpose for which George himself required the vase. It seems, therefore, that since most people would have bought the vase for its aesthetic appreciation, the fact that it was not a 'Xing' vase did not make the vase unfit for aesthetic appreciation which, despite its value being so much lower than the price, did not mean that the goods were of unsatisfactory quality.

We are told that George subsequently discovers that the vase leaks when he uses it to display a bunch of flowers. Can George claim that this rendered the vase of unsatisfactory quality? Before the 1994 amendments to **s 14**, there was authority that the term as to merchantable quality did not require that the goods were reasonably fit for all the purposes for which goods of that description were commonly supplied, and that it was sufficient if they were fit for one of those purposes (*Aswan v Lupdine* (1987)). Now, however, **s 14(2B)** provides that one aspect of the quality of the goods is their fitness for all the purposes for which goods of that kind are commonly supplied. Certainly, vases are commonly supplied for use as display containers holding fresh flowers and water. It is difficult to know whether that is one of the purposes for which 'Xing' vases are commonly supplied. If it is, then the fact that the vase leaks suggests that it is not of satisfactory quality. If such vases are, however, commonly supplied for only one purpose, aesthetic appreciation (without containing fresh flowers), then the fact that it leaks will not make it of unsatisfactory quality.

FITNESS FOR PURPOSE

Section 14(3) provides that where goods are required for a particular purpose which has been made known to the seller, there is an implied term that the goods should be reasonably fit for that purpose. This will not apply if George did not rely or it was unreasonable for George to rely on China Emporium's skill and judgement in supplying the goods. In relation to the problem, two questions therefore need to be asked. First, did George make known to China Emporium the exact purpose for which the vase would be required? Second, if so, was it reasonable for him to rely on China Emporium's skill and judgement? The answer to the first question seems likely to be 'yes', as George is a well-known dealer and it is therefore reasonable to assume that if China Emporium is aware of this, it would also know that George would have bought the vase for resale as an antique item. The answer to the second question, however, is likely to be 'no', because, as was discussed in relation to 'description' (above), as between the parties George was the expert in 'Xing' vases and it would be unreasonable for him to rely on China Emporium's skill and judgement. It seems, therefore, that China Emporium is not liable under **s 14(3)**.

MISREPRESENTATION

The false statement that the vase was a 'Xing' vase may amount to an actionable misrepresentation, entitling George to rescind the contract and claim damages. The requirements of an actionable misrepresentation are that there was a statement of an existing fact by one party which induced the other party to enter the contract. It must be a statement of fact and not opinion, although an opinion which is not honestly held at the time or is based on facts which the maker of the statement ought to have known may be actionable.

It is clear from this question that the shop assistant did describe the vase as a 'Xing' vase. George's reliance on this description does not have to be reasonable (*Museprime Properties v Adhill* (1990)). The court held in the *Museprime Properties* case that the reasonableness of the reliance was relevant to determining whether there was actual reliance, but that the test of reliance is subjective (the more unreasonable the reliance, the less likely the court is to believe that it did actually affect the buyer's decision to enter into the contract). It is also clear that the statement does not have to be the sole reason for entering into the contract: it is sufficient that it was one reason (*Edgington v Fitzmaurice* (1885)). It may be, therefore, that George has a stronger claim in misrepresentation than under the implied conditions under the **Sale of Goods Act**.

Once it has been established that an actionable misrepresentation has been made, the remedies will depend on whether the misrepresentation was made innocently, negligently or fraudulently.[3] It is unlikely that the shop assistant will have made the statement that it was a 'Xing' vase fraudulently. Either he made it innocently (that is, in genuine ignorance of the fact that it was untrue) or negligently (that is, he had no reasonable grounds for believing that the statement was true) under **s 2(1)** of the **Misrepresentation Act 1967**.[4] If the misrepresentation was made innocently, George will be entitled to rescission of the contract. If the misrepresentation was made negligently, George will be entitled not only to rescission, but may recover for all losses caused by the misrepresentation, unrestricted by the rules of remoteness (*Royscot Trust Ltd v Rogerson* (1991)). Moreover, following *Parabola Investments v Browallia* (2009), he will be entitled to lost profits.

One final point which needs to be made is that whether George decides to pursue the matter for breach of contract or for misrepresentation may depend on the fact that it was some three weeks after he bought the vase that he tried to reject the goods against China Emporium. Any action for breach of contract is subject to the rules of acceptance under **s 35** of the **Sale of Goods Act** which, *inter alia*, deems the buyer to have accepted the

....

3   A detailed knowledge of misrepresentation is not usually required on commercial law courses, but bear in mind that the examiner is entitled to test you on the general principles of contract law.

4   It is possible, of course, to bring the action under the common law, that is, under the rule in *Hedley Byrne v Heller* (1964). Since the **Misrepresentation Act 1967**, however, s 2(1) is the preferable cause of action because then the burden of proof is on the defendant to show that there were reasonable grounds for believing that the statement was true.

goods if, after a lapse of reasonable time, he retains the goods without intimating to the seller that he rejects them. In *Bernstein v Pamson Motors* (1987), a period of three weeks was regarded as beyond a reasonable time in which to examine a motor car. Since then, **s 35** has been amended and a reasonable period now will normally include a reasonable opportunity for the buyer to examine the goods for the purpose of ascertaining whether they conform to the contract. This may well mean that the reasonable period of time before the buyer is taken to have accepted the goods will be longer than previously (*Clegg v Andersson* (2003)). George had in fact had the vase for over three weeks before giving notice of rejection. Furthermore, he discovered after two weeks that it was not a 'Xing' vase. Assuming that that is a breach of condition, it is arguable that keeping it a further week afterwards before rejecting it amounts to acceptance. If, however, he was using that week in order to have experts examine it to confirm whether or not it was a 'Xing' vase (although we are told nothing to suggest that he was), that would have the effect of lengthening the reasonable period of time (*Truk v Tokmakidis* (2000)). If he has accepted the goods, then his only remedy for breach of contract would be a claim for damages, the amount of which would depend greatly on whether, on the one hand, he could establish a breach of contract arising out of the description 'Xing' vase or, on the other, was able only to rely on the fact that the vase leaked.

An action in misrepresentation is not subject to the acceptance rules and a buyer is only deemed to have lost his right to rescind if he has affirmed the contract which, after three weeks, it may be held that he has done. If it were established that the misrepresentation were fraudulent, then time would begin to run only from when George discovered the truth. It seems that George knew of the lack of authenticity of the vase around 14 March and it was only a week later that he contacted China Emporium. Thus, if it was a fraudulent misrepresentation, George would be able to rescind the contract. He would in any case be entitled to damages for misrepresentation, unless China Emporium could show that it had reasonable grounds to believe it was a 'Xing' vase.

QUESTION 9

Janet wants to buy a washing machine. She walks into a branch of Machines-R-Us Ltd and asks Fred, the sales assistant, for his advice. She tells him that she needs a machine that has a quick wash cycle. Fred recommended the Helper because, on average, it requires just 30 minutes for a wash cycle at 50 degrees Celsius. The machine is delivered later that day.

It turns out that for a wash cycle at 50 degrees Celsius the machine in fact requires 60 minutes. Two weeks later, the machine is beginning to make funny noises and starts belching smoke. The load it is washing at the time is completely destroyed. When Janet phones Fred to ask for her money back, Fred tells her that the contract Janet signed included a clause stating: 'All conditions relating to the quality or condition of any machine are hereby excluded. The seller accepts no liability in respect of any statements made prior to the contract unless such statements have been put in writing.'

▸ **Advise Janet.**

Answer Plan

The issues raised in this question are:

❖ liability for breach of the conditions as to satisfactory quality and fitness for purpose;

❖ liability (for an express term and/or misrepresentation) arising out of the statement about the washing machine needing only 30 minutes for a wash cycle;

❖ the remedies available to the buyer and, in particular, whether there has been acceptance of the goods so as to preclude rejection;

❖ the exclusion clause. The method of dealing with it is, after quickly acknowledging that it was incorporated into the contract, to deal with the interpretation of the clause and then the effect of the **Unfair Contract Terms Act 1977** and the **Unfair Terms in Consumer Contracts Regulations 1999**.

ANSWER

This question raises issues of liability for express and implied terms of the contract and the extent of any remedies available to Janet, bearing in mind the seller has purported to exclude liability.

EXPRESS TERM

When Janet told Fred she needed a washing machine capable of a quick wash cycle, he recommended the Helper because, he said, it needed just 30 minutes for a wash cycle. This may have amounted to an express term. Assuming it was an express term of the contract, it is clear that that express term was broken in Janet's case because the wash cycle, in fact, took 60 minutes.

SATISFACTORY QUALITY

Because Machines-R-Us sells in the course of business, terms regarding satisfactory quality and fitness for purpose are implied as conditions into the sale contract with Janet. Under **s 14(2)** of the **Sale of Goods Act 1979** there is an implied condition that goods sold should be of satisfactory quality. No reasonable person would regard the washing machine as satisfactory if after such a short period of time (two weeks) it makes funny noises and starts belching smoke. It is unlikely that Fred specifically drew this defect to Janet's attention before the contract was made. We are not told whether Janet made a pre-purchase examination of the washing machine, as regards any defect which 'that' examination ought to have revealed. Even if she did examine the machine, it is unlikely this would have revealed the defect. It seems therefore that Janet can rely upon the condition in **s 14(2)**. The machine belched fumes, ruining the load it was washing at the time. A reasonable person would not regard the machine as satisfactory, taking account of any description given to the goods, the price and any other relevant circumstances (**s 14(2A)**). We are not told what price Janet paid for the machine nor whether it was bought as new or second-hand goods. The general approach is that the higher the price paid, particularly for new goods, the higher the standard the buyer can expect. However, in Janet's case, the defects are sufficiently serious to render even second-hand goods of less than satisfactory quality.[5] Therefore, it is submitted that Janet has a valid claim under **s 14(2)**.

FITNESS FOR PURPOSE

Janet's claim in respect of the defects discussed above might equally be made under **s 14(3)**. Since the description of the goods ('washing machine') points to one purpose only, the washing machine must be fit for that particular purpose (*Preist v Last* (1903)) and it is clear that the defects already being relied upon under **s 14(2)** render the washing machine not reasonably fit for that purpose and this a breach of the implied condition in **s 14(3)**. In addition, Janet told Fred that she needs a machine that has a quick wash cycle. The machine recommended to her was not capable of this. Since it is reasonable for Janet to place reliance upon Fred's skill and judgement in respect of his recommendation, Janet will have a claim under **s 14(3)**.

EXCLUSION CLAUSE

Like any exclusion clause, the clause in this case will not have any effect unless it satisfies each of the following requirements:

❖ it was incorporated into the contract;
❖ as a matter of interpretation, the wording of the clause is effective to exclude liability which otherwise the seller would incur;
❖ the clause is not rendered invalid by either the **Unfair Contract Terms Act 1977** or the **Unfair Terms in Consumer Contracts Regulations 1999**.

Clearly, in the present case, the first of these requirements is satisfied as we are told that Janet had signed the contract (*L'Estrange v Graucob* (1934)).

---

5   *Crowther v Shannon Motors* (1975).

INTERPRETATION OF THE CLAUSE

As regards the second requirement, the first half of the clause would clearly exclude liability for breach of the implied condition as to satisfactory quality in **s 14** of the **Sale of Goods Act 1979**. The words of the clause are clear and there is no longer any presumption (at common law) that the clear words of a clause are not to be given effect, and that is so even if they clearly purport to exclude what used to be referred to as a fundamental breach of contract (*Photo Productions v Securicor Transport* (1980)). Does it also exclude liability for the condition of fitness of purpose? The *contra proferentem* rule of construction which the courts use in construing exclusion clauses requires that, where a clause is truly ambiguous, the meaning which gives the clause the lesser effect is adopted. This is the rule as applied over the years in such cases as *Wallis and Wells v Pratt and Haynes* (1911) and *Andrews v Singer* (1934). Nothing in the *Photo Productions* case does away with the *contra proferentem* rule in cases of true ambiguity. Referring to the wording of the clause, the condition as to fitness is excluded if it relates to the 'quality or condition' of a machine. Clearly, on the facts of the problem given, it is the quality that is in issue and, undoubtedly, the quality of a washing machine can affect its fitness for a particular purpose. However, the fitness for purpose condition implied by **s 14(3)** is not confined to matters of quality or condition. A machine can be of excellent quality and in excellent condition and still not be fit for a particular purpose for which the buyer has indicated she wants it. Here, Janet told Fred that she wants a machine capable of quick wash cycles. If the clause in issue here were held to exclude the condition as to fitness for purpose, it would rule it out in the latter situation, as well as where the unfitness is caused by defects in quality or condition. Applying the *contra proferentem* rule, therefore, it seems likely that a court would hold that the fitness for purpose condition was not excluded.

It appears then that the first sentence of the clause, as a matter of interpretation, does exclude liability for breach of the condition as to satisfactory quality, but may well not do so as regards the condition of fitness for purpose.

Let us turn to the matter of Machines-R-Us's possible liability in respect of the pre-contract statement about the washing machine being capable of a 30-minute wash cycle. The latter part of the clause would appear to exclude that liability, since there is no indication that Fred's statement was put into writing. There is, however, an argument which might prevent such a conclusion. It is possible that Fred's words might give rise to liability for breach of an express term of the contract (*Andrews v Hopkinson* (1957)). The clause refers to statements made 'prior to the contract'. It does not refer to statements which are part of the contract itself, which an express term – even one not reduced to writing – would undoubtedly be. So it might be argued that the clause was not intended to exclude express terms. The point is clearly an arguable one, since it could alternatively be said that the intention of the clause is to exclude all liability in respect of pre-contract statements, including terms of the contract itself, unless those terms are in writing.

UNFAIR CONTRACT TERMS ACT 1977

Assuming that the clause is effective at common law to exclude at least some possible liabilities, is it robbed of that effect by the **Unfair Contract Terms Act (UCTA) 1977**? This Act applies differently to different heads of liability. **Section 6** deals with the clause insofar as it purports to exclude liability for breach of the implied conditions in **s 14** of the **Sale of Goods Act 1979**. Since Janet dealt as a consumer in buying the washing machine, neither of those implied terms can be excluded.

Let us turn to the effect of the **UCTA** on the clause insofar as it purports to exclude liability for breach of unwritten express terms of the contract. The clause is subject to the requirement of reasonableness. This is provided for by **s 3** of the **UCTA**. **Section 3** will apply since it appears that the clause in question is one of Machines-R-Us's standard terms. Technically, **s 3** does not refer to **Sched 2** which offers guidelines as to whether or not a clause is reasonable. However, there is little doubt that similar considerations will be applied. The court is very likely to consider the clause as a whole in deciding whether it satisfies the requirement of reasonableness.

In any case where that requirement is under consideration, account needs to be taken of the factor, highlighted in the cases, that a clause which does not merely limit liability but purports totally to exclude it is much less likely to satisfy the requirement of reasonableness (compare *Mitchell v Finney Lock Seeds* (1983) and *Ailsa Craig Fishing v Malvern Fishing* (1983)). It has already been said that perhaps the clause in Janet's case will, on its wording, be held not to exclude liability for the condition as to fitness for purpose or for breach of an express term of the contract. Even so, in relation to those liabilities which it does purport to exclude, its exclusion of liability is complete. This fact strengthens the argument that the clause fails to satisfy the requirement of reasonableness.

UNFAIR TERMS IN CONSUMER CONTRACTS REGULATIONS 1999

Because Janet has contracted as a consumer, the **1999 Regulations** will apply to her contract with Machines-R-Us (**reg 4**). The effect of these Regulations will render the exclusion clause of no effect since, contrary to a requirement of good faith, the clause causes a significant imbalance in the parties' rights and obligations to the detriment of the consumer. The exclusion clause in question is likely to be declared 'unfair'.

REMEDIES

For any breach of contract, there is a right to claim damages. Because the **Sale and Supply of Goods to Consumers Regulations 2002** are in force, Janet has additional rights if an item purchased is not of satisfactory quality or not reasonably fit for its purpose. She is in principle entitled to claim a remedy of repair or of replacement of the item, unless such a claim would be disproportionate. If such a claim would be disproportionate or, alternatively, if such a claim is made and not complied with within a reasonable time, then Janet is entitled to a reduction in the price or to rescind the contract. It appears that these additional rights are not what Janet wishes to claim for. We are told that she wants to reject the machine. Assuming that there was breach of the implied term in either **s 14(2)** or **s 14(3)**, Janet undoubtedly has a right of rejection, since both of those terms are implied *conditions*. The same is not necessarily true of the express term (that the wash cycle is complete in 30 minutes), since it would have to be decided whether the parties intended it to be a condition, that is, a term any breach of which would give Janet the right to reject the goods and regard the contract as repudiated. The tendency of the courts is not to regard as a condition any express term (other than one as to the time of delivery), unless the parties have very clearly indicated it (*Cehave v Bremer, The Hansa Nord* (1976)). Thus, the test of whether Janet had any right of rejection/repudiation for breach of the express term depends upon whether the breach was sufficient to deprive Janet of substantially the whole of the benefit of the contract (*Hong Kong Fir v Kawasaki Kisen* (1962)). It is possible that the fact that the machine needs more than 30 minutes to complete the wash cycle was not sufficiently serious.

Assuming that Janet was, because of the breach of the conditions in **s 14**, within her rights in rejecting the machine and demanding the return of the price, she will nevertheless have lost that right if, by the time she phones Fred, she had already 'accepted' the machine within the meaning of **s 35**. Janet rejected the machine about two weeks after taking delivery. After a similar period of time, the buyer in *Bernstein v Pamson Motors* (1987) was held to have accepted a car. Even under the law as it then stood, that decision was controversial. Since then, however, **s 35** has been amended so that, in determining what is a reasonable length of time, it is relevant to ask whether the buyer has had a reasonable opportunity to examine the goods for the purpose of ascertaining whether they comply with the contract. It is thus arguable that Janet had not, in just two weeks, had the washing machine long enough to have examined it for that purpose.

CONCLUSION

In conclusion, whatever interpretation is held to be the correct construction of the clause, it seems very likely that the clause will not satisfy the requirement of reasonableness in the **Unfair Contract Terms Act** nor 'fair' under the **Unfair Terms in Consumer Contracts Regulations**. It will therefore be of no effect. Consequently, Janet is entitled to the return of the machine's purchase price. She may also claim damages, in particular for the load the machine was washing but which was completely destroyed. Such damages would not be too remote under the rule in *Hadley v Baxendale* (1854).

QUESTION 10

Katie, in the course of her business, agreed to buy from Bennet '2,000 Christmas trees, Scots Pine, five feet to six feet high, fair average quality for the season, packed 50 to a pallet, delivery to Katie's premises on 10–12 December'. The contract contained an exclusion clause which satisfied the requirement of reasonableness in the **Unfair Contract Terms Act 1977** and which excluded liability for any breach of the statutory implied conditions as to satisfactory quality and fitness for purpose. On 12 December, Bennet tenders delivery to Katie.

Consider the legal position on 12 December in each of the following alternative situations:

(a) 90% of the trees are between five feet and six feet high but 5% of them are slightly less than five feet and 5% are slightly over six feet high;

(b) a number of the trees are unevenly tapered in shape and are thus not 'fair average quality for the season';

(c) the trees are packed 75 to a pallet;

(d) the delivery tendered is of 2,020 trees.

Answer Plan
This question, with its exclusion clause, plainly effective to exclude the implied conditions as to satisfactory quality and fitness for purpose, is clearly concentrated on the implied condition as to description and to the (often) related issues that arise in relation to delivery of the wrong contract quantity or of contract goods mixed with non-contract goods. A simple approach here is to deal with each numbered part of the question in turn, taking care to refer back where necessary to an answer already given rather than to repeat issues that are the same in relation to the different parts of the question.

ANSWER

(A)
The fact that 10% of the trees are outside the definition of 'five feet to six feet high' could cause the seller to be in breach of the condition, implied by **s 13** of the **Sale of**

Goods Act 1979, that the goods must correspond with their description. So far as we are informed, the shortness or extra length does not render the trees of any less quality or likely to be less fit for any purpose for which Katie had indicated to Bennet that she wanted them. It seems clear that the description 'five feet to six feet high' was part of the contract description and thus any failure to comply would be a breach of the condition in **s 13**. We are not told how short of five feet or how much in excess of six feet the non-conforming trees measured, except that we are told that the deviation was 'slight'. Bennet might seek to invoke the maxim *de minimis non curat lex* and thus argue that any deviation was so small that it ought to be ignored. However, the measurements of five feet to six feet, given in the contract description, are precise measurements and it has been held by the House of Lords that a contract requirement on the seller to supply staves 'half an inch thick' was exactly that and that supplying staves up to nine-sixteenths of an inch thick was a breach of the implied condition implied by **s 13** (*Arcos v Ronaasen* (1933)). If the seller had wished for a margin, he should have stipulated for it in his contract. In the present case, that reasoning can be taken further by the observation that there *was* a margin stipulated for in the contract, that is, anything from five to six feet high. Thus, it seems that Bennet is in breach of the condition in **s 13**.

Normally, a breach of condition entitles the buyer to reject the goods. In the case of a breach of the conditions in **ss 13–15** of the **Sale of Goods Act**, however, this is subject to an exception which applies where (like Katie) the buyer is not dealing as a consumer. This exception means that Katie will not be entitled to reject the goods if the breach was so slight that it would be unreasonable for her to reject them (**s 15A**). Although we are told that some of the trees were 'slightly' over or under the contract height, we are not given enough facts to know if **s 15A** does apply – and it is for Bennet, the seller, to show that it does. If it does not apply, then Katie has a whole range of options open to her. Firstly, she could waive her right to reject the goods (which would leave her in exactly the same position as if **s 15A** does apply) and simply claim damages for her loss, if any, arising from the fact that some of the trees were too short and some too long. If she suffered no damage or loss because of that, then she would be entitled only to nominal damages. Secondly, she could reject the whole consignment and, assuming that Bennet is unable to supply a complete consignment of complying trees by the end of the contractual delivery deadline (12 December), she could claim damages which would be assessed on the difference between what she was contracted to pay Bennet and the market price (if higher) on 12 December of 1,000 trees matching the contract description (**s 51**). Thirdly, Katie could accept those trees which did conform to the contract description and reject some or all of the 10% which did not (**s 35A**). In this scenario, she must pay for those she accepts *pro rata* at the contract rate. She will also be able to claim damages in relation to the 10% she rejects, the damages being the difference between the contract price for the number of rejected trees and, if higher, the market price on 12 December for that number of trees conforming to the contract description.

(B)

Given the facts that (i) Katie was not dealing as a consumer, and (ii) the exclusion clause satisfies the requirement of reasonableness, the implied conditions as to satisfactory quality and fitness for purpose cannot be relied upon by Katie. Unless there is some special statutory provision relating to Christmas trees or to trees, there are no other implied conditions as to quality (s 14(1)). That leaves two possible causes of action available to Katie. The first is that Bennet is in breach of the condition as to description, in that the trees do not conform to the contract requirement that they be of 'fair average quality for the season'. However, it seems unlikely that the court would regard those words as part of the contract 'description' (*Ashington Piggeries v Hill* (1972)). This is because the contract description does not normally include quality requirements but is confined to those elements in the contractual requirements which help to 'identify' the goods. The result of this, combined with the exclusion clause, is that reliance on the implied conditions as to description and quality is ruled out. This means that Katie is thrown back on her other possible cause of action, namely, a claim for breach of an *express* term of the contract, that is, a term that the trees be of fair average quality for the season. This term is unlikely, however, to be regarded by the court as a condition of the contract since the parties have not, it appears, indicated that it was their intention that any breach of the term would entitle Katie to regard the contract as repudiated. That being so, the term is only a warranty (or intermediate term) of the contract and Katie could not regard the contract as repudiated by a breach of that term unless the breach deprived Katie of 'substantially the whole benefit' of the contract (*Hong Kong Fir v Kawasaki Kisen* (1962); *Cehave v Bremer* (1976)). We are told of neither the severity of the poor shape of the trees nor of the number affected. If more than half are affected and they are severely misshapen and if, as a result, Katie cannot sell them without damaging her own commercial reputation, then the court would very likely be prepared to regard the breach as a repudiatory one. If the breach is sufficiently severe to amount to a repudiatory breach, then Katie is entitled to accept those which conform to the contract and to reject some or all of those which do not. Whether Katie refuses to accept all or just some of the goods, the risk for her is that the court may subsequently hold that the breach did not deprive her of substantially the whole benefit of the contract. In that case, then, Katie would herself be in breach of contract for refusing to take delivery and would be liable to Bennet for non-acceptance of the goods. The measure of damages would be the difference between the contract price for the number of trees rejected and the market price, if lower, on 12 December. Katie should therefore be advised to consider accepting the trees and reselling them for whatever she can get. She would in those circumstances be able to claim damages for breach of the express term that the trees be of fair average quality for the season. Her measure of damages would, *prima facie*, be the difference in the value to her of the trees actually delivered and the higher value they would have had if they had been of fair average quality for the season (**s 53(3)**).

(C)

Even if the fact that the trees are packed 75 instead of 50 to a pallet renders them of unsatisfactory quality or unfit for their purpose, Katie will be unable to rely upon the implied conditions in **s 14** of the **Sale of Goods Act**, for the reasons just given in relation to the contract requirement that the trees be of fair average quality for the season. Again, therefore, Katie has two possible causes of action. The first is for breach of an express term of the contract and the second is for breach of the implied condition as to description. As regards the former, again, it seems unlikely that the court would construe the express term as a condition of the contract and therefore, again, any right of Katie to regard the contract as repudiated (and, hence, to reject the goods) must depend upon whether the breach (the trees being packed 75 instead of 50 to a pallet) deprives Katie of substantially the whole benefit of the contract. Unless there are some unusual facts which are not disclosed by the words of the problem as set, it seems unlikely that Katie has suffered such a breach. Thus, Katie's only right is to claim damages for breach of the express term, on the same basis as just explained in relation to the requirement that the trees be of fair average quality for the season. That is so, unless she can claim that Bennet is in breach of the condition as to description in **s 13**. Such a claim depends upon the requirement 'packed 50 to a pallet' being accepted by the court as being part of the contract 'description'. In *Re Moore and Landauer* (1921), a somewhat similar requirement was accepted by the Court of Appeal as being part of the contract description. This has the result that any deviation (even if quite a small one) from the requirement is a breach of condition and entitles the buyer to reject the goods. In *Re Moore and Landauer*, the buyer was held entitled to reject a consignment of tinned fruit because although the correct contract quantity had been delivered, some of them were packed in cases of 24 tins instead of (as the contract required) in cases of 30 tins. That decision has, however, since been doubted in the House of Lords (*Reardon Smith Line v Hansen Tangen* (1976)). It is clear now that the courts are unlikely to find that an express term of the contract comprises part of the contract description unless it helps to 'identify' the goods. This means that the court is highly unlikely to regard the requirement that the trees be packed 50 to a pallet as anything other than a warranty (or intermediate term) of the contract. Furthermore, **s 35A** has been added to the **Sale of Goods Act 1979** by the **Sale and Supply of Goods Act 1994** with the result that, even if there has been a breach of condition, Katie has no right to reject the goods if the breach was so slight that it would be unreasonable for her to reject them. Katie therefore should be advised not to reject the trees but to accept them and to claim damages for any loss as a result of the trees being packed 75 to a pallet.

(D)

This question seems no more than a straightforward example of the seller tendering more than the contract quantity. However, it must also inevitably be that the trees are not all 'packed 50 to a pallet', since 2,020 is not divisible by 50! For a discussion of that aspect of the matter, see the answer to (c) above. Leaving that issue aside, there remains the matter of the extra quantity. The normal rules on over-supply are as follows. Firstly, Katie can reject all the goods for breach of the condition to supply 2,000 trees (s 30(2)). Secondly, she can accept the contract quantity and reject the surplus ten (s 30(2)). Thirdly, she could accept the lot and pay for the extra *pro rata* at the contract rate (s 30(3)). However, the operation of s 30 is subject to any custom and practice between the parties and to any usage of the trade (s 30(5)). Even if there is no such relevant custom, practice or usage, the court may well regard the over-supply of 20 trees (that is, a mere 1% of the contract quantity) as *de minimis*. In that case, Katie has suffered no breach and will be required to pay nothing for the extra ten trees.

> ### Common Pitfalls ✕
> This question includes a lot of points. A good answer must acknowledge each of the points raised and must not concentrate on some of the issues to the exclusion of the others.

QUESTION 11

Shakespeare agreed to sell to Watson 900 pine desks. The contract required delivery to be made in three equal instalments on 20 January, 25 January and 30 January. It also contained the clause 'This entire contract is governed by English law'. On 20 January, Shakespeare delivered 280 pine desks, mistakenly including 20 teak desks in the consignment. Today is 25 January and Shakespeare has delivered 295 pine desks. Watson has now found a cheaper supplier and wishes to return all the desks delivered so far and to cancel delivery of the third consignment.

▶ Advise Watson.

What difference, if any, would it have made to your advice if today is 3 February and Shakespeare has only just delivered the second consignment?

Answer Plan

There are two particular issues in the question which, on the facts given, it is impossible to determine for sure. These are 'has Watson accepted the first consignment within the meaning of **s 35** of the **Sale of Goods Act 1979**?' and 'is the contract severable or entire?'. Because of this, it is important not just to point these things out, but also to identify the position in the different possible eventualities. Thus, it is essential to use that wonderful word 'if', which is so often useful to examinees in law examinations.

As the question gives a story of two defective deliveries, the structure adopted for the answer here is to deal with them each in turn and then, at the end, to deal with the rider to the question.

ANSWER

It is proposed to deal initially with the effect of the defective first delivery five days ago and then with the effect of today's defective delivery.

THE FIRST DELIVERY

When Shakespeare delivered the first consignment, he was in breach of contract in one or both of two respects. First, 20 of the desks were not pine and therefore did not comply with what must have been part of the contract description. That put Shakespeare in breach of the condition implied by **s 13** of the **Sale of Goods Act 1979**. Secondly, one can say that Shakespeare delivered too small a quantity of the contract goods (that is, pine desks). Either way, there has been a breach of condition, giving the buyer the right to reject the goods (see **s 30(1)** of the **1979 Act**) and this, we are told, is what Watson wishes to do. There are, however, two problems with that. Firstly, it is not clear whether the contract is a severable one. If it is, the defective first delivery may not give Watson the right to reject the later two consignments. Secondly, it is possible that Watson may have lost his right to reject the goods because he may be held to have 'accepted' the first defective delivery.

To take the second of these issues first, a buyer who accepts the goods or part of them is precluded from rejecting the goods (**s 11(4)** of the **Sale of Goods Act 1979**). **Section 35** of the **1979 Act** states three things which will amount to acceptance. The problem simply gives us no information on the first two; we are therefore unable to state whether Watson has either intimated to Shakespeare his acceptance of the goods or else done any act inconsistent with rejecting them. As to the third thing (**s 35(4)**) listed in **s 35**, it is debatable whether a lapse of a reasonable length of time has occurred.

Watson has had the desks for five days. It is true that a reasonable period of time will not have elapsed if Watson has not had the goods long enough to have been able to examine them to see if they conform with the contract. However, it must have been fairly obvious almost immediately upon delivery that: (a) 20 of the desks were missing; and (b) 20 of those which were delivered were teak and not pine. It is arguable in those circumstances that five days is more than a reasonable period of time in which to reject. Certainly, three weeks was held to be more than a reasonable period of time in the first instance decision (on the very different facts of a defective motor car) in *Bernstein v Pamson Motors* (1987). We are not told what were the provisions of the contract regarding the time of payment. If a period of, say, one month was allowed for Watson to pay, then it may be that a reasonable period of time would be held to last at least until the deadline for payment (*Truk v Tokmakidis* (2000)).

Since **s 35** was amended, there is now a right of partial rejection which would allow Watson to reject the desks which do not conform to the contract and to accept the rest (the other 260). However, it is clear from the facts that Watson would prefer to reject the lot. Thus, assuming that Watson has not 'accepted' the first consignment, he will have the right to reject that consignment (the whole of it). Whether that gives him the right to reject the later consignments also depends upon whether the contract is an entire contract or is a severable one. If it is not severable, then the breach of condition entitles Watson to reject all consignments. The test of whether a contract is severable is one of construction (interpretation) of the contract, that is, one is trying to discover from the words of the contract what was the intention of the parties. Was it their intention that a breach in relation to one consignment should entitle the purchaser to reject all? If not, then the contract is severable – see generally *Jackson v Rotax Motor and Cycle Co* (1910). The fact that the desks were to be delivered in instalments is some evidence that the contract was severable. We are not told, however, whether under the contract, the consignments were each to be paid for separately. If they were, then that would be strong evidence that the contract was severable. It may be argued that the parties had themselves clearly labelled the contract as not being severable but as being entire, because of the clause in the contract which read that the 'entire' contract was governed by English law. It is submitted, however, that this clause is nothing more than a choice of law clause and that the word 'entire', in the particular context of that clause, does not bear upon whether the contract was severable, but merely means that all of the contract, as opposed to part of it, was to be governed by English law.

If Watson has not 'accepted' the first consignment and if the contract is not severable, then he is entitled to reject all the goods, including the later two consignments. If he has not 'accepted' the first consignment and the contract is severable, then he may still be able to regard the whole contract as repudiated and thus be able to reject the two later consignments. Whether the whole contract is repudiated depends upon the following two factors: (a) the ratio that the breach bore quantitatively to the whole contract; and (b) the likelihood of the breach being repeated in later instalments (*Maple Flock Co v Universal Furniture Products* (1934)). This is not so easy to determine. At the time that the breach occurs, one cannot tell anything about the second of these factors. As to the first, it could be said that the breach is fairly small in relation to the whole contract. First, it relates to only one consignment out of the three and, within that consignment, it affects only a small proportion of the total quantity of the desks.

Thus, based on the first defective delivery, one's advice to Watson would be cautious since: (a) he may have 'accepted' the goods; (b) the contract may be severable; and if it is, the *Maple Flock* test may not be satisfied so as to allow him to regard the whole contract as repudiated.

THE SECOND DELIVERY

The breach in relation to the second delivery is simply a delivery of too small a quantity. The missing five desks would appear too many for the courts to be prepared to ignore the breach on the *de minimis non curat lex* principle. Thus, it is a breach of condition.

If the contract was not severable and Watson has not 'accepted' the first consignment, then he is entitled to reject all three consignments because of the breaches of condition in relation to the first two consignments. If the contract was not severable and Watson has 'accepted' the first consignment, then the position is clouded by the fact that the effect of s 11(4) and the new s 35A is not entirely clear. **Section 35A** introduced the concept of partial rejection, allowing the buyer to reject some or all of the non-conforming goods, provided he accepted all of the conforming goods. One thing which does seem clear is that **ss 11(4)** and **35A** do not allow the buyer to reject any goods (whether conforming or not) which he has actually accepted. Thus, if the contract is not severable and Watson has 'accepted' the first consignment, he cannot now reject any of the first consignment (though he may claim damages in respect of the breaches relating to the first consignment). As regards the second consignment, he is entitled to reject any non-conforming goods, but not conforming goods. However, there are no non-conforming goods, since the only breach relating to the second consignment is a shortfall in the number of desks. **Section 30(1)** entitles the buyer to reject all the goods if a quantity less than the contract quantity is tendered. The buyer appears, however, to be precluded from exercising this right by his acceptance of the first consignment. This is the effect of s 11(4) in the case of a non-severable agreement. Although s 11(4) is subject to s 35A, the latter is of no help to the buyer in this instance. **Section 35A(1)** applies only where it is non-conforming goods which are being rejected. **Section 35A(2)** also appears to be of no help, since it applies only where the buyer has a right to reject an instalment, and that is the very issue which we have to determine (that is, does the buyer have a right to reject the second instalment?). If this seems an odd result, it is explicable on the basis that the agreement is not severable. In the case of a non-severable agreement, acceptance by the buyer of any conforming goods precludes rejection of any goods. Perhaps this makes it more likely that the courts will regard contracts for delivery in instalments as severable contracts.

If the contract was severable, then Watson would certainly be entitled to reject the second consignment because of the breach of condition in relation to that consignment, and that is so even if he had 'accepted' the first consignment; s 11(4) does not apply to severable contracts. In the event that the contract was severable, then the *Maple Flock* test again needs to be applied to determine whether Watson is entitled to reject the third instalment as well. This time, however, it seems much more likely that the test is satisfied. This is because, on two out of the three instalments, Shakespeare has made a non-conforming delivery. Thus, the ratio that the breach(es) bear quantitatively to the whole contract is much higher and would also seem to suggest a higher probability that he will repeat this with the third and last delivery. On that interpretation, Watson is entitled, even if the contract is severable, to regard the whole contract as repudiated and thus to reject the third consignment as well as the second. Whether that entitles him also to reject the first consignment is debatable. Although on its wording s 11(4) does not apply to severable contracts, it would seem unlikely that the law is such as to allow rejection of any goods which have actually been accepted. Of course, if Watson has not 'accepted' the first instalment, then the breaches relating to the first two instalments entitle him, for the reasons just given, to regard the whole contract as repudiated, to reject all the goods delivered under the first two instalments and to refuse to accept the third.

THE RIDER

Would it have made any difference if the second delivery had been made only on 3 February? This would affect the consideration of two issues discussed above. Firstly, the time lapse between the first delivery and today would be longer (that is, from 20 January to 3 February) and that would increase the likelihood that Watson would be held to have accepted the first consignment and thus be precluded from rejecting that consignment or, if the contract was not severable, any of the consignments. Secondly, it would increase the seriousness of the breach in relation to the second consignment, which would suggest that there is a greater degree of breach compared to the contract as a whole, for there would be no doubt that the breach in relation to the second consignment did indeed affect the whole of that consignment. Thus, if the contract is severable, it would be much more likely that by the time the second delivery has come, several days late and with five desks short, Shakespeare has committed a breach entitling Watson to regard the contract as repudiated and therefore to reject the third consignment immediately.

Passing of Property and Risk

INTRODUCTION

This chapter covers the passing of property and risk. It incorporates the topic of retention of title clauses, and also deals with perishing goods.

QUESTION 12

Dragonyarns plc sells silk to various garment makers on terms that require payment 30 days after delivery. About 50% of its sales are to regular customers and the rest are to 'one-off' customers. Some of its customers resell the silk, whereas other customers use it in the manufacture of dresses and other garments which are then stored or sold.

▶ Advise Dragonyarns plc on why it ought to consider incorporating a retention of title clause into its standard terms of sale and what protection such a clause might provide.

Answer Plan

The question invites an explanation of the purpose of retention of title clauses and a discussion of the effects and effectiveness of them. You should approach the question as follows:

- ❖ explain the purpose of retention of title clauses;
- ❖ deal with the passing of risk;
- ❖ state the requirements for an effective clause;
- ❖ explore the limits on effectiveness without being registered where:
  - (a) the buyer sub-sells the goods (and can the seller take an interest in the proceeds of the sub-sales?);
  - (b) the buyer pays for the goods (and what if he only makes part-payment or if the buyer owes other money to Dragonyarns plc?);
  - (c) the goods lose their identity.

ANSWER

The reason why Dragonyarns plc ought to consider incorporating a retention of title clause into its standard terms of sale is to protect itself against the risk of one of its customers becoming insolvent and hence going into liquidation before the customer has paid Dragonyarns plc for the silk supplied. Without a retention of title clause or some other form of security, Dragonyarns plc would in that event be a mere unsecured creditor of the insolvent buying company and would be lucky to get more than a small proportion of the debt owed to it. The purpose of a retention of title clause would be to put Dragonyarns plc in a stronger position in the event of the buyer going into liquidation – that is, if the goods had not been paid for, to enable Dragonyarns plc to retake possession of the goods (Dragonyarns plc's goods) and to do so irrespective of how many other creditors the insolvent buyer might have.

PASSING OF RISK

Before dealing with the effectiveness of a retention of title clause to protect Dragonyarns plc, a warning should be given about the passing of risk. A retention of title clause, when it works, will result in title (that is, ownership, or what the **Sale of Goods Act 1979** terms 'property') being retained by Dragonyarns plc (that is, not passing to Dragonyarns plc's buyer) for some considerable time after delivery. However, by **s 20(1)** of the **Sale of Goods Act**, the goods will, unless the contrary is agreed, remain at the seller's risk until the property in them passes to the buyer. Thus, Dragonyarns plc would be well advised, when including a retention of title clause in its conditions of sale, either to include also a clause stating that the goods will be at the buyer's risk from the moment of delivery, or else to see that Dragonyarns plc is covered by its own insurance for loss or damage caused after delivery by accident, act of God or act of a third party.

EFFECTIVENESS WITHOUT BEING REGISTERED

By a properly drafted retention of title clause, Dragonyarns plc can ensure that it retains property in the goods supplied until one of three events occurs. As soon as one of these events occurs, property will pass (that is, Dragonyarns plc will lose title to the goods). Those three events are: firstly, that the goods are sold by the buyer and property passes under that contract to the buyer's sub-buyer; secondly, that the buyer pays Dragonyarns plc; thirdly, that the goods, although still unsold by the buyer, lose their identity on becoming incorporated in something else. The point is that, until one of these events occurs, Dragonyarns plc will have *retained* title to the goods and will be able, on the buyer going into liquidation, to retake the goods, thereby enforcing its rights of ownership. Such a right does not have to be registered as a charge, because the requirement (in **s 860** of the **Companies Act 2006**) to register applies only to charges *created* by the buying company. Thus, both the Court of Appeal (in *Clough Mill v Martin* (1985)) and the House of Lords (in *Armour v Thyssen* (1990)) have held that retention of title clauses are enforceable without being registered. Attention will now be paid in turn to each of the three possibilities that will cause Dragonyarns plc to lose ownership in the goods even where there is a retention of title clause.

BUYER SELLS THE GOODS

Dragonyarns plc may think that it would be wise to retain title until the goods have been paid for and to ensure that if they have not been paid for, Dragonyarns plc still retains title even if the buyer sells the goods. This, however, would be unrealistic. It is very likely that Dragonyarns plc's buyer needs to be able to sell the goods in order to maintain its own cash flow and thereby to be able to settle its debts, including those owed to Dragonyarns plc. On the other hand, if that buyer were unable to pass on good title to a sub-buyer to whom it sold the goods, it would be very unlikely to be able to find willing sub-buyers. In any case, even if the retention of title clause were to purport to retain title for unpaid goods even after they had been sold on to a sub-buyer, there is always the risk that the sub-buyer, if unaware of the retention of title clause, would claim nevertheless to obtain title by virtue of one of the exceptions to the principle *nemo dat quod non habet* – in particular, the one in **s 25(1)** of the **Sale of Goods Act 1979**. Therefore, a sensibly drafted retention of title clause will authorise the buyer to sub-sell the goods (see the *Romalpa* case) so that the buyer in sub-selling the goods will, *vis-à-vis* the sub-buyer, be selling as a principal and, *vis-à-vis* Dragonyarns plc, be selling as an agent of Dragonyarns plc. Technically, of course, Dragonyarns plc would not lose ownership and the sub-buyer would not acquire ownership until, according to the terms of the sub-sale, property passes from the buyer to the sub-buyer.

If then, as seems inevitable, Dragonyarns plc is not to retain ownership after the time when property is to pass to the sub-buyer, is there any way that Dragonyarns plc can continue to protect itself against the subsequent insolvency of the buyer? The answer, confirmed by the decision in the *Romalpa* case, is that an appropriately worded clause *may* give Dragonyarns plc an interest in the proceeds of sale received by the buyer from the sub-buyer. For such a result to be achieved, the clause will need to make it clear that in having possession of and sub-selling the goods, the buyer is agent of, bailee of, fiduciary of, and selling for the account of the seller. Then, if the buyer has kept any such proceeds of sale in a separate account, Dragonyarns plc will, in priority over the buyer's other creditors, be able to take those proceeds of sale to satisfy the outstanding debt due to Dragonyarns plc. If the proceeds have been mixed by the buyer with other monies, then Dragonyarns plc would be able to trace according to the equitable principles of tracing (*Re Hallett's Estate* (1880)). It is important that the clause complies with the requirements set out above. Even then, there is uncertainty surrounding clauses aimed at securing to the seller (here, Dragonyarns plc) an interest in the proceeds of sub-sales by the buyer. Some of this uncertainty was exposed in *Pfeiffer GmbH v Arbuthnot Factors* (1988), where the clause authorised the buyer to sub-sell and required the buyer to pass on to the seller all the buyer's rights under those sub-sales contracts, requiring this to be done up to the amount of the buyer's indebtedness to the seller. It was held in the High Court that this was a charge created by the buyer and was void because it was not registered under the **Companies Act**. There were two significant distinctions between the clause here and that in *Romalpa*. Firstly, the clause providing that the buyer in sub-selling was doing so for the account of the seller was expressly limited to the amount of the outstanding debts owed by the buyer to the seller. Secondly, it failed expressly to state that the buyer was, in selling the goods, a fiduciary of the seller. One possibly significant uncertainty in all of this is that in *Romalpa*, the one case where a seller has successfully claimed an interest in the proceeds of sub-sales, the decision rested on a concession made by counsel for the buyer's receiver, namely, a concession that the relationship of seller and buyer was that of bailor and bailee. Advice to Dragonyarns plc is therefore to include in the contractual retention of title provisions a clause which deals with the proceeds of sub-sales and satisfies the requirements indicated above, but to recognise the uncertainty over its legal effect, if not registered as a charge created by the buyer.

BUYER PAYS DRAGONYARNS PLC

For those customers of Dragonyarns plc that are 'one-off' customers, the clause need retain title only until the purchase price has been fully paid. The effects of such a clause were set out in *Clough Mill v Martin* (1985) (partly *ratio* and partly *obiter*). If the buyer goes into liquidation before paying for the goods, then Dragonyarns plc can retake the goods. Dragonyarns plc can then resell the goods itself, since they are its property. If Dragonyarns plc sells them for more than the original price that the buyer had agreed to pay, then Dragonyarns plc will make a profit which it would not have made if the buyer had paid for the goods before going into liquidation; Dragonyarns plc will be entitled to retain that profit. If Dragonyarns plc is able to resell the goods only for a lower figure than the buyer had agreed to pay, then Dragonyarns plc will have a claim for damages against the buyer for the consequent loss; however, Dragonyarns plc will be unlikely to recover much of that loss, in respect of which it will be merely an unsecured creditor of the insolvent buyer. If, at the time when the buyer had gone into liquidation, the buyer had paid *part* of the purchase price to Dragonyarns plc, and if Dragonyarns plc, having repossessed the goods, is able to sell them for the same price that the buyer had agreed to pay, Dragonyarns plc will be under a duty to refund the buyer's part-payment. If, however, Dragonyarns plc has been able to resell the goods only at a lower figure than the buyer had agreed to pay, then Dragonyarns plc will be able to deduct that loss from the amount of any refund.

For Dragonyarns plc's regular customers, the clause should, in the interests of Dragonyarns plc, be an 'all liabilities' clause; it should retain title until the buyer has satisfied all his liabilities to Dragonyarns plc, whether arising under this or any other contract. That such a clause can be effective was confirmed by the House of Lords in the Scottish case of *Armour v Thyssen* (1990), and it is not thought that the law is any different in this respect in England. Indeed, the reasoning in that case would seem also to legitimise a clause which retains title to Dragonyarns plc until all debts owed to Dragonyarns plc by the buyer *or by any subsidiary or associated company of the buyer* have been paid.

GOODS LOSE THEIR IDENTITY

It has been established in various cases that a retention of title clause will cease to be effective once the goods have lost their identity by becoming incorporated in something else. This usually occurs in the buyer's manufacturing process, for example, resin becoming incorporated in chipboard (*Borden v Scottish Timber Products Ltd* (1981)), or pieces of leather becoming incorporated into handbags made by the buyer (*Re Peachdart Ltd* (1984)). It seems that Dragonyarns plc cannot retain title to the silk once that silk has been used in the manufacture of other products, such as suits, jackets, bedspreads, etc. It seems unlikely that the silk (unlike the engines in *Hendy Lennox v Grahame Puttick Ltd* (1984)) could be incorporated in something else without losing its identity. Thus, Dragonyarns plc cannot protect itself where the silk has been incorporated in something else in the buyer's manufacturing process, without registering a charge created by the buyer over the manufactured product.

CONCLUSION

Dragonyarns plc would be well advised to include retention of title provisions in its contracts, which, if carefully drafted, should serve to give some security against the risk of the buyer becoming insolvent. Without being registered as a charge, those provisions should be effective in the case of unmixed goods and, possibly, the proceeds of sale of unmixed goods.

Common Pitfalls ✖

Students need to categorise the goods in order to ascertain where property in the goods is vested so that risk can be considered.

QUESTION 13

Balls Wines Ltd is a wine merchant. Its stock in its warehouse a month ago was:

- ❖ 100 bottles of 1960 Château Magret;
- ❖ 200 bottles of 1970 Château Pouilley which, unknown to Balls Wines Ltd, were the last bottles of that vintage remaining unconsumed anywhere in the world;
- ❖ 350 bottles of 1980 Château Darcey;
- ❖ assorted other wines.

In the last month, Balls Wines has made and received no deliveries of wine, but has made the following agreements to sell wine:

- ❖ '100 bottles of 1960 Château Magret' to Pugwash;
- ❖ '200 bottles of 1970 Château Pouilley' to Barnabas;
- ❖ '300 bottles of 1980 Château Darcey, currently in Balls Wines' warehouse' to Tom;
- ❖ '50 bottles of 1980 Château Darcey' to Jake.

As regards payment: Pugwash paid Balls Wines when he made the contract; Barnabas agreed to pay upon collecting the goods from Balls Wines' warehouse; Tom and Jake each agreed to pay upon delivery by Balls Wines to their respective premises.

Yesterday, Balls Wines despatched to Jake 50 bottles of 1980 Château Darcey. Unfortunately, the lorry (Balls Wines' own) crashed en route and all the wine on board was lost. Last night, a fire destroyed Balls Wines' warehouse and its contents.

▶ Advise Pugwash, Barnabas, Tom and Jake.

Answer Plan

This question is plainly concerned with the issue of whether risk had passed from the seller to the buyer. However, the answer must not be confined to that, because it is important to know whether the contracts are still binding and, if not, what the position is.

ANSWER

Each of the buyers will be advised as to whether the risk in the goods had passed to him and, if not, whether the contract is still binding.

We are not told whether the contracts contained any provision stating when risk was to pass to the buyer or when property was to pass. It will be assumed that there was no such provision. In any case, even if there were a provision that property was to pass to the buyer at a particular stage, that provision could not, in the case of a contract for the sale of unascertained goods, come into effect until those goods were ascertained (s 16 of the **Sale of Goods Act 1979**).

In the absence of contrary agreement, and subject to a couple of provisos, risk passes with property (**s 20**). Subject to the rule in **s 16** just mentioned, property passes when the parties intend it to (**s 17**) and, unless a different intention appears, property passes according to the rules in **s 18**. The application of these rules depends upon whether the contract in question was for specific goods or unascertained goods.

SPECIFIC OR UNASCERTAINED GOODS?

The time for determining whether goods are specific or unascertained goods is that at which the contract is made. If the contract is for goods which are 'identified and agreed upon' at the time the contract is made, then it is one for the sale of specific goods (**s 61(1)**). The agreement which Pugwash has is not one for specific goods, since, even if the parties had expected that Pugwash's contract would be fulfilled from Balls Wines' stock, there was apparently no contractual agreement to that effect, but simply an obligation on Balls Wines to deliver '100 bottles of 1960 Château Magret'. Thus, if Balls Wines chose to keep for itself the 100 bottles in its stock at the time of the contract or if it chose to supply them to another customer, it could still comply with its contractual commitments to Pugwash by getting hold of 100 other bottles of 1960 Château Magret and supplying those to Pugwash. That makes it a contract for the sale of unascertained goods, since the contract did not identify the 100 bottles in Balls Wines' stock as the contractual bottles (*Re London Wine Shippers* (1986)).

Similarly, the contract with Barnabas did not identify the 200 bottles of 1970 Château Pouilley in Balls Wines' stock as being the contractual bottles. Had it been possible to do so, Balls Wines could have bought a further 200 bottles and used those to fulfil its contract with Barnabas. It is submitted that it is irrelevant that it would in fact have been impossible to buy more such bottles. It may be argued that a contract to buy 'a painting of the *Mona Lisa* by Leonardo da Vinci' is no different from a contract to buy 'the painting of the *Mona Lisa* by Leonardo da Vinci', since there is only one such painting. However, in the present case, Balls Wines was unaware that the bottles in its warehouse were the only ones in existence and, in those circumstances, it cannot be said that the 1970 Château Pouilley bottles were 'identified and agreed upon at the time the contract was made' as being the contractual goods, since, so far as the parties were concerned, the contract allowed other goods to be supplied which corresponded with the contract description. Thus, Barnabas' contract also was for the sale of unascertained goods.

The contract with Tom did identify Balls Wines' stock as the source from which Tom's bottles must come. However, it did not identify which of the 350 bottles in its stock were to be supplied to Tom. Thus, Tom's contract was also a contract for the sale of unascertained goods (*Re Wait* (1927)).

Jake's contract, apparently, did not even require his bottles to be supplied from Balls Wines' current stock. So, for the same reasons as applied to Pugwash's contract, Jake's was a contract for the sale of unascertained goods.

SECTION 20A

Section 20A provides for the buyer to obtain an undivided share of goods in unascertained goods from an identified bulk. There is, however, no question of **s 20A** applying to any of the goods in this problem. There is only one lot of goods which are to come from a bulk which is identified by the parties, either in the contract or subsequently. Those are the 300 bottles that Tom has agreed to buy. **Section 20A** does not apply to these goods, because it comes into operation only when the buyer pays for the goods and Tom is not due to pay until delivery occurs. It follows that the passing of ownership and risk will be determined by reference to what the parties may have agreed and, failing that, by reference to **ss 16–19**.

PASSING OF PROPERTY

It may be that, in the case of Pugwash, the parties intended property to pass at an early stage, since Pugwash paid for the goods at the time of making the contract. However, nothing was done to ascertain which bottles were to be supplied to Pugwash. Therefore, no property ever passed to Pugwash, since no property can pass in goods until they are ascertained (**s 16**).

Where, after the making of the contract, goods become ascertained, property will not pass (unless a contrary intention appears) until goods are unconditionally appropriated to the contract by one party with the assent of the other (**s 18 r 5**). In the case of Barnabas, so far as we are told, nothing was done to appropriate the goods to the contract. Therefore, there being nothing to indicate a contrary intention on the part of the parties, property never passed to Barnabas.

If, contrary to the opinion advanced above, the sale to Barnabas was in fact a sale of specific goods, then, assuming that the contract was an 'unconditional' one[1] and that the wine was in a deliverable state, property will have passed to Barnabas at the time

---

1 Ie, the contract does not contain a condition preventing s 18 r 1 from applying. In *Varley v Whipp* (1900), since the seller did not own the goods which were the subject of the contract, it was held that this was a conditional contract, ie a contract with the condition that the seller needed to acquire the goods first before property could pass to the buyer.

the contract was made. At least, that is so according to **s 18 r 1**, which states that it is immaterial that payment or delivery or both are postponed. However, the application of that rule coupled with the rule in **s 20** would mean that risk had passed to Barnabas even though the goods were still in Balls Wines' warehouse. That would be an unsatisfactory result to achieve unless the parties had very clearly indicated it to be their intention, as it would be quite likely that Balls Wines was covered by insurance for the loss of or damage to its goods on its premises, and quite unlikely that a buyer would expect to have to take out insurance cover for goods of which he had yet to take delivery and for which he had yet to make payment. Maybe it was for that sort of consideration that Diplock LJ said in *Ward v Bignall* (1967) that in the case of specific goods, very little is needed to give rise to the inference that the parties intended property only to pass upon payment or delivery. If the court found the parties' intention by that means, then **s 18 r 1** would not apply, since the **s 18** rules apply only where the intention of the parties is not apparent. Therefore, it is submitted that even if the sale to Barnabas were of specific goods, the property was intended to pass only upon delivery and payment and that therefore no property in the wine passed to Barnabas.

It could be that, in the case of Tom, his 300 bottles became ascertained by exhaustion (see *Karlshamns Olje Fabriker v Eastport Navigation Corp, The Elafi* (1982)). This is because the contract requires his bottles to be supplied from the 350 in stock and as soon as the 50 are despatched to Jake, Tom's have become ascertained as being the remaining 300. However, although no property can pass before the goods become ascertained, it does not follow that the parties intended that property should pass as soon as the goods became ascertained. Unless the intention of the parties appears otherwise, the property has not passed unless there is unconditional appropriation of the goods to the contract. It might be argued that Balls Wines made the unconditional appropriation by despatching the 50 bottles to Jake, since Balls Wines was thereby effectively committing itself to delivering the remaining 300 to Tom. In that case, however, it would seem that Balls Wines was unconditionally appropriating the 50 bottles to Jake. But was it really? Certainly, it would have been had it consigned the 50 bottles to an independent carrier to deliver to Jake (see **s 18 r 5(2)**). Is this still the case when it sends its own lorry? If this was an unconditional appropriation of the 50 bottles to Jake, then it is submitted that there was an unconditional appropriation of the remaining 300 to Tom. In that case, it seems likely that we can infer that Tom impliedly assented in advance to that appropriation (as is possible; see *Aldridge v Johnson* (1857)), since he must have assumed that Balls Wines was free to dispose of all but 300 of its stock of 1980 Château Darcey. It is arguable, however, that consigning the goods to Jake on Balls Wines' own lorry did not amount to an unconditional appropriation and that such an appropriation would occur only upon delivery by Balls Wines' lorry to Jake. If the lorry had been recalled, for example by Balls Wines calling the driver via a mobile telephone in the lorry's cab, then Balls Wines would still have 350 bottles from which to select Tom's. Thus, the despatch of 50 bottles in Balls Wines' own lorry did not, it is argued, demonstrate an intention to attach those 50 irrevocably to Jake's contract, or the remaining 300 irrevocably to Tom's. It is submitted that, therefore, property did not pass to either Tom or to Jake. Even if the despatch to Jake did amount to an unconditional appropriation, it would still be the case that no property would have passed to Jake (as opposed to Tom), since there is nothing from which to infer Jake's assent given in advance to such an appropriation and thus his assent would only be given upon delivery to him, which never occurred because of the lorry crash.

PASSING OF RISK

It has been argued that no property passed to any of the buyers in the problem. It follows that no risk passed to them either (**s 20**) unless delivery was delayed for any of their faults (**s 20(2)**). It is possible that delivery to Barnabas was delayed through his fault, depending upon whether he has taken more than the agreed (or else a reasonable) time in coming to collect his wine. If he did, then the 200 bottles of Château Pouilley were at Barnabas' risk, since their loss in the fire is certainly something that might not have happened if he had collected them earlier (**s 20(2)**).

Risk not having passed (except possibly to Barnabas), Balls Wines is not excused from having to deliver to Pugwash and to Jake wine which corresponds to the descriptions in their respective contracts. Nothing has rendered their contracts impossible to perform, because they were contracts for the sale of purely generic goods. If Balls Wines does not carry out those contracts, it will be liable to the buyers for non-delivery.

On the other hand, both Barnabas' and Tom's contracts have become impossible for Balls Wines to carry out: Barnabas' because there is no more of that wine left in the world and Tom's because the contract provided for the goods to come from a particular source and that source is now void (*Howell v Coupland* (1876)). The contracts being for unascertained goods, **s 7** will not apply, but the contracts are frustrated at common law, assuming the frustration was not self-induced, that is, that the fire was not Balls Wines' fault. That being so, Balls Wines is not liable for non-delivery and nor are Tom and Barnabas liable to pay the price. Even if (that is, in Barnabas' case) the contract had been for the sale of specific goods, the result would have been the same (that is, provided that risk had not passed) by virtue of **s 7**.

If risk had passed to Barnabas, that is, if delivery was delayed because he was contractually late in collecting, then Barnabas' contract will not be terminated or void for frustration, but instead he will be liable for the price.

QUESTION 14

(a) 'The rules in the **Sale of Goods Act 1979** relating to the passing of risk do not always place the risk upon the party who should sensibly bear it.'

▶ Discuss this statement.

(b) James enters into a contract for the sale to Finnegan of 600 bags of feveroles out of the 800 bags of James' feveroles currently stored in Peter's warehouse. On receiving a cheque for the purchase price, James gives Finnegan the invoice and written delivery authority. A month later, when Finnegan goes to collect the feveroles, it is discovered that, since the contract was made, 400 of James' bags have been stolen. Finnegan is offered delivery of the remaining 400 bags and seeks your advice.

▶ Advise Finnegan.

Answer Plan

Many law examiners do not indicate how many marks are allocated to each half of the question. The only safe guide to adopt in such a case is that either the (a) and (b) parts carry equal marks, or else there will not be a very great disparity between the marks allocated to each part. It is certainly unreasonable to assume that, because the question in (a) is shorter, the answer should be.

The answer to (a) is to some extent a matter of taste. There is certainly no right answer. One could mount a good case for the rules being sensible. The approach taken in this model answer is to attack the rules on the basis that if you can come up with some plausible criticisms of the area of law under scrutiny, it is usually easier to attack the state of the law than it is to defend it.

Part (b) is a typical problem on the passing of risk. The most common cause of students throwing away marks on problems on this topic is a failure to do any more than consider who bears the risk, that is, a failure to spell out the consequences, such as a possible frustration of the contract and whether the buyer still has to pay the price. The plan adopted in (b) is to consider on whom the loss of the theft falls, and then to consider the possible consequences of it falling on James or Finnegan.

ANSWER

(A)

Apart from the addition of **ss 20A** and **20B** in 1995, the rules referred to in the question have remained virtually unchanged since the first **Sale of Goods Act** was passed in 1893.

That Act was itself a codifying Act which simply sought to put into statutory form rules that had been arrived at by judges deciding individual cases. Thus, they do not result from a considered comprehensive approach to the whole range of issues that ought to bear upon a piece of legislation. They do, however, reflect the basic 'freedom of contract' philosophy which imbued the decisions in commercial cases by nineteenth-century judges. This accounts for the opening words of **s 20** ('unless otherwise agreed') which allow the parties to determine the rules within their own contract. To that extent, the comment in the question is certainly unjustified, since it is surely sensible to have risk borne by the party who it has been agreed in the contract should bear it.

Where the matter is more debatable is in those cases where the contract is silent as to who bears the risk. In this situation, apart from two exceptions specifically catered for in **sub-ss (2)** and **(3)**, the basic approach adopted is to tie the passing of risk to the passing of property. This approach is flawed because the passing of property is significant for other purposes as well as for determining the passing of risk – those other purposes including the seller's right to maintain an action for the price (see **s 49**) and the right of the relevant trustee in bankruptcy to take the goods in the event of one or other of them becoming bankrupt. The rules on the passing of property are themselves subject to the freedom of contract principle which allows the parties to agree when they intend property to pass. In that case, the rules on the passing of risk and the passing of property are not lacking in sense, since the parties can presumably remember to cater for the one when making a specific provision for the other. It would certainly be quite absurd of the parties to include a retention of title clause whereby the seller retains title (that is, property) long after delivery to the seller without also including a clause stating that the risk passes with delivery.[2]

It is where the parties do not remember or think to include express provisions on these matters that the rules in **s 20** (on the passing of risk) and the related rules in **ss 16–19** (on the passing of property) appear particularly flawed. The plain fact is that it would be logical (apart from the clear justice of the exceptions in **s 20(2)** and **(3)**) to link the passing of risk with physical delivery of the goods, unless the parties have expressly agreed otherwise. There are two very sound reasons for this. First, it is obvious that in the vast majority of cases, it is the person in possession who has the greatest ability to take care of the goods to see that they are not stolen, burnt, damaged, etc. If he has to bear the risk of any loss, then he has the consequent incentive to exercise that care. The second reason is that it is likely to be much easier to secure insurance cover for goods on your own premises or otherwise within your own possession. Of course, it is possible to secure insurance cover when they are

---

2   See Question 12 on retention of title clauses.

elsewhere. One does wonder, however, how many businesses fail to insure goods of which they are not in possession but for which they are bearing the risk. The notion of insuring goods where, although the risk of loss or damage is borne by the insured, the property in the goods is with someone else may raise problems of whether the insured had in law an insurable interest. If that is a problem, then the law on insurable interest needs changing. Not only do the rules in **ss 16–20** not tie the passing of risk and of property to the transfer of possession of the goods, they expressly recognise that the passing of property and/or risk can occur independently of whether delivery has occurred – see the wording of **s 18 r 1** and **s 20**. There is undoubtedly something inconsistent about saying, as **s 20** does in its principal rule in **sub-s (1)**, that it is immaterial whether delivery has been made or not and then saying in an exception to that rule that where delivery is delayed due to the fault of one of the parties, any loss which might not have occurred but for the delay is to be borne by the party at fault.

There is, however, a further difficulty which would more commonly arise if the rule tying the passing of risk to the passing of property in the absence of contrary agreement were abolished. This is the absurdity where, while the risk is with one party and the property is with the other, the goods are destroyed or damaged by the negligence of a third party; the party who suffers the loss is unable to maintain an action for damages against the culprit (*Leigh and Sillivan v Aliakmon Shipping Co* (1984)).

Finally, it must be acknowledged that the somewhat complicated rules relating to the sale of a specified quantity of unascertained goods out of an identified bulk were a sensible amendment to the law. They were introduced in 1995 and are stated in **ss 20A** and **20B**. They were designed to deal with the situation where the buyer has paid for the goods and where they are still unseparated from the identified bulk at the time when the bulk is damaged or lost in whole or in part. Now, unless the parties have agreed something to the contrary, the buyer will no longer be a mere unsecured creditor in the event of the seller's insolvency. So far as risk is concerned, the seller's proportion of the bulk will be assumed to have perished or been damaged first, but if the loss or damage goes beyond that, each buyer will have to bear the risk of loss or damage to his share of the bulk.

(B)

The question requires us to establish, if possible, at whose risk the goods were when 400 bags were stolen. Much depends upon whether they were stolen before or after Finnegan paid for the goods (that is, gave over his cheque to James). If they were stolen after that point, then **ss 20A** and **20B** are relevant. These sections apply where there is a sale of a specified quantity (here, 400 bags) out of a bulk which is identified in the contract (here, James' feveroles stored in Peter's warehouse). Their effect is that, upon payment of the price, the buyer (Finnegan) acquires property in an undivided share of the bulk. From that point onwards, there is a possibility that loss of or damage to the bulk will to some extent fall upon Finnegan. Where only some of the bulk is lost or damaged, then that loss is taken first of all to have fallen on that share of the bulk retained by the seller, James. The problem does not state that there is any other buyer to whom James has agreed to sell any of the bulk. It appears therefore that after Finnegan paid the price of his 600 bags, the bulk of 800 bags comprised 600 for Finnegan and 200 retained by James. The loss occasioned by the theft of 400 thus falls first on James' 200 and thereafter on Finnegan's 600. Thus, after the theft, there are none of James' left and only 400 bags of Finnegan's left. These remaining bags will then have become Finnegan's by a process of exhaustion. He is entitled to the remaining 400 bags, but is not entitled to recover any of the purchase price he paid.

The result whereby the loss is taken to have fallen first on James' share of the bulk is challengeable by James if he can rely on **s 20(2)** or if it can be said that the arrangement over giving the delivery authority to Finnegan indicated that the parties intended risk to pass on the handing over to Finnegan of the delivery authority. In either of those two eventualities, Finnegan and James would bear the loss in the proportions of their respective interests in the bulk: 75% and 25%. As regards **s 20(2)**, we are told that Finnegan went to collect the feveroles 'a month later', that is, presumably a month after being given the written delivery authority. It is quite possible that a month was an unreasonable delay and that therefore one could describe delivery as having been delayed through Finnegan's 'fault'. If so, Finnegan has to bear the consequences of the theft if that loss might not have occurred if he had collected the goods within a reasonable period of time (say, within a week). We are not told when the theft occurred. If it is established that it occurred before the lapse of what would have been a reasonable length of time for Finnegan to turn up to collect the goods, then James cannot rely on **s 20(2)**. If it occurred after a lapse of that length of time, or if it might have done, then it is a loss which 'might' not have occurred if Finnegan had collected on time and **s 20(2)** applies. Alternatively, the arrangement over the giving of the delivery authority, and Finnegan thus taking on the task of collecting the goods, could well be something which a court would take as indicating the intention of the parties that risk should pass to Finnegan upon the handing over to him of the delivery authority (*Sterns v Vickers* (1923)). In the situation where either **s 20(2)** applies or else the theft occurred after the parties intended risk to pass (for example, on the handing over of the delivery note), the result is as in *Sterns v Vickers*, namely, that all 800 bags were *pro rata* (that is, 75%) at Finnegan's risk. This is because he had agreed to buy 75% of the 800 bags. In that case, he has to bear 75% of the loss of 400 bags, that is, the loss of 300 bags. In that case, he is entitled to take delivery of a further 300 bags, but must pay the full contract price. In this scenario, there is no possibility that the contract has become frustrated by virtue of the theft, since the only way to make sense of the rule that Finnegan has to bear the risk is to make him pay for the goods, despite the fact that some of them have been stolen.

We now consider the situation if James had agreed to sell the remaining 200 bags to another buyer (B2) who had also paid for them before the theft from Peter's warehouse. In that situation, both Finnegan and B2 would have an undivided share in the bulk in the proportions 75% and 25% respectively, and they would bear the loss in those proportions. This would mean that they would suffer the loss as follows: Finnegan would lose 300 bags and B2 would lose 100. This would mean that they would each be entitled to take from the remaining bulk 300 and 100 bags respectively. In that scenario, Finnegan would be entitled to 300, not 400, of the remaining bags. He would not, however, be entitled to any repayment of the price he has paid.

We now turn to the situation where the theft occurred before Finnegan paid James. In that situation, Finnegan had not at that time acquired any property or any undivided share in the goods. Thus, the risk will have at that time been with James. In that case, frustration becomes a possibility. **Section 7** of the **Sale of Goods Act 1979** will not apply because it refers only to contracts for the sale of specific goods. It is possible, however, for the contract to be frustrated at common law if it is a contract for the sale of unascertained goods out of a specific bulk (*Howell v Coupland* (1876)). This would certainly be the case where the whole of the bulk was lost or stolen. In that case, James would not be liable for non-delivery and Finnegan would not be liable to pay the price. However, the court may infer an intention on the part of the parties that, where only part of the bulk has been lost, the contract should not be regarded as frustrated, but that there was an implied term that: (a) the seller was excused from his obligation to deliver the whole contract quantity of 600 bags; and (b) the buyer was to have the option of buying what was left at a *pro rata* proportion of the contract price (*Sainsbury v Street* (1972)). The solution adopted in this latter case would leave Finnegan with a choice as to whether to take the remaining 400 bags at two-thirds of the contract price or to decline to take any at all. The solution adopted in *Sainsbury v Street* might not be quite so simple for a court to adopt in James' and Finnegan's case if James had in fact also made a contract to sell the other 200 bags to someone else. In that case, the option allowed to the two buyers, Finnegan and the other one, would presumably be an option to take a proportion (in Finnegan's case, 75%) of the remaining 400 bags and pay for them *pro rata* at the contract rate. Or could it be that, in the event of the other purchaser not wanting to take his proportion of the 400 bags, Finnegan would be given the option of taking all 400? These are some of the possible difficulties in the court adopting a *Sainsbury v Street* approach and could lead the court instead simply to decide that the contract is frustrated. In the latter case, Finnegan would have no right to take any of the remaining 400 bags, but might be able to negotiate a new contract with James about them.

Nemo Dat Quod Non Habet

INTRODUCTION
This chapter covers the *nemo dat* principle and the exceptions to it.

QUESTION 15

Alf left his car for repair at Maidstone Garage, carelessly leaving the car's registration document in the glove compartment which was unlocked. While the car was at Maidstone Garage, Maidstone telephoned Alf and informed him that another customer had seen the car and wished to buy it for £3,000. Alf said that he had not intended to sell the car, but that If Maidstone were to receive an offer in excess of £4,500, he would be interested. Without again contacting Alf, Maidstone sold the car for £3,500 to Jenny, handing over the registration document and the ignition key.

▶ Consider the legal position.

Answer Plan

This question requires an understanding of the *nemo dat quod non habet* rule and the exceptions to it, in particular, the estoppel exception and the case law on **s 2(1)** of the **Factors Act 1889**. Sometimes, examiners allow you in the examination to refer to the statutory provisions. Without a knowledge of the case law, those provisions will take you only so far. Indeed, the question requires consideration of some possible distinctions between the facts of the problem set and those of a couple of the cases.

The sensible layout of an answer is very straightforward indeed. It is to consider first who now owns the car (no definite answer, however, can be given to that). That involves considering the two relevant exceptions to the *nemo dat* principle. Many candidates answering this type of question are content to leave it there. The question does, however, ask you to consider the legal position and that must also involve setting out the rights of the parties *vis-à-vis* each other in the light of the conclusion (or different possible conclusions) you come to as to who now owns the car. It is often important in questions such as this to consider possible claims in conversion and claims under s 12 of the **Sale of Goods Act 1979**.

ANSWER

It is necessary first to establish who now owns the car, and then to advise the parties as to the legal position flowing from that.

TITLE

The first issue is who owns the car now? Alf, we are told, owned it to start with and since he has never agreed to sell it, he is still the owner unless one of the exceptions to the *nemo dat* principle applies. The *nemo dat quod non habet* principle states that someone who lacks title to goods (for example, Maidstone) cannot transfer that title. Only if one of the exceptions to that principle applies will Maidstone have conferred good title upon Jenny. Two such possible exceptions present themselves for discussion: estoppel and the mercantile agent exception. The first of these can be quickly dismissed, since it is now clearly established that the mere act of the owner of letting someone have possession of his goods is insufficient to enable an estoppel to be raised against him. The position is still the same even if the owner (here, Alf) has parted not only with possession of the goods (here, a car), but also the ignition key and the registration book; the registration book is not a document of title (*Central Newbury Car Auctions v Unity Finance* (1957)).

Does the mercantile agent exception apply? There are a number of requirements, each of which must be complied with before this exception, in **s 2(1)** of the **Factors Act 1889**, will apply. Firstly, Maidstone must have been a mercantile agent, that is, someone having, in the customary course of his business as an agent, authority to sell. On the given facts, it seems likely that Maidstone as a car dealer had such customary authority, including the customary authority to sell the goods in his own name (*Rolls Razor v Cox* (1967)). Secondly, Maidstone must have been in possession of the goods (or documents of title) with the consent of the owner (Alf) at the time of the sale to Jenny, which he clearly did, since he had possession of the car. Maidstone must have also been at that time in possession of the car in his (Maidstone's) capacity as mercantile agent. There is some ambiguity about this in the question, since originally Alf left his car with Maidstone for repair and therefore not with a view to Maidstone selling it, or seeking offers for it. However, after Maidstone's telephone call, Alf could be said to have left the car with Maidstone in two different capacities, one as a repairer and one as a factor (that is, authorised to seek and/or consider offers). This is because Alf in that telephone call clearly contemplated the possibility of Maidstone receiving further offers. **Section 2(1)** does not require that Maidstone 'obtained' possession with the consent of the owner, merely that he was (that is, at the time of the disposition to Jenny) in possession with that consent. The same presumably applies to the judicial gloss on the section which requires him to have been in possession in his capacity as a mercantile agent. Furthermore, there does not seem to be any logical reason why Maidstone should not have been in possession in two capacities at the same time.

There is, however, a problem over the registration document. It is not a document of title but, for the mercantile agent exception to operate, the seller (here, Maidstone) must be in possession of the goods, not just in his capacity as a mercantile agent, but also in such a way as to clothe the seller with apparent authority to sell; in the case of a motor vehicle, that really requires the seller to be in possession not just of the vehicle, but also of its registration document (*Pearson v Rose and Young* (1951)). This also ties in with the further requirement for the exception to apply, namely, that the seller in selling acts in the normal course of business of a mercantile agent. It was said in *Stadium Finance v Robbins* (1962) that selling a car without its registration document would not be a sale in the ordinary course of business. On the given facts, Maidstone was in possession of the registration document which, together with the ignition key, he handed over to Jenny. However, it was held in *Pearson v Rose and Young* that not only must the seller be in possession of the registration book as well as the car, but also he must be in possession of the registration book (as well as of the car) *with the consent of the owner*. In *Pearson v Rose and Young*, the seller was in possession of the registration book, but did not have the consent of the owner to that possession, since the seller had obtained possession of it by a trick he played upon the owner. This was taken one stage further in *Stadium Finance v Robbins*, where it was held that the owner accidentally leaving the document locked in the glove compartment did not amount to the seller having possession of it with the consent of the owner. The only possible distinctions between that case and the present problem are: firstly, that in Alf's case, the document was in an *unlocked* glove compartment; secondly, that very possibly the key to the glove compartment in Alf's car was the same as the ignition key which Alf presumably left with the car; thirdly, that possibly (although we do not know) something was said in the telephone conversation between Maidstone and Alf which alluded to the registration document and indicated Alf's 'consent' to Maidstone's possession of it.

Subject to what has just been said about the registration book, it seems that all the requirements of the exception have been satisfied, including the requirement that Jenny took the car in good faith without notice of Maidstone's lack of authority to make the sale. There is nothing in the stated facts of the problem to indicate that

Jenny should have been 'put on notice'; at least, that is so provided the sale price of £3,500 was not so low as itself to be a cause of suspicion. If there is a substantial doubt about Jenny's good faith, that could cause her a problem, since the burden of proof to show that she took in good faith is upon Jenny (*Heap v Motorists Advisory Agency* (1923)).

CONSEQUENCES

Assuming that all the requirements of **s 2(1)** of the **Factors Act** are satisfied, then Jenny now has good title to the car. That means of course that Alf, in any action for conversion, would fail against Jenny. Alf would, however, have a good claim for conversion against Maidstone. This is a tort of strict liability and, since Maidstone has effectively disposed of the car to Jenny, could not result in an order for the goods to be returned to Alf, but only in an award of damages. The *prima facie* measure of damages to which Alf is entitled would be the value of the car at the time of the sale to Jenny. This would be a matter of evidence, but presumably Alf will try to insist that it was worth at least £4,000, since that was a figure he would have been interested in. The value, however, is not necessarily the car's value to Jenny, but its market value. It is of course possible that, before selling the car, Maidstone had carried out the repairs. In that case, the cost of the repairs will need to be taken into account in one way or another, either by a set-off of their cost or by deduction of an improvement allowance by virtue of the provisions of the **Torts (Interference with Goods) Act 1977**. That allowance might well be less than the cost of the repairs, since it is the proportion of the value of the car (that is, at the time of the sale to Jenny) which is attributable to the improvement effected by the repairs.

If Jenny did not satisfy the requirements of **s 2(1)** of the **Factors Act**, she will not have acquired good title. In that case, Alf would be entitled to succeed against Jenny in an action in conversion. It is assumed that the car was not unique. Therefore, the result of such an action would not be to compel Jenny to return the car, but would be an award of damages (with Jenny perhaps being given the option of returning the car). The damages would be calculated as in the case of the claim against Maidstone just discussed. Thus, the improvement allowance (due to the repairs by Maidstone – assuming Maidstone had effected those repairs) would be deducted. If Jenny chose to return the car to Alf, Alf would be liable to pay the improvement allowance to Jenny.

If Jenny were to be held liable to Alf in the way just outlined, Jenny would have a claim against Maidstone for breach of the condition as to title in **s 12** of the **Sale of Goods Act 1979**. She would be entitled to the return of her purchase price, but would have to give credit for any improvement allowance received by her from Alf. The entitlement to the return of the purchase price is based upon the notion that, since Jenny never got title, she has suffered a total failure of consideration. Thus, according to the controversial decision in *Rowland v Divall* (1923), Jenny is entitled to the return of the full purchase price (minus, if applicable, the improvement allowance) even if she has had some months' use of the car before having to surrender it to Alf, for example if it was some considerable time before the truth was discovered and the car's whereabouts traced to Jenny.

QUESTION 16

Annalisa owns a jewellery shop in Bromley. Roberto came into the shop, selected a ruby bracelet and paid for it. Roberto explained to her that he had an appointment to play football that afternoon and asked if it would be all right to leave the bracelet with Annalisa until after his football game. A little later that same afternoon, Lopez, who looked the very image of Rafael Nadal, the famous tennis player, and had a strong Spanish accent, came into the shop and selected the very same bracelet (which by an oversight Annalisa had failed to remove to be kept for Roberto). Annalisa let Lopez pay the £1,000 price by cheque, which Lopez did – signing himself Rafael Nadal. Subsequently, the cheque was dishonoured and Annalisa informed the police, who traced the bracelet to Danny's shop in Croydon. It has turned out that Lopez has a stall at Bermondsey market in South London and that he sold the bracelet (for £200) early one morning to Danny, a jewellery dealer, who considered at the time that he had a real bargain.

▶ **Advise Annalisa.**

Answer Plan

The question deals with certain 'exceptions' to the *nemo dat* rule, namely:

❖ the position where a seller sells goods which the seller has already sold to an earlier buyer;

❖ when a buyer misrepresents (or a seller is mistaken as to) the buyer's identity;

❖ the rule (in s 25 of the **Sale of Goods Act 1979**) dealing with a buyer in possession who sells the goods.

Also expected is the knowledge that the exception relating to market overt has been abolished. It is logical to deal with the transactions in chronological order. In that way, the passing of title can be traced through those transactions. As always in this sort of examination question, certain key facts are not given, with the result that the examinee cannot always be sure if an exception does or does not apply. This requires, as the answer progresses, copious use of the expressions 'if' or 'assuming that'.

ANSWER

As there is nothing in the question to suggest otherwise, it will be assumed that Annalisa was at the outset the owner of the bracelet. Therefore, each of the transactions (the sales to Roberto and to Lopez and the sale by Lopez to Danny) must be examined to see whether it operated to pass title.

ANNALISA'S SALE TO LOPEZ

The sale by Annalisa to Lopez appears to have been affected by fraud on the part of Lopez, who passed himself off as being Rafael Nadal. Whether or not he said anything to that effect, he certainly made a representation of it by signing himself as Rafael Nadal. The effect of this was either to render the contract between himself and Annalisa void for unilateral mistake or to render it voidable for fraud. In one case on somewhat similar facts (*Ingram v Little* (1961)), it was held that the contract was void for unilateral mistake. That case, however, is now generally regarded as having been decided on its own special facts. The law presumes that, as the parties were dealing face to face, Annalisa intended to deal with the person there in the shop, albeit that she was mistaken as to that person's identity (*Lewis v Averay* (1972)). This is not a situation, like that in *Shogun v Hudson* (2001), where the parties were not face to face but contracted via an intermediary. Thus, there was an agreement between Annalisa and Lopez which, however, was a voidable contract, that is the agreement was valid unless and until Annalisa avoided the contract for fraud. This was the result achieved in a case on remarkably similar facts, involving a sale of a ring by a jeweller (*Phillips v Brooks* (1919)). Thus, assuming for the moment that Annalisa had title, good title passed to Lopez, unless and until such time as Annalisa rescinded the contract. In circumstances like those in the present case, it is impractical to suppose that the seller (Annalisa) can contact the buyer (Lopez) in order to rescind (set aside) the contract, since Annalisa does not actually know who Lopez was. If, however, the seller, when she realises the fraud, does her best to rescind the contract, for example, by informing the police, that will be regarded as rescinding the contract (*Car and Universal Finance v Caldwell* (1965)). This is what Annalisa did. Giving such notice to a third party with an intention to rescind operates to rescind it and thus to cause the title to revert to the seller (Annalisa). However, it will not have that effect if, as in *Phillips v Brooks*, the rogue buyer (Lopez) has already sold the goods to a purchaser who was ignorant of the fraud and who bought in good faith. We are not told whether Lopez sold the bracelet to Danny before or after Annalisa informed the police of the fraud upon herself. If it was afterwards, then Annalisa's informing of the police will have operated to rescind her contract with Lopez and to cause title to the bracelet to revert to Annalisa. If Lopez sold the bracelet to Danny before Annalisa informed the police, then, since Lopez had title at that time, Danny will have received title and, assuming that he was ignorant of the fraud and a purchaser in good faith, his title will be unassailable by Annalisa. The fact that the price which Danny paid was low would not seem to prevent him having been a purchaser in good faith. Indeed, one would expect prices in a street market to be significantly less than in, say, a Central London jewellers.

ANNALISA AS SELLER IN POSSESSION

The position relating to the sale by Annalisa to Lopez is complicated by the fact that the bracelet in fact belongs to Roberto. If the transaction between Annalisa and Lopez was not avoided for fraud before Lopez sold the bracelet on to Danny, the question arises as to whether that transaction operated to transfer title from Annalisa who did not have title so as to defeat the title of Roberto. Annalisa was a seller (she had sold to Roberto) and she continued in possession of the goods with the consent of the buyer (Roberto). In those circumstances, if she sold and delivered the goods to another person who received them in good faith and without notice of the previous sale to Roberto, that transaction has the same effect as if Annalisa had been expressly authorised by Roberto to make it (**s 24** of the **Sale of Goods Act** and **s 8** of the **Factors Act 1889**). Thus, it would operate to transfer Roberto's title to the innocent buyer. The question then arises as to whether Lopez was 'in good faith'. In one sense, he very clearly was not acting in good faith because he was himself fraudulent. **Section 24** is clearly intended not to allow someone who takes in bad faith to benefit from the section. The difficulty is that if the absence of good faith prevents the sale from Annalisa to Lopez transferring title to Lopez, it is not Lopez who suffers but the person (Danny) to whom Lopez sold. The requirement of good faith may possibly simply relate to the matter of the previous sale (in this case, to Roberto). It may mean that the buyer is not acting in good faith – and **s 24** does not operate – if the buyer (even though he may not have 'notice' of the previous sale) has reason to suspect that there is a previous sale. If that is what it means, then Lopez was (in that limited sense) presumably acting in good faith (that is, without the slightest suspicion of any earlier sale of the bracelet by Annalisa). In that case, if the sale by Lopez to Danny took place before Annalisa informed the police, Lopez (and, through Lopez, Danny) will have secured good title by virtue of **s 24**. In that case, Roberto will have lost title.

LOPEZ'S SALE TO DANNY

It is necessary now to consider the position if the sale by Lopez to Danny occurred after Annalisa informed the police. In those circumstances, Lopez was selling something to which he did not have title and, according to the *nemo dat quod non habet* principle, he will not have conferred title upon Danny. However, there is one exception to that principle which might have relevance. This is the possibility of Danny relying upon **s 25** of the **Sale of Goods Act**. First, however, it must be pointed out that the exception which used to exist in relation to any sale in market overt no longer exists, since **s 22** of the **Sale of Goods Act** was repealed in 1995. Thus, the fact that it was in Bermondsey market that Lopez sold the bracelet is of no significance.

SECTION 25

It is possible that Danny can claim good title by virtue of **s 25**, which is virtually identical in its wording to **s 9** of the **Factors Act 1889**. Assuming, as has been argued above, that the sale by Annalisa to Lopez was a voidable (and not a void) contract, then Lopez was someone who had 'bought or agreed to buy'. He was in possession of the bracelet with the consent of the seller (Annalisa) and he delivered the bracelet under a sale to Danny. That all being so, the conditions of **s 25** were all satisfied, apart from the requirement that Danny received the bracelet in good faith. It would seem that Danny's belief that he had a good bargain would not cast doubt on his *bona fides* unless the price of £200 was so low that it ought to have put him on notice. Once the conditions of the section are satisfied, the sale and delivery of the bracelet by Lopez to Danny has the same effect as if Lopez were a mercantile agent in possession of the goods with the consent of Annalisa. This wording of **s 25** taken literally means that even if all the conditions of **s 25** were satisfied, Danny will have obtained good title only if the conditions for the passing of title by a mercantile agent (that is, under **s 2(1)** of the **Factors Act 1889**) were also satisfied. This means that **s 25** will operate to pass good title only if the buyer in possession (here, Lopez) sells the goods in the normal course of business of a mercantile agent – that is, even if he was not in fact a mercantile agent. This seems to have been the approach adopted by the Court of Appeal in *Newtons of Wembley v Williams* (1965), where the buyer in possession sold the goods (a car) in a street market where mercantile agents commonly sold cars. It was held in that case that **s 25** did operate to pass good title in circumstances (such as those in the present problem) where the buyer in possession had acquired the goods under a contract which was voidable for his own fraud, and which had in fact been avoided before the sale by the buyer.

However, **s 25** is probably of no use to Danny unless he can use it to defeat the title of Roberto as well as that of Annalisa, since we have seen that Roberto appears to have obtained good title prior to Annalisa's agreeing to sell the bracelet to Lopez. We are here dealing with the situation where it is after Annalisa contacted the police that Lopez sold the bracelet to Danny. In that situation, **s 25** is of no use to Danny, because **s 25** can be relied on to defeat the title only of the original owner (Annalisa) who entrusted the goods to the buyer (Lopez) who has then sold them on to the innocent purchaser (Danny) (*National Mutual General Insurance Association v Jones* (1988)).

Thus, Annalisa is advised that Roberto obtained title by virtue of having bought the bracelet from her. If Annalisa informed the police and thus avoided her contract for fraud with Lopez before he sold the bracelet to Danny, then Roberto still has that title. The sale to Danny will not operate to transfer title to Danny because: (a) the market overt exception to the *nemo dat* rule had been abolished; and (b) **s 25** cannot operate to transfer to the buyer (Danny) any title other than that of the person (Annalisa) who entrusted goods to the seller (Lopez). It will not operate to defeat Roberto's title. In those circumstances, Roberto could then demand return of the bracelet from Danny and, failing its return, would be entitled to succeed in an action against Danny in conversion. If Annalisa did not inform the police before Lopez sold the bracelet to Danny, then (subject to the correct interpretation of the expression 'in good faith' in **s 24**) Danny will have obtained good title by virtue of having bought from someone (Lopez) who obtained good title by virtue of **s 24** of the **Sale of Goods Act**. In those circumstances, Annalisa will be liable in conversion to Roberto for having sold his bracelet.

Making and Cancelling a Credit Agreement

[Assume that the EU Consumer Credit Directive 2008/48/EC 23 April 2008 is fully in force.]

INTRODUCTION

This chapter deals with the common law and statutory provisions, both under the domestic law contained in the **Consumer Credit Acts 1974–2006**, and where relevant the **EU Consumer Credit Directive 2008/48/EC** relating to the advertising and marketing of credit, the position of credit-brokers if they do not hold a valid licence from the OFT, the making of a credit agreement, pre-contract disclosure and formalities, including coverage of the triangular scenario involving a customer, a garage and a finance company and cancellation of credit agreements.

Checklist ✔

The following topics should be prepared in advance of tackling the questions:

- definition of 'credit';
- definition of a 'regulated agreement' – **ss 8** and **9** of the **Consumer Credit Act 1974** (as amended by **ss 1–4** of the **Consumer Credit Act 2006**);
- definition of a regulated consumer hire agreement **s 15** of the **Consumer Credit Act 1974**;
- Office of Fair Trading's powers to impose requirements on licensees and civil penalties (**ss 38–43** and **ss 52–54** of the **CCA 2006**);
- effects of unlicensed trading – **s 40** of the **Consumer Credit Act 1974** as amended by **s 26** of the **Consumer Credit Act 2006**;
- criminal controls on false and misleading credit advertising – **s 44** of the **Consumer Credit Act 1974** and the **Consumer Protection from Unfair Trading Regulations 2008**;

- pre-contract disclosure requirements – **s 55 & ss 55A-C 1974**;

- **ss 60–65** of the **Consumer Credit Act 1974** on the documentation formalities;

- **ss 66A–74** of the **Consumer Credit Act** on cancellation;

- **Cancellation of Contracts made in the Consumer's Home or Place of Work etc Regulations 2008/1816**;

- **s 56** of the **Consumer Credit Act 1974** on the agency of the dealer and the position at common law;

- the responsibilities of credit intermediaries **s 160A CCA 1974**.

QUESTION 17

On Monday, about three weeks ago, John visited Sellapup's garage where he test-drove a second-hand Webb's Wonderful car. Sellapup told him: 'It has done 40,000 miles.' John, who had an old car to give in part-exchange, asked for hire purchase terms. Sellapup produced one of Fleece You Finance Ltd's hire purchase proposal forms. John and Sellapup agreed upon the following terms:

❖ £8,000 cash price for the Webb's Wonderful car;
❖ 30 monthly instalments of £250 each;
❖ a total hire purchase price of £10,000;
❖ an initial payment of £500;
❖ a part-exchange allowance of £2,000.

Sellapup completed the proposal form accordingly and John signed it. John left the initial payment with Sellapup, who informed him that he would be able to take delivery of the Webb's Wonderful (and at the same time leave his old one) when Fleece You Finance Ltd had confirmed its acceptance. All the relevant pre-contractual disclosure provisions in **ss 55, 55A, 55B & 55C CCA 1974** had been complied with as well as the formality and copy requirements provisions.

On Friday last, John telephoned Sellapup and informed him that he now wanted to back out of the whole deal. That same day, John learnt two things: Sellapup had become bankrupt, and the Webb's Wonderful had in fact done over 80,000 miles. The very next day, last Saturday, John had received from Fleece You Finance Ltd its acceptance of his proposal together with a copy of the fully executed agreement; this had been posted to John the day before, Friday. Since then, John has not taken delivery of the Webb's Wonderful and still has his old car.

▶ Advise John.

Answer Plan

The agreement in this case does not appear to be cancellable. Thus, the issues are:

❖   Did John's telephone call to Sellapup work to revoke his offer (that is, his offer to enter the hire purchase agreement with Fleece You Finance Ltd)? This involves discussing whether notice to Sellapup was sufficient and whether the revocation came before acceptance.

❖   If John's revocation was effective, what are the consequences?

❖   Can John use the new right of unilateral withdrawal?

❖   If the revocation was not effective, what remedies, if any, has John got against Fleece You Finance Ltd in respect of the misrepresentation?

❖   If none of the above is available, should he take advantage of the statutory right of termination in relation to hire-purchase and conditional sale agreements?

ANSWER

The agreement in this case appears to be a regulated consumer credit agreement, since John is an individual and is not a 'high net worth' individual or buying for business purposes (**ss 1–4** of the **Consumer Credit Act 2006**, which removes the £25,000 upper limit on regulated agreements). The amount of credit in this agreement is £5,500, being £8,000 (the cash price) minus £2,000 (the part-exchange allowance) and the initial payment (£500). This leaves the interest as £2,000, which appears to be the only item in the total charge for credit. Clearly, from his telephone message to Sellapup, it can be seen that John wishes to back out of the whole deal. Advice will therefore be given to him on whether he can and, if he can, the consequences of doing so. Advice will also be given to him on any remedies he may have for Sellapup's false statement that the car had covered only 40,000 miles and, briefly, on his rights under **s 99** of the **Consumer Credit Act 1974**.

WITHDRAWAL

The hire purchase agreement in this case is not a cancellable one within **s 67** of the **Consumer Credit Act** since, although there were (at Sellapup's garage) antecedent negotiations including oral representations, John signed the agreement (it appears) at Sellapup's garage and therefore the requirement that he sign it away from certain business premises is not satisfied (*Moorgate Services v Kabir* (1995)). Nor is the agreement cancellable under the **Cancellation of Contracts Made in the Consumer's Home or Place of Work etc Regulations (2008)**, which would cover both unilateral visits or those at the request of John, since it was not made during or following a visit by a trader to anybody's home or to John's place of work. Thus, John's chances of getting out of the agreement depend upon: (a) whether his telephone message to Sellapup was effective to withdraw his offer to enter the hire purchase agreement; or, failing that, (b) whether he can rescind the agreement because of the misrepresentation made to him of the car's mileage. The latter possibility will be discussed later. Alternatively John may be able to exercise the unilateral right of withdrawal under s 66A of the **Consumer Credit Act 1974**. Failing any of those possibilities, John could exercise his statutory right of termination under s 99 of the **Consumer Credit Act**.

WITHDRAWAL FROM THE PROSPECTIVE AGREEMENT

Sellapup was an agent of Fleece You Finance Ltd for the purpose of receiving notice of cancellation. That is so at common law (*Financings v Stimson* (1962)), a rule confirmed in the case of a regulated agreement by s 57(3). Thus, the telephone conversation on Friday in which John informed Sellapup that he wanted to back out of the deal will have the same effect as if that conversation was between John and Fleece You Finance Ltd. **Section 57(2)** and **(3)** makes it clear that the agency rule just mentioned applies equally to oral as to written notice, which 'however expressed' indicates John's intention to withdraw from the agreement. However, it is important to see whether John's withdrawal came in time. He was able to withdraw only from a 'prospective agreement'. This brings into play the operation of the rules of the law of contract in order to discover whether, at the time of John's telephone call to Sellapup, the hire purchase agreement had already been made or was still only a prospective agreement. We are informed that on that same day (Friday), Fleece You Finance Ltd posted to John its acceptance of his offer. Presumably, it was reasonable to expect the post to be used as the medium of communication and, assuming that the acceptance letter was properly stamped and addressed (as seems likely, since John got the letter the following day), then the rule in *Henthorn v Fraser* (1892) applies; thus, Fleece You Finance Ltd's acceptance took effect upon posting. The result is, therefore, that John's position depends upon the relative timings, on Friday last, of the posting by Fleece You Finance Ltd of its acceptance and of John's withdrawal, that is, his telephone call to Sellapup. If the acceptance was posted first, then the contract between John and Fleece You Finance Ltd was made. In that case, John is not, on the facts given in the question, able to back out of it, other than by exercising his unilateral right of withdrawal under s 66A **Consumer Credit Act 1974**, or by virtue of Sellapup's misrepresentation or by exercising his statutory right of termination under s 99 of the **Consumer Credit Act 1974**. If John's withdrawal occurred before the acceptance was posted, then John no longer has an option: he will effectively have withdrawn from the prospective agreement.

Assuming that John's withdrawal came in time, his withdrawal, although it in fact came *before* the acceptance, nevertheless has the effect laid down in **s 57**. The effect is as if the agreement had been a cancellable one within **s 59**, had been made and then had been cancelled. This in turn has the effect of applying **ss 69–73** to the agreement. According to **s 69**, the agreement is cancelled and, on the facts of the problem set, there are not many complications, since John still has his old car and has not taken delivery of the new one. That is now the position, which John is entitled to maintain. John has, however, parted with the £500 initial payment, which he paid to Sellapup. That sum is now repayable to John (**s 70(1)**). Primarily, that sum is repayable by the person (Sellapup) to whom John made it, which is unfortunate for John because Sellapup is bankrupt. If the agreement had been one which fell within **s 12(b)**, that is, within **s 11(1)(b)**, John could have claimed the return of the money from Fleece You Finance Ltd, which would have been liable to John for it, jointly and severally liable with Sellapup, by virtue of **s 70(3)**. However, John's hire purchase agreement falls within **ss 12(a)** and **11(1)(a)**, and that rule in **s 70(3)** therefore does not apply to it.

However, it may be that John can recover the £500 from Fleece You Finance Ltd on a different basis, namely, on the ground that it is money had and received on a total failure of consideration. Presumably, one could say that a prospective agreement which is deemed to have been made and then immediately cancelled reveals a total failure of consideration. Even so, to succeed with such a claim, John would need to show that the money had been *received* by Fleece You Finance Ltd. If, when Fleece You Finance Ltd accepted John's offer, it also accepted Sellapup's offer to sell the car to Fleece You Ltd and if, in doing so, Fleece You Finance Ltd sent to Sellapup a cheque in payment of the cash price, £8,000, and if that cheque was in fact only for £7,500, that is, because Sellapup had been paid £500 by John, then it would be said that Fleece You Finance Ltd had received the £500, that is, by deducting it from the sum paid to Sellapup (see *Branwhite v Worcester Works Finance* (1969)). Certainly, that would be the case if the cheque to Sellapup had been cashed. If Fleece You Finance Ltd has not received the £500 in the way just discussed, then it can still be said to have received it, if it can be established that Sellapup was, when he received it, Fleece You Finance's agent. At common law, unless there was something expressly done or said to make Sellapup its agent, Sellapup would not be regarded as such (*Branwhite v Worcester Works Finance*). However, it is very likely that by virtue of **s 56(2)** of the **Consumer Credit Act**, Sellapup is to be treated as having been its agent. Undoubtedly, the negotiations between Sellapup and John were antecedent negotiations within **s 56(1)(b)**. There is an argument that perhaps **s 56(1)(b)** and **56(2)** does not apply to a prospective agreement unless and until it is made. However that may be, John can here rely on the fact that the agreement was made and then cancelled, that is, by virtue of the deeming provisions of **s 57**. Thus, John has good grounds for saying that Fleece You Finance Ltd has received the £500 and therefore is liable to return it to him.

UNILATERAL RIGHT OF WITHDRAWAL

The problem of an offer before it has been accepted by the creditor or trying to argue that the agreement is cancellable has been considerably reduced by the introduction of a new unilateral right of withdrawal by virtue of **Article 14 EU Consumer Credit Directive 2008/48/EC** implemented in UK law by **s 66A Consumer Credit Act 1974**.

John could withdraw from a regulated credit agreement without giving a reason, either orally (in the manner specified in the agreement) or in writing, provided he does so within 14 days of the relevant date, which in this problem would be the later of:

❖ the day on which the agreement was made; or
❖ the day on which he received the relevant statutory copy of the agreement.

If the withdrawal right is exercised, the agreement shall be treated as never having been entered into and related ancillary service contracts, such as insurance or a payment protection policy, will also be cancelled. This would appear relatively straightforward here, as the car has not been delivered. As the agreement is deemed never to have been entered into, John is entitled to his £500 back and would presumably advance the same agency arguments as discussed in relation to the 'Withdrawal from prospective agreement' section. It has to be said that the right of withdrawal does not seem to operate very clearly in relation to the hire-purchase and conditional sale – talking as it does about the repayment of credit received – but of course the hirer does not actually receive any money, but merely a product which he pays for over the period. John has not received the car and not 'received' any credit and it would appear therefore that under **s 66A(9) & (11)** he has nothing to repay. It is unclear how things stand between the creditor and Sellapup Garage – in all probability the car will have been sold to the finance company and therefore is their property and could be the subject of another hire-purchase agreement with another consumer. Recourse and warranty arrangements with Sellapup would seem to be of little use to them as Sellapup is bankrupt, but the finance company may have bad debt insurance if they cannot make a claim under any recourse right they have against Sellapup.

MISREPRESENTATION

Now consider the position if John's withdrawal came *after* Fleece You Finance Ltd's acceptance was posted or he had failed to or is unable to exercise his right of withdrawal. The hire purchase agreement would in that case be effectively made. John would, however, have a claim against Fleece You Finance Ltd in respect of the claim made by its agent (see **s 56**), Sellapup, that the car had covered 40,000 miles. John would be entitled to rescind the agreement for misrepresentation.

Arguably, he did just that when he telephoned Sellapup telling him that he was backing out of the agreement. The difficulty with that is that Sellapup would not have been Fleece You Finance Ltd's agent for receiving that notice. **Section 56(2)** would not apply as that only applies to 'antecedent' negotiations and presumably, once the agreement is made, those have come to an end. **Section 102**, which expressly makes the person who was the negotiator in antecedent negotiations agent of the creditor for the purpose of receiving notice of rescission, would not apply either; this is because 'notice' according to **s 189(1)** is confined to 'notice in writing'. So, whether John can rescind the contract depends upon whether he has by some other means already communicated to Fleece You Finance Ltd his intention to rescind and, if not, whether he is still within a reasonable period of the making of the agreement, since the equitable remedy of rescission depends upon no unreasonable delay and, unless the misrepresentation can be proved to be a fraudulent one, time runs from that of the making of the agreement (*Leaf v International Galleries* (1950)). It is likely that John is still in time, since the agreement was only made on Saturday last. Irrespective of any claim to rescind the contract, John can claim damages under **s 2(1)** of the **Misrepresentation Act 1967**, unless Fleece You Finance Ltd can prove that there were reasonable grounds to believe, and that up to the time the contract was made, it (or perhaps, rather, Sellapup) believed, that the car had only done 40,000 miles. The damages may be assessed as in the tort of deceit (*Royscot Trust v Rogerson* (1991) and *Pankhania v Hackney LBC (Damages)* (2004)), although if John succeeds in rescinding the contract, it is difficult to see what damage he will have suffered.

It is just possible that as an alternative to, or in addition to, a claim for misrepresentation, John could make a claim for damages (and to reject the goods and repudiate the contract) for breach of the condition as to description, which is implied by **s 9** of the **Supply of Goods (Implied Terms) Act 1973** (that is, the equivalent in a hire purchase agreement to **s 13** of the **Sale of Goods Act 1979**). For this, however, he would have to assert that the goods were bailed (that is, contracted for) by description and that that description included the statement that the car had covered 40,000 miles (*Dick Bentley Productions Ltd v Harold Smith (Motors) Ltd* (1965)). Unless that statement was repeated in writing in the agreement, it might be difficult to show that it was part of the contractual description.

If John's withdrawal did not occur before Fleece You Finance Ltd posted its acceptance, and if he has lost his right to rescind for misrepresentation (for example, through lapse of time), then he does have a statutory right to terminate the agreement under **s 99** of the **Consumer Credit Act**. The consequences of exercising such a right are set out in **s 100** and would be costly, making it a very unattractive option for him. It should, however, be an unnecessary one, since on the facts given, even if John's withdrawal was too late to be an effective withdrawal from the prospective agreement, he should either be able to exercise the right of withdrawal or still be able to rescind the agreement for misrepresentation.

NOTE

For a discussion of whether **s 56** operates only in the case of agreements that have actually been made, see an article by AP Dobson, 'Consumer credit – finance company's liability for dealer's default' (1975) JBL 208, at p 212.

QUESTION 18

Bert, in partnership with his two brothers, runs a sub-post office and is worried about the continued viability of their postal business. The brothers agree that to try and stimulate business beyond core postal services, they need added value services to entice customers in. Bert is approached by Reg, a self-employed salesman, who acts for a variety of firms, including Stingray Photography, who specialise in placing photography booths in shops and other public areas. Reg is very experienced and has been dealing with Stingray Photography for over 10 years. The booth is equipped with computerised printing facilities, which allow customers to produce prints of various sizes and to carry out touching up of their photographs. Reg informs Bert that the hire is £300 per month and that the minimum duration of a hire agreement is 36 months, and he must give three months' notice of termination. Reg assures Bert that based on his considerable experience, and taking into account the location of the sub-post office, annual takings are likely to be of the order of £10,000. The partnership enters into a hire contract and the booth is installed. After six months Bert is extremely unhappy because takings from the machine are barely covering half the monthly hire fee; the computerised printing facilities are very temperamental and are continually jamming, and so he wants to terminate the hire contract, which Stingray Photography the owners of the booth are refusing to do.

1   Advise the partnership; and
2   Would your advice differ if instead of hiring the machine, the partnership had licensed Stingray Photography to place the booth in their shop, agreeing to account for the takings on a monthly basis to Stingray Photography minus a 10% commission for doing this, dealing with customer queries and minor maintenance such as removing jams in the print facility?

Answer Plan

The question requires you to consider the scope of the **CCA 1974** in relation to hire agreements (and in the second scenario, site licence agreements); the status of Reg and whether he is a principal in his own right or an agent, and if the latter, whether **s 56 CCA** applies; whether there is any liability for his misleading opinion about potential takings; whether there is a right to reject if the equipment is not working satisfactorily; and the position in relation to breach and termination if the equipment is not found to be unsatisfactory.

ANSWER

SCOPE

This is a hire agreement with a business partnership requiring minimum payments of £10,800 over 36 months. The title of the **Consumer Credit Act 1974** was misleading, in that it protected all debtors other than corporate debtors (and even those might be partially protected if there was a joint credit agreement with individual debtors – **s 185** of the **CCA 1974**). As part of an exercise in deregulation, the **CCA 2006** redefines 'individual' to include 'a partnership consisting of TWO or THREE persons not all of whom are bodies corporate and an unincorporated body of persons which does not consist entirely of bodies corporate and is not a partnership'. The effect is that generally only small partnerships and not large-scale partnerships will benefit from the protections of the Act. The financial limit in **s 15(1)(c)** excluding hire agreements where the required hire payments would exceed £25,000 has been repealed (**ss 1** and **2** of the **CCA 2006**). However, consumer hire agreements for wholly or predominantly business purposes where the required hire payments will exceed £25,000 are treated as exempt agreements under **s 16** of the **CCA 1974** (**s 4** of the **CCA 2006**). The agreement here is therefore a regulated consumer hire agreement.

AGENCY

The partnership may be able to take advantage of the statutory agency in relation to Reg's statements under **s 56** of the **CCA 1974**. The statutory agency' is very precisely defined and it is necessary to check whether the facts of a consumer credit or hire transaction fall within one of the three 'sub-categories of agency' in **s 56(1)(a)–(c)** – see *Black Horse Ltd v Langford* [2007] *EWHC 907 (QB)*. The statutory agency does not apply to consumer hire agreements unless the statements are made by the creditor or owner himself (which can include his employees and agent) and not by third party credit-brokers or suppliers (*Moorgate Mercantile Leasing Ltd v Gell & Ugolini Dispensers* (1985) and *Lloyds Bowmaker Leasing Ltd v MacDonald* (1993)). It would be a question of fact whether at common law Reg is the agent of Stingray Photography, though the courts have been reluctant to create an agency in relation to intermediaries in credit transactions (*Branwhite v Worcester Works Finance* (1969)). If he were an agent, then as principal, Stingray Photography would be held liable for the statements of Reg if they gave rise to any legal liability as either misrepresentations or terms of the contract. The statements by Reg would probably be regarded as 'antecedent negotiations' made in relation to a regulated agreement, even though not directly concerned with the hire payments element, and such liability would be non-excludable (**s 56(1)(a)**, **(3)** and **(4)** – see *Forthright Finance Ltd v Ingate & Carlyle Finance* (1997)). If Reg were deemed to be not an agent but a freestanding principal, then **s 56** of the **CCA 1974** would not apply. The joint liability provisions in **s 75** of the **CCA 1974** do not apply to consumer hire agreements.

MISREPRESENTATION

On the face of it, Reg's remarks as to likely revenue from the booth look to be a mere opinion, but given his status and experience, the courts would probably imply a statement of fact that he had a reasonable basis for his opinion and if this did not exist, then potential liability might arise for misrepresentation. If he is an agent of Stingray Photography, an action for statutory negligent misrepresentation would be available under **s 2(1)** of the **Misrepresentation Act 1967**, with the added advantage that the onus of proving a reasonable factual basis for Reg's opinion would lie on Stingray Photography (*Howard Marine & Dredging Co Ltd v A Ogden & Sons (Excavations) Ltd* (1978)). If Reg is a free-standing principal **s 2(1)** would not apply, as the consumer hire contract would not be with him but Stingray Photography, but here a common law tort action for negligent misstatement might lie, based on the principle in *Hedley Byrne v Heller & Partners* (1964), on the basis that Reg is aware that Bert is relying on his skill and judgement in relation to potential revenues and it is fair and just to impose liability on him.

IMPLIED TERM

If the computerised printing facilities keep breaking down and this is attributable to a defect in the equipment, there is the potential for the termination of the contract for breach of the implied term of satisfactory quality under **s 4** of the **Supply of Goods and Services Act 1982** even though Bert has had the booth for three months (see *UCB Leasing v Holtom* (1987) and *Farnworth Finance Facilities v Attryde* (1970)).

TERMINATION

Unfortunately for Bert, the statutory right of termination of consumer hire agreements provided in **s 101** of the **CCA 1974** will not apply as the annual payments exceed £1500 and the agreement is for business purposes (**s 101(7)** of the **CCA 1974**). In the absence of any contractual right of early termination, the partnership would be bound by the minimum hire period of 36 months.

BREACH AND DAMAGES

In the absence of any contractual right to reject for breach of the condition of satisfactory quality, or contractual right of early termination, then the partnership would be in breach of contract if they sought to terminate the hire before the 36-month minimum period had elapsed and could, assuming proper default procedures had been followed (**ss 87–89** of the **CCA 1974**), face an action for damages for breach of contract or face a demand for immediate payment of the hire charges under a valid acceleration clause (*Wadham Stringer Ltd v Meaney* (1981)), as well of course as the return of the photography booth to Stingray Photography. It is quite probable that as this is a business contract there will be a liquidated damages clause in the hire contract, and provided this is a reasonable pre-estimate of the owner's loss, will be upheld by the courts even if the amount payable under the clause exceeds the actual loss on this occasion (*Robophone Facilities Ltd v Blank* (1966)). The statutory rebate provision in **s 94** of the **CCA 1974** does not apply to consumer hire agreements. It is unlikely on the facts that the hirer could claim relief under **s 132** of the **CCA 1974** on grounds that it is just that he be relieved from some or all of his future hire payments and recover any part of instalments already made.

LICENSING AGREEMENT

In the second scenario, the partnership merely license Stingray Photography to place the machine in their shop and to account for any proceeds received for use of the machine, minus a commission. It follows from this that if no one used the machine, they would not be required to pay any money to Stingray Photography. The question then arises whether it is still a regulated consumer hire agreement within **s 15** of the **CCA 1974**. The answer to that question appears to be no, as a result of the decision in *TRM Copy Centres (UK) v Lanwall* (2008), where it was held that for a bailment to fall within the scope of the Act, there must be an element of payment involved, and where in that case, involving a photocopier, in a post office the owner of the shop only had to account for the proceeds of use of the copier minus a commission, it was held that as there were no mandatory hire charges, it was not a regulated consumer hire agreement. The outcome here is then that in the second scenario it would be an unregulated credit agreement governed by the common law and it would depend on the terms of the licence whether and under what conditions the partnership could terminate the licence – presumably if the machine did not work they might, in absence of any express provision, rely on an implied term to give business efficacy to the contract that the licensed equipment actually work satisfactorily (*Liverpool City Council v Irwin* (1977)).

Aim Higher ★

A candidate looking to secure a first class mark will have picked up the more limited impact of the **Consumer Credit Act** regime on regulated hire agreements as opposed to regulated consumer credit agreements – in particular in relation to operation of **ss 56 & 101 CCA 1974**. Another key element in this and a number of other questions on consumer credit is to be able to apply the known **CCA 1974** dimensions – in this question in particular the scope and operation of the **Misrepresentation Act 1967** and the relevant common law provisions on breach and liquidated damages clauses in relation to hire agreements, to use a modern phrase, to 'think outside the box'. In other words, not all the aspects of a question will be dealt with by the **Consumer Credit Act 1974** regime – examiners will give extra credit for this broadness of vision.

> ## Common Pitfalls ✗
>
> Often marks may be lost by simple errors such as confusing pure hire agreements with hire-purchase agreements and for example incorrectly applying the agency provisions in **s 56 CCA 1974** and the termination provisions in **s 99 & 100 CCA** instead of the correct provision in **s 101 CCA 1974**. Another error is to fail to realise that the **CCA 1974** can apply to some business credit contracts in particular with small partnerships – the weak candidate will not have taken on board the narrowed definition of an '*individual*' in the amended **s 189(1) CCA 1974**. Another common oversight is failure to consider whether – which will commonly be the case – there is a valid liquidated damages clause in a business hire agreement. In relation to the second fact scenario, a weak student may not appreciate the parameters of the definition of a regulated hire agreement in **s 15 CCA 1974** and the impact of the House of Lords decision in *TRM Copy Centres (UK) v Lanwall* (2008).

QUESTION 19

Steve is facing serious financial problems, having recently lost his job, and he also owes money to a variety of creditors, including a number of credit card companies. Steve sees an advertisement in the *Newtown Gazette* by Access Brokers offering to arrange debt consolidation loans at affordable interest rates for people with concerns about multiple debts. Steve visits Access Brokers and signs a proposal form to enter into an unsecured £30,000 consolidation loan, repayable over five years at 21% APR with Newtown Loans Ltd. The loan is to be used to pay off his existing loans and leave him with about £5,000 for his personal use. He is given a copy of the unexecuted agreement by Access Brokers and five days later receives a copy of the executed loan agreement from the creditor, Newtown Loans Ltd. Three months later he receives written notice advising him that the interest rate is to be raised to 28% APR. The letter states that this is because of adverse credit conditions caused by the so-called credit crunch. Steve also learns that Access Credit do not hold a credit brokerage licence under the **Consumer Credit Act 1974**. He is also concerned that the interest rate he is being asked to pay is not affordable, and the advertisement gave no indication of the rates involved in the proposed consolidation loans. A friend has also told him he should have received another copy of the loan agreement and therefore he can stop repaying the loan.

Advise Steve on the following:

1   whether the credit agreement is enforceable as the introduction to the creditor was made by an unlicensed credit broker;
2   whether any criminal offence has been committed by the brokers in relation to their advertisement in the Newtown Gazette;
3   whether he has received the appropriate pre-contract advice and whether the agreement copy formalities have been carried out and, if not, is the loan agreement enforceable;
4   whether Newtown Loans can unilaterally vary the interest rate;
5   whether he could withdraw from the agreement having reflected that it is not good value for him.

Answer Plan

The question requires the candidate to be aware of the licensing provisions relating to credit brokers and the effect on the principal credit agreement if the credit-broker is unlicensed; the criminal regulation of false and misleading credit advertisements, and the key requirement in cases where lenders are trying to entice over-extended or indebted consumers into debt consolidation arrangements to give a typical APR; the copy requirements in the **CCA 1974**, how specific the creditor has to be about the circumstances in which a variable interest rate may be adjusted, and whether there is any limitation on the variation power at common law or under the **CCA 1974** and **CCA 2006**.

ANSWER

INTRODUCTION TO CREDITOR BY UNLICENSED BROKERS

Credit brokerage is an 'ancillary credit business', and the carrying on of such a business requires a licence granted by the OFT (**ss 145** and **147** of the **CCA 1974**). As the £25,000 limit no longer applies to consumer credit agreements with non-high net worth individuals for non-business purposes, the introduction here is for entry into a regulated consumer credit agreement (**s 2** of the **CCA 2006**). An introduction by an unlicensed credit-broker means that the principal credit agreement is unenforceable without a validation order from the OFT even if the principal creditor does hold a valid licence (**s 148** of the **CCA 1974**). Either the credit-broker or the creditor can seek to apply for such an order and the OFT can deem the credit-broker to have been licensed at the time when the agreement was entered into with Steve. In deciding whether to grant such an order, the OFT will take account of the degree of prejudice to the debtor and the degree of culpability involved: was it merely an administrative oversight, or deliberate fraud on the part of the credit-broker? The OFT will also take account of the degree of culpability of the principal creditor in not ensuring that credit-brokers they dealt with were licensed.

WHETHER ANY ADVERTISING OFFENCES WERE COMMITTED

Truth in lending is a core principle of the **CCA 1974**. The Act created a general offence of issuing a false and misleading credit advertisement in **s 46** of the **CCA 1974** and more detailed positive content requirements by the statutory instrument made under **s 44** of the **CCA 1974**. On 26 May 2008, **s 46** was repealed, and false or misleading credit advertising is now dealt with under the **Consumer Protection from Unfair Trading Regulations 2008**. On the assumption that the credit crunch was not foreseen, and so the advertisement was placed in good faith, it would have to be argued that the use of the word 'affordable' was misleading and that it would deceive the average consumer – one who is deemed to be reasonably well informed, reasonably observant and circumspect (**reg 2(2)** of the **CPUTR 2008**). It would have to be argued that the advertisement is misleading under **reg 5** of the **CPUTR 2008**, and it caused or would be likely to cause the average consumer to take a transactional decision they would not otherwise take. It is very doubtful whether the use of word 'affordable' of itself would be enough, and given that the consumer must receive a copy of the draft agreement and a pre-contractual notice setting out material terms which would indicate the annual percentage rate, or at least an estimated rate based on assumptions that it would be reasonable to make (**Consumer Credit (Disclosure of Information) Regs 2004**), it is hard to argue that the advertisement alone would cause the consumer to enter the loan of itself. It is unlikely therefore that the advertisement breaches **reg 5** of the **CPUTR 2008** which could lead to a criminal prosecution for breach of a strict liability offence under **reg 9** of the **CPUTR 2008**. It might be argued that the omission of the typical interest rates was a material omission under **reg 6** of the **CPUTR 2008**, in that the information would be needed by an average consumer to take an informed transactional decision in the context. As the pre-contract information document and the draft credit agreement would clearly set out the annual percentage rate and total charge for credit, it is difficult to argue that their omission in a general advertisement of itself would be a misleading omission.

A more likely route to conviction is that the credit broker has breached **reg 8** of the **Consumer Credit (Advertisements) Regulations 2004** in advertising the ability to arrange debt consolidation loans without specifying the typical annual percentage rates for such loans, which generally means those available to at least 66.66 per cent of customers – this is the case, as the advertisement appears to be directed to those who might be expected to believe that their recourse to fresh credit is restricted because of current debt problems (**s 151(1)**, **s 167** and **Sched 1** of the **CCA 1974**). Breach of the regulations is a strict liability offence and if Newtown Loans were referred to in the advertisement, they would be deemed to be an advertiser as well (**s 189** of the **CCA 1974**) and could face prosecution as well, unless they were able to bring themselves within the due diligence defence in **s 168** of the **CCA 1974** – that the offence was due to the act or default of access loans and they had taken all reasonable precautions and exercised all due diligence to avoid the commission of the offence.

WERE PRE-CONTRACT PROCEDURES PROPERLY CARRIED OUT?

What Access Brokers do for Steve is not explicitly stated in the question but they appear to be acting as a '*credit intermediary*' within the terms of **s 160A CCA 1974** – certainly they have made available a prospective regulated credit agreement to him and probably done other preparatory work (**s 160A (1)–(2) CCA 1974**). It will be an offence for them not to disclose whether they are acting independently or exclusively with a creditor and must disclose any financial consideration they are receiving from the creditor in relation to making the arrangements for the loan (**s 160A (3)(4) CCA 1974**).

The agreement entered will be improperly executed if Steve does not receive the key information about the loan in the form of a pre-contractual disclosure notice (**s 55 CCA 1974** and **Consumer Credit (Disclosure of Information) Regulations SI 2010/1013**). Either the credit intermediary or the creditor must also have ensured that either orally or in writing Steve has received an 'adequate explanation' of the key pros and cons of the proposed agreement (**s 55A CCA 1974**). Steve's '*creditworthiness*' must be assessed before the agreement is entered into (**s 55B CCA 1974**). Under **s 55C** Steve must be given a copy of the draft agreement or such part of it that has been reduced to writing. It is not immediately clear what the sanction for breach of **s 55A & B** is. Breach of **s 55C** is actionable as a breach of statutory duty. Steve would have had an opportunity to take away the pre-contractual information for consideration if he had wished (**s 55A(1)(b) CCA 1974**).

WAS PRINCIPAL CREDIT AGREEMENT PROPERLY EXECUTED?

One of the key elements of the **CCA 1974** regime is to ensure the debtor receives full information about his commitments both in the agreement itself and by the provision of appropriate copies (**ss 60–65** of the **CCA 1974**). Failure to do this will mean that the agreement is improperly executed and only enforceable either by the free and informed consent of the debtor given at the time enforcement is sought or by an enforcement order from the court (**ss 65, 127** and **173(3)** of the **CCA 1974**). It is important to note that the agreement is not void or voidable, merely civilly unenforceable in a court, and if the debtor makes all payments and performs the agreement no further redress will normally be available. Here the debtor has been given a copy of the unexecuted agreement at the premises of the broker as required by **s 61A** of the **CCA 1974**; in the terms of the executed agreement, no further copy of the executed agreement need be supplied – merely a letter from the creditor confirming that the two agreements are identical. As the agreement is not cancellable, and a copy of the executed agreement, and any other document referred to in it (signed and accepted by the creditor – the debtor being the one who has made the offer) has been sent to him by post within seven days of the agreement being executed, then it appears the correct formalities in relation to copies have been carried out and the agreement is properly executed (**ss 61 & 61(A)** of the **CCA 1974**).

EXERCISE OF THE RIGHT OF WITHDRAWAL

However, provided he acts promptly, Steve may be able to take advantage of the unilateral right of withdrawal in **s 66A CCA 1974**. Oral or written notice must be given within 14 days of the latest of the following:

- ❖ the day on which the agreement is made;
- ❖ in the case of an agreement to which **s 61A** … applies, the day on which the debtor receives a copy of the agreement under section or on which the debtor is informed as specified in **subsection (3)** of that section (**s 66A(1)–(3) CCA 1974**).

The agreement must set out the manner in which the oral notice is to be given (**s 66A(4)**). Written notice can be given in hard copy form or electronically (**s 66(A5) & (6)**). If right of withdrawal is validly exercised, the principal credit agreement is treated as if it had never been entered into and also any related 'ancillary service contract'. Specifically included are insurance and payment protection policies (**s 66A(13) CCA 1974**). However, the main practical obstacle that Steve may encounter is that within 30 days, beginning with the day after the day on which the notice of withdrawal was given, Steve must repay the credit provided along with any accrued interest but is not otherwise required to pay any compensation, fees or charges (**s 66A(9)–(10)**). A lot will depend on how promptly Steve decides better of this agreement, and he can recover sums paid to prior debtors.

VALIDITY OF UNILATERAL VARIATION CLAUSE

Variable interest loans are quite common – often linked to the Bank of England base rate or some other index. At common law, the courts are generally unwilling to imply a term that any interest variation clause must be operated in a fair or reasonable manner, or that the creditor is required to adjust the interest rate downwards when the base rate falls. The minimum requirement is that the interest rate is set in good faith, and not in an arbitrary, capricious or dishonest manner (*Nash v Paragon Finance* (2002) and *Paragon Finance v Pender* (2005)). Furthermore, in *Lombard Tricity Finance*

Ltd v Paton (1989) it was held that the creditor need not outline each and every circumstance which might lead to an adjustment of an interest rate: it was sufficient to state that it was 'subject to variation by the creditor from time to time on notification as required by law'. It might be possible to argue that a unilateral increase of the rate of interest by 25% a year by the creditor means 'the way in which the creditor has exercised or enforced any of his rights under the agreement' has created an unfair relationship (**s 19** of the **CCA 2006**) and permit the court to reduce the rate. There is nothing in the question to indicate that Steve has not been sent a copy of the modified agreement as required in **s 82 CCA 1974** because until that is done the increased rate of interest would not be enforceable.

Default and Termination of Credit Agreements

[Assume that the EU Consumer Credit Directive 2008/48/EC, 23 April 2008 is fully in force.]

INTRODUCTION

This chapter covers the termination of hire purchase agreements as well as other regulated agreements; challenges by the debtor to an allegedly unfair credit agreement; and the use of the Financial Ombudsman Service instead of the courts in the event of a dispute with the creditor.

Checklist ✔

The following topics should be prepared in advance of tackling the questions:

- need to issue arrears and default notices and arrears and default information sheets under **ss 8–12** of the **Consumer Credit Act 2006**;
- need for and effect of a default notice under **s 87** of the **Consumer Credit Act 1974**;
- non-default notice under **ss 76** and **98**;
- time orders under **s 129** of the **Consumer Credit Act**;
- liability of surety in relation to regulated agreements;
- protected goods provision in **s 90** of the **Consumer Credit Act**;
- accelerated payments clauses;
- hire purchase customers' right of termination under **s 99** of the **Consumer Credit Act**;
- claim by owner against a third party to whom a hire purchase customer has sold or bailed the goods;
- the consumer credit jurisdiction of the Financial Services Ombudsman under **ss 59–61** of the **Consumer Credit Act 2006**;

- the jurisdiction to intervene in an 'unfair relationship' between the creditor and the debtor **ss 19–22** of the **Consumer Credit Act 2006** replacing extortionate credit bargain provisions in **ss 137–40** of the **Consumer Credit Act 1974**;

- guidance on irresponsible lending set out in 'Irresponsible Lending' OFT Guidance for Creditors (OFT 1107, March 2010) and **Articles 8 & 9 EU Consumer Credit Directive 2008/48/EC**;

- the provisions of the **EU Consumer Credit Directive 2008/48/EC, 23 April 2008** and their implementation in the **Consumer Credit Act 1974**.

QUESTION 20

Just over five months ago, Fred traded in his old car in part-exchange for a new car which he acquired from XYZ Finance under a regulated hire purchase agreement. The hire purchase agreement showed the following details:

❖ a cash price of £21,000;
❖ a total hire purchase price of £24,000;
❖ a part-exchange allowance of £4,000.

Under the agreement, Fred agreed to make an initial cash payment of £2,000 and 36 monthly instalment payments of £500.

Upon trading in his old car and taking delivery of the new one, Fred paid the initial payment of £2,000 and has since paid the first three of the £500 monthly instalments. However, he is now two months in arrears with his instalments and a week ago wrote to XYZ Finance, informing it that he was temporarily out of work and unable to keep up his payments.

Advise Fred as to his legal position now that he has received a default notice which complies with the requirements of the **Consumer Credit Act 1974** and states that unless he pays off his outstanding arrears within seven days, XYZ Finance will regard the agreement as terminated.

Answer Plan

This question demands a consideration of the area of termination of a hire purchase agreement. The plan is to consider the following:

❖ have the procedures in relation to dealing with arrears been followed?
❖ has a terminating event occurred?

❖   what are the consequences of termination arising from Fred's breach?
❖   can Fred avoid those consequences, for example by paying off the debt before expiry of the default notice, or applying for a time order (and how in all of that does the fact that the goods are 'protected goods', if indeed that is what they are, help Fred)?
❖   is it worthwhile for Fred to exercise his own right of termination?
❖   is there any other way out of the mess for Fred, for example selling the car or refinancing the debt?

ANSWER

The question states that the hire purchase agreement is a regulated one. No information is given about whether the formalities and documentation requirements of the **Consumer Credit Act 1974** have been satisfied, and it is assumed in this answer that they have been.

The problem requires a discussion of whether the agreement has been, or can be, terminated and the possible consequences of that for Fred.

ARREARS INFORMATION AND ARREARS NOTICE

The creditor would have to check whether it had to serve a notice of 'sums in arrears' under **s 9** of the **CCA 2006** which will be the case where the debtor is required to have made more than two payments under the agreement and the amount of the shortfall is no less than the sum of the last two payments which Fred is required to have made before the relevant time. This applies here, and within 14 days of these conditions being satisfied under a fixed-sum credit agreement, an arrears notice must be served and with this notice a copy of an OFT-issued 'arrears information sheet' must be given which is designed to inform debtors who receive an arrears notice of what steps they might take and the consequences of taking remedial action (**s 8** of the **CCA 2006** and see copy on OFT website: http://www.oft.gov.uk/shared_oft/consumer_leaflets/credit/OFT965a.pdf). Failure to give such a notice will mean that while this default continues, the creditor may not enforce the agreement and the debtor will not be liable for interest or any default sum during the non-compliance period (**s 11** of the **CCA 2006**).

TERMINATING EVENT – FRED'S BREACH

Has a terminating event occurred? There is no doubt that Fred is in breach of his agreement by becoming in arrears. There are three alternative ways in which this could be argued to be a terminating event. The first is if it amounts to a repudiation by

Fred. On the facts, that argument would be difficult to sustain, since there is no outright refusal by Fred to honour the agreement and his failure to pay two instalments, coupled with Fred's letter referring to him being *temporarily* out of work, hardly signifies a repudiation.

The second way that Fred's breach could be argued to be a terminating event is if the agreement expressly gives to XYZ Finance a right to terminate the agreement, for example if Fred falls into arrears exceeding seven days' delay in making any payment. The third way is if the agreement expressly stipulates that prompt making of payments by Fred is 'of the essence' of the contract (see *Lombard North Central v Butterworth* (1987)).

Even if one of the last two possibilities proves to be the case, XYZ Finance would not be able to treat the agreement as terminated until the expiry of the default notice (**s 87**) The default notice issued under **ss 87–89** of the **CCA 1974** will also have to contain information required by a 'default notice' under **s 12** of the **CCA 2006** – the contents of which will be prescribed by statutory regulation; default interest will not be payable until the lapse of 28 days after the issue of the notice and interest on default sums can only be calculated on a simple interest and not a compound interest basis, eg no interest on interest, only on the outstanding principal (**ss 13** and **18** of the **CCA 2006**). It is also important to note that under **s 88(4A)**, to be valid notice a default information sheet must be included which will advise Fred on how he might deal with the default issue (see copy on OFT website: http://www.oft.gov.uk/shared_oft/consumer_leaflets/credit/OFT966a.pdf). If Fred makes good his default and pays off his arrears (together with any default interest) before the expiry of the default notice (and under **s 88** amended by **s 14** of the **CCA 2006** Fred must be given at least 14 days from the date of the service of the notice to rectify the breach), then Fred's breach will be treated as not having occurred (**s 89**) and therefore XYZ Finance will have no right to treat the contract as terminated.

CONSEQUENCES OF TERMINATION UPON FRED'S BREACH

If Fred's breach is a terminating event, what will be the consequences of termination (that is, assuming also that Fred does not pay off his arrears before expiry of the default notice)?

If the termination arose because the agreement gave XYZ Finance a right of termination upon the debtor falling into arrears, then the consequences of that termination would be those indicated in *Financings v Baldock* (1963). These would be that Fred would lose the right to keep the car and would be liable for the arrears due up to termination; assuming that the agreement imposed upon him a requirement to take reasonable care of the vehicle, he would be liable also for any loss caused by any failure of his to take that care.

If the termination arose because the agreement made Fred's prompt payment of instalments 'of the essence', then XYZ Finance would be entitled to regard the termination as having come about as a result of a repudiation by Fred and would be able to claim not only the return of the car, but also damages assessed on a *Waragowski* (1961) basis, which would allow XYZ Finance to claim not only the arrears already fallen due, but also all the outstanding instalments minus the value of the vehicle recovered and minus a deduction to reflect the fact that XYZ Finance was getting early payment of some instalments. This deduction would be assessed on a rather rough-and-ready basis at common law (*Overstone v Shipway* (1962)) but, under the **Consumer Credit Act**, would be calculated according to the regulations (under **s 95**) governing the rebate for early payment.

It has been said that if termination on either basis just discussed occurred, then XYZ Finance would be entitled to recover the goods. That is in principle true, and at common law an owner is entitled simply to help himself to his own goods – at least if he can do so without trespassing (see *Bowmakers v Barnet Instruments* (1945)). However, XYZ Finance would not be able simply to help itself to the car, for example from the street, if the car was 'protected goods' within the meaning of **s 90**. In this case, the goods will be protected goods if Fred has made or tendered payments totalling one-third (that is, £8,000) or more of the total price (of £24,000). Fred has actually paid a £2,000 initial cash payment, plus £4,000 trade-in allowance plus three instalments of £500, which totals only £7,500. If he were to tender payment of one more instalment, the goods would become protected goods. In that case, XYZ Finance would have to bring court proceedings for a return order (under **s 133**) in order to recover the car. If Fred does not offer that further payment, the goods will not be within the definition of protected goods. It would still be the case, however, that XYZ Finance would not be entitled to trespass to recover the car (for example, if it was in a garage on Fred's premises) (see **s 92**). Fred could, of course, waive the protection afforded by **ss 90** and **92** by giving permission to XYZ Finance to recover the goods – provided that that consent is given at the time of the repossession (**s 173(3)**). Even then, the consent would not be effective if Fred had not been informed of what his rights would be if he refused that consent (*Chartered Trust v Pitcher* (1987)), although it is thought that the default notice is likely to have given Fred that information. Fred would be well advised not to give that consent. The ability or otherwise of XYZ Finance to recover possession of the goods without having to bring court proceedings could well be significant, since if it recovers possession of the goods – and especially if it then subsequently sold them, it would be very difficult in any later court proceedings for the court to keep Fred's hire purchase agreement alive. If, on the other hand, XYZ Finance has to bring court proceedings to recover the car, Fred will have a meaningful option to apply under **s 129** for a time order. If evidence of his means is sufficiently convincing, the court could then allow Fred extra time to pay off his arrears (*Southern and District Finance v Barnes* (1995)). Furthermore, this being a hire purchase agreement, the court would have power in making a time order to reorganise the future payment pattern in relation to instalments which have not yet fallen due: **s 130(2)**. In the event that the car is not within the definition of protected goods and is kept on the highway, then Fred might well consider applying immediately for a time order, so as to try to pre-empt any attempt by XYZ Finance to recover the goods. As a default notice has been served on him, Fred has the right to apply for a time order under **s 129** without waiting for proceedings to be commenced against him. Under **s 16(2)** of the **CCA 2006**, after being served with an 'arrears information sheet' and an 'arrears notice' (**ss 8** and **9** of the **CCA 2006**) Fred can apply for a time order but must give the creditor at least 14 days' notice of his proposed schedule of payments.

FRED'S RIGHT OF TERMINATION

A different option open to Fred, rather than to await termination taking place upon his own breach of the agreement, is to exercise the right himself to terminate the agreement under **s 99**, which he could do simply by serving upon XYZ Finance a written notice to that effect. The effects of him doing that are laid down in **s 100**. He would have to return the car and would be liable to pay the arrears which have already fallen due: £1,000.

Also, he may be liable to pay such further sums as would be required to bring his payments up to one-half of the total price unless the loss suffered by the creditor is less than that amount. After payment of his arrears, his payments to date will be £8,500. Thus, the final sum to be paid by Fred (in addition to the £1,000 arrears) could be up to £3,500, which would bring the £8,500 up to £12,000 (which is the total price of £24,000). This figure of £3,500 would be reduced to such sum, if any, stipulated in the agreement as payable upon termination. Normally, an agreement will state a formula which will produce exactly the same figure as, in this case, the £3,500; if the agreement fails to stipulate any sum as payable upon termination, the figure of £3,500 is reduced to zero. Assuming that the sum of £3,500 is stipulated in the agreement, the court still has discretion under **s 100** to reduce the £3,500 to such lesser figure as it considers sufficient to compensate XYZ Finance. It might do this if, for example, the value of the car when recovered by XYZ Finance proved still to be very high (that is, over £12,000).

CONCLUDING ADVICE

Which is the better (or least negative) option outlined above largely depends upon two things. The first is the likelihood of Fred getting back into work which will enable him to resume full payments; this would certainly make an application for a time order look an attractive option if XYZ Finance can be prevented from helping itself to the car. Failing the first, the second is the value of the car at present. If it is still of a high value, exercising the s 99 right of termination might prove quite expensive and, even if Fred sat back and let XYZ Finance terminate the agreement, it might be galling to have to return a car when he has already paid £7,500 towards it and when he would still be liable for the £1,000 arrears. Of course, if he can summon up the financial resources, he could pay off the arrears before expiry of the default notice and thus put off the problem until he is next in arrears.

Otherwise, Fred might consider a different possibility. He could ask XYZ Finance for a settlement statement, thus discovering how much is required for him to pay off the whole of the outstanding debt (that is, getting the benefit of a rebate of charges under s 95), and then he could discover how much he could sell the car for. It may be that Fred would be better off selling the car and using the proceeds to pay off the debt to XYZ Finance than if he either simply let XYZ Finance terminate the agreement or he terminated it himself under s 99. If Fred could find a willing buyer at the right price, he has only either to get that buyer to pay direct to XYZ Finance the outstanding balance owed by Fred or else himself to pass that amount on to XYZ Finance. Either way, as soon as XYZ Finance is paid off, Fred will acquire title to the goods, which title would of course be 'fed' straight on to Fred's purchaser (*Butterworth v Kingsway Motors* (1954)). If Fred cannot sell the car for a figure which would help him out of his difficulties, he could possibly make a different use of his right (under ss 94 and 95) to pay off the debt early and earn the rebate of charges for doing so. That is, he might find that his bank is willing to make him a loan agreement at a significantly lower rate of interest than the hire purchase agreement is costing him. Because Fred is out of work, his credit rating may make the bank wary of any such agreement, but the possibility of refinancing the agreement could at least be investigated (note any firm advising him on how to 'clean up' his credit rating and remove anything likely to impede future granting of credit will need to be licensed as a provider of 'credit information services': s 25 of the **CCA 2006**).

QUESTION 21

Harley had longed for a motorcycle which he had seen in the window of Cycles Sellers Ltd. On his 17th birthday, Harley acquired the motorcycle under the terms of a regulated hire purchase agreement which he made with Davison Finance. Davison Finance had refused to make the agreement until Harley's father, Gullible, had provided a guarantee of Harley's liabilities under the hire purchase agreement. Davison Finance also has a recourse agreement with the dealer, Cycles Sellers Ltd. The hire purchase agreement provided for an initial payment of £3,000 and 36 monthly payments of £200 each. After making the initial payment and paying one of the monthly instalments, Harley stopped making payments. Davison served a default notice upon him at a time when he was two instalments in arrears and, upon expiry of the default notice without Harley having paid off his arrears, Davison Finance terminated the agreement and repossessed the cycle, helping itself to it from outside Gullible's house where Harley had left it. That was yesterday. The motorcycle is now worth £3,000 and Harley has no assets.

▶ **Advise Davison Finance.**

What difference, if any, would it make if at the time when Harley fell into arrears, he had already paid three of the monthly instalments and if the agreement which Gullible signed was expressed as an indemnity?

Answer Plan

This question tells us that Harley has no assets and thus it requires us to consider any claims Davison Finance may have against Harley's father and the dealer. The fact that the agreement signed by Gullible is a guarantee means that we cannot avoid examining what claims in law Davison Finance may have against Harley. Since we are not told of the terms of the recourse agreement, it seems sensible first to consider the claim against Gullible. It is assumed that the correct procedures have been followed in relation to the issuing of any required arrears notice and default notice (s 9 of the **CCA 2006** and s 87 of the **CCA 1974**).

ANSWER

GULLIBLE'S LIABILITY

Since Harley has no assets, Davison Finance will not be advised to consider any proceedings against Harley. It is nevertheless necessary to ask what is the legal liability of Harley because the liability of Gullible, if not of the dealer, may well depend upon it. The most obvious issue is that Harley was, at the time of the making of the contract, a minor. This might well make the contract unenforceable against Harley. Even if that is so, however, that particular defence will not be available to someone, here Gullible, who has guaranteed Harley's liability. If the only reason that the principal debtor is not liable is that he was a minor at the time of the contract, then that will not prevent someone who has guaranteed that liability from being liable on his guarantee (s 2 of the **Minors' Contracts Act 1987**). Apart from that exception, Gullible, as Harley's guarantor, cannot be liable to any greater extent than Harley.

So, ignoring the fact that Harley was a minor, what is the extent of Harley's liability? The hire purchase agreement made by Harley was, we are told, a regulated consumer credit agreement. It provided for a total hire purchase price of £10,200. At the time of the termination, Harley had paid £3,200, which is less than one-third of the total price. In those circumstances, the motorcycle was not 'protected goods' within the definition in **s 90** of the **Consumer Credit Act 1974**. That being so, once the contract had been validly terminated, Davison Finance had a right to possession of its own goods irrespective of whether the contract stated so in express terms (*Bowmakers v Barnet Instruments* (1945)). We are told that the cycle was repossessed from outside Gullible's house. We are not told if this means that it was in the street, that is, the public highway, or in Gullible's garden. If the latter was the case, then despite the fact that Davison Finance was entitled to possession of the cycle, it was not entitled to trespass in Gullible's garden in order to retrieve it (**s 92**) and is liable to Gullible for breach of statutory duty (**s 92(3)**). There is no other sanction for the entry onto Gullible's premises (if that is what occurred) to recover possession of the cycle. It will thus have no bearing upon Gullible's liability under his guarantee, other than to afford him a counterclaim in any proceedings that Davison Finance may bring against him.

Harley's liability, and hence Gullible's, would certainly include a liability to pay off the £400 of arrears already due before the termination occurred. Beyond that, the liability depends upon the terms of the hire purchase agreement. If it provided that prompt payment of all instalments under the agreement was 'of the essence' of the agreement, then that would result in a liability for the whole outstanding balance of the hire purchase price (*Lombard North Central v Butterworth* (1987)). From that would be deducted the value of the cycle when recovered (£3,000) and any rebate due for the consequent earlier payment of the outstanding instalments.

The mathematical process is thus as follows:

1	Ascertain the total HP price	£10,200
2	Deduct from the total HP price all sums already paid	£3,200
3	That leaves the outstanding balance	£7,000
4	Divide the outstanding balance into:	
	(a) arrears owing at termination	£400
	(b) future payments owing	£6,600
5	Deduct from future payments owing, both:	
	(i) value of vehicle repossessed	£3,000
	(ii) amount of rebate for early settlement	£X
6	The total due is then:	
	(a) arrears owing at termination	£400
	(b) future payments owing minus the items at 5(i) and (ii) above	£3,600 *less £X*
7	The total due thus is	£4,000 *less £X*

£X is the statutory rebate for early payment of outstanding instalments.

If, however, the contract contained no provision making prompt payment 'of the essence' of the contract, then there will be no liability beyond an obligation to pay off arrears due before termination together with damages (if any) for any failure by Harley to take reasonable care of the cycle (*Financings v Baldock* (1963)). This is because, on the facts given, there is no evidence of Harley having committed a repudiation of the contract. In this situation, there is no question of Gullible being held liable to any greater extent than Harley would be, for example, for the outstanding instalments. This is because, apart from the exception which deals with the fact that Harley was a minor, a guarantor cannot be liable to any greater extent than the debtor whose debts or obligations he has guaranteed.

DOCUMENTATION

So, can Gullible be held liable to the extent indicated above? The answer is probably yes, but there are some documentation requirements which need first to be considered. The guarantee given by Gullible is 'security' within the meaning of the **Consumer Credit Act** (see **s 189(1)**). Thus, it needs to be determined (the question does not tell us) whether the necessary documentation requirements were complied with, both in the making of the hire purchase agreement between Harley and Davison Finance, and also in the making of the guarantee agreement. So far as the first of these is concerned, any defence available to Harley because of any failure to observe the documentation requirements is equally available to Gullible. This is a result of the nature of a guarantee and is reinforced by **s 113** of the **Consumer Credit Act**. The court has a discretion whether to grant an enforcement order even when the documentation requirements have been infringed (see **s 127**, **s 15** of the **CCA 2006** has repealed **s 127(3)–(5)** so there are no longer any cases where the infringement of the documentation requirements automatically renders the credit and/or security agreements permanently unenforceable and also reverses the effect of the House of Lords decision in *Wilson v First County Trust (No 2)* (2003)). There are documentation requirements which should have been observed in the making of the guarantee (see **s 105**), which include a requirement that Gullible receive a copy of Harley's hire purchase agreement. Again, however, the court has a discretion, under **s 127**, to grant an enforcement order against Gullible even if the requirements were not complied with (*Hurstanger Ltd v Wilson* (2007)).

There is, however, one further documentation requirement to be mentioned. It is that Gullible should have been (we are not told whether he was) served with a copy of the default notice served on Harley (**s 111**). If he was not, then again the court has a discretion (under **s 127**) nevertheless to grant an enforcement order against Gullible. It is to be observed, however, that in exercising its discretion in all the above-mentioned cases, the court must take into account not only the culpability (that is, of Davison Finance) for the infringement, but also any prejudice caused by it. If there was a failure to serve Gullible with a copy of the default notice, then, unless Harley informed Gullible about Harley having received the default notice, the degree of prejudice to Gullible could have been very severe. Had he been served with the default notice, then he might well have paid off the arrears owing and thus prevented the termination of the hire purchase agreement.

LIABILITY OF CYCLES SELLERS

We are informed that Davison Finance has a recourse agreement with Cycles Sellers. We are not told anything of its terms. It is usual, however, for these agreements to be expressed as indemnities and definitely not as guarantees. Thus, Cycles Sellers will have taken on a primary liability and, unlike Gullible, will not automatically have available to it any defence available to Harley. Also, the recourse agreement will not be within the definition of 'security' in **s 189(1)**, since it is virtually certain that the recourse agreement was not entered by Cycles Sellers at the request (express or implied) of Gullible. Indeed, it is highly likely that Harley and Gullible will never have known anything of the existence of the recourse agreement. Thus, the agreement is not subject to the documentation provisions, nor to **s 113**, discussed above in relation to Gullible. Furthermore, since the recourse agreement is not (we can be reasonably sure it is not) a guarantee, it is possible for Cycles to be liable to a greater extent than Harley himself. Thus, for example, if Harley's hire purchase agreement did not make prompt payment of the instalments 'of the essence' and therefore Harley's liability was limited to *Financings v Baldock* damages, it is nevertheless possible for Cycles Sellers to be held liable for more than that if, by the terms of its recourse agreement, it had agreed to indemnify Davison Finance against any loss the latter might suffer as a result of Harley not paying the full hire purchase price (*Goulston Discount v Clark* (1967)).

THE RIDER

If the agreement between Gullible and Davison Finance had been written as an indemnity instead of a guarantee that would make no difference at all to the answer above. The agreement would still have been 'security' within the meaning of the Act (**s 189(1)**). That being so, it would have been subject to exactly the same documentation requirements as those already referred to. Furthermore, **s 113** would apply and that section has the effect of rendering an indemnity (which is security within the meaning of the Act) of exactly the same effect as a guarantee. Thus, Gullible cannot be liable to any greater extent than Harley (ignoring for this purpose that Harley was a minor).

The fact that Harley had made three instalment payments before falling into arrears would considerably alter the advice given. This is because in that case, Harley would, at the time the contract was terminated, already have paid over one-third of the hire purchase price, namely, £3,600 (the initial payment of £3,000 plus three instalments of £200 each). £3,600 is more than one-third of £10,200. Thus, the cycle was protected goods within **s 90**. It does not appear that Harley gave his permission to the repossession at the time the cycle was repossessed, and there is no suggestion in the facts that Harley had disposed of the cycle or had abandoned it. Thus, the repossession of the goods was an infringement of the protected goods provisions and Harley (and therefore also Gullible) are relieved of any further liability under the agreement (**s 91**). For the same reason, Davison Finance is liable to repay to Harley all payments he has made under the agreement.

QUESTION 22

'The **Consumer Credit Act 2006** has in three key respects strengthened the protection for vulnerable debtors borrowing in the sub-prime market: first, strengthened licensing controls, secondly introduced a wider regulation of unfair credit transactions, and thirdly a new alternative dispute resolution mechanism.'

▶ **Critically discuss the above statement.**

Answer Plan

The vulnerability of debtors who are offered unsuitable loans and forced to borrow, often on disadvantageous terms, from unscrupulous lenders in the so-called sub-prime market, has been an issue of concern to the Office of Fair Trading and other consumer groups for some years. The question requires candidates to consider three areas of reform introduced by the **Consumer Credit Act 2006**:

1. the enhanced licensing powers granted to the Office of Fair Trading in relation to applicants for, and current holders, of consumer credit licences by ss 38–54 of the **CCA 2006**;
2. new provisions to regulate unfair credit transactions in **ss 19–22** of the **CCA 2006**;
3. the extension of the powers of the Office of the Financial Services Ombudsman, set up under the **Financial Services and Markets Act 2000**, to cover consumer credit disputes; and
4. the new focus on prevention of irresponsible lending.

The candidate should seek to assess whether these changes, taken together, will provide more effective protection for such vulnerable debtors, than those provided for in the **Consumer Credit Act 1974**.

ANSWER

INTRODUCTION – CONTEXT OF REFORMS

At the time of its passage, the **Consumer Credit Act 1974** was hailed as the most sophisticated and comprehensive consumer credit regime in the world. However, in the intervening period there have been massive changes in the amount of credit granted and the structure of the consumer credit market. One area of concern, however, has proved stubbornly resistant to effective legal remedy, and that is the problem of poorer vulnerable debtors who borrow from sub-prime lenders, sometimes known as non-status lending (see *OFT Guidelines – Non-Status Lending: Guidance for Lenders and Brokers* (1997) OFT 192). A sub-prime loan is simply one made outside the prime market, which comprises mainstream lenders such as the major clearing banks and their subsidiaries. People who cannot borrow in the prime market are often forced to borrow in the sub-prime market on more expensive terms, in terms of both interest rates and expensive default charges, and often at the mercy of more unscrupulous lenders. In some cases these lenders will be unlicensed, and thus committing a criminal offence (**s 39** of the **CCA 1974**). Illegal actions such as threats of violence, harassment and seizure of benefit books as security are not uncommon. Trading standards authorities have found it very difficult to assemble evidence in relation to such activities and to persuade frightened debtors to come forward and give evidence. One of the aims of the reforms introduced by the **CCA 2006** is to address these issues.

LICENSING

Part III of the **CCA 1974** required those operating a consumer credit, consumer hire or ancillary credit business to hold either a standard licence or be subject to a group licence. Unlicensed lending is a criminal offence (**s 39** of the **CCA 1974)** and is civilly unenforceable without a validation order from the OFT (**s 40** of the **CCA 1974)**, but these deterrents often had little effect on fringe lenders. These provisions remain in force but the objective now is for the Office of Fair Trading to aim for more focused, targeted and effective enforcement of the licensing provisions, with added enforcement powers. The majority of licences will now be granted for an indefinite period, and will not need to be renewed every five years so, releasing resources for more targeted enforcement against abuses (**s 34** of the **CCA 2006**). The fitness criteria set out in **s 25** of the **CCA 1974** are expanded to allow the OFT to take into account the applicant's skills, knowledge and experience in relation to the relevant credit business and the practices and procedures the applicant proposes to implement in the conduct of the business (**s 29** of the **CCA 2006**), thus allowing perhaps greater focus on the proposed business plan and compliance mechanisms of sub-prime lenders. **Sections 44–51** of the **CCA 2006** give the OFT greater enforcement powers, in particular in relation to acquiring information from the business and increased powers to enter premises to acquire information about breaches of the law. In addition to the rather cumbersome current procedure of revoking, varying or suspending a licence, the OFT is given more flexible powers under **ss 38–43** of the **CCA 2006** to impose *requirements* on licensees. The powers are very wide: the OFT can impose requirements if dissatisfied with the way a regulated business is, has been or is proposed to be carried on by a licensee or by an associate or former associate of the licensee. Dissatisfaction is not defined, although the OFT must publish guidance on when *they might be minded to impose requirements* (**s 42** *of the* **CCA 2006**. The OFT can require the doing or ceasing from doing any act in relation to the licensee's business or proposed business (**s 38** of the **CCA 2006**). Extensive supplementary powers are granted for the OFT to specify the time or period within which the required action is to be taken). An example is the *Requirements Notice imposed on Creation Consumer Finance Ltd* (OFT Press Release 65/10, 17 June 2010: http://www.oft.gov.uk/news-and-updates/press/2010/65-10); this notice required the firm to stop issuing proceedings against Scottish debtors in English courts. The OFT regarded this practice as unfair because of the unfamiliar law and procedure involved in a court claim in a different jurisdiction, and any associated travel costs might deter consumers from defending such action. This practice was in breach of the OFT's Debt Collection Guidance.

A licensee who is unhappy with the imposed requirements can appeal to the First Tier (Consumer Credit) Tribunal, which is part of the General Regulatory Chamber of the Tribunal Service – the appeal will be by way of a full rehearing on the merits, and there is a further right to appeal to the Administrative Appeals Chamber of the Upper Tier Tribunal on a point of law (replacing the Consumer Credit Appeals Tribunal created by **ss 55–58** of the **CCA 2006** under the unification of the Tribunal Service appeals structure created by the **Tribunal Courts and Enforcement Act 2007**). The OFT, again subject to a right of appeal to the First Tier (Consumer Credit) Tribunal, may impose a civil penalty of up to £50,000 for failure to comply with the requirement (**ss 52–55** of the **CCA 2006**). However, before imposing a penalty, the OFT must give the licensee the reasons for the imposition of the penalty, and give them a chance to respond. It is hoped these extended powers and the more flexible penalties should allow a more effective enforcement regime by the OFT. In *EEC Ltd v Office of Fair Trading* (Decision 01, 23 November 2009), the First Tier Tribunal ruled that the onus of proving that it was legitimate to revoke a licence once granted rested on the OFT: http://www.consumercreditappeals.tribunals.gov.uk/Documents/decisions/ecisiononpreliminaryissueson23November2009inEECLtdvOfficeofFairTradingwithdirectionsandNCN_dec09.pdf (see also *QSolvency Ltd* (Decision 07, June 2009 – rejection of an appeal against OFT's refusal to grant a licence in relation to an internet-based debt counselling service, based on acting before receiving a licence, lack of appropriate experience and misleading statements on the proposed website: http://www.consumercreditappeals.tribunals.gov.uk/Documents/decisions/0007_QSolvencyRowley.pdf)

UNFAIR CREDIT RELATIONSHIPS

Sections 137–140 of the **CCA 1974** gave the courts a very wide discretion to reopen extortionate credit bargains, which were agreements that required the debtor to make payments which were grossly extortionate or which otherwise grossly contravened the principles of fair dealing. The provisions, however, were not a great success, partly because they relied on the individual debtor taking legal action or raising the provisions by way of a defence, which few did, and the bar for court intervention was set at too high a level. The credit agreement did not merely have to be unfair or unreasonable but grossly exorbitant or grossly extortionate, which was a difficult hurdle to surmount. The **CCA 2006** repeals these provisions, and by **ss 19–22** of the **CCA 2006** introduces new powers for the intervention if the agreement is unfair to the debtor. Unfairness is not defined but analogies may be drawn to the **Unfair Terms in Consumer Contract Regulations 1999** (see *Director General of Fair Trading v First National Bank* (2001)). In one key respect these provisions are wider, in that they cover both core and non-core terms, so can be used in relation to excessive interest rates. The court can take account of the whole relationship between the debtor and creditor arising out of the principal credit agreement and any related agreement (such as a brokerage or payment protection plan) and is unfair because of any of the terms of the agreement or of any related agreement or by the way in which the creditor has exercised or enforced any of his rights under the agreement or related agreement. The powers are also wider than those in the **CCA 1974** in that the courts can look not only at the position when the agreement is entered into but how the agreement is being enforced. The court can take account of any relevant factor relating to the debtor or creditor. Extensive powers are given to set aside the agreement, vary it, reduce or discharge any sum payable or set aside any security given. It is also important to note that if the collective interests of debtors are being affected by the use of unfair agreements the Office of Fair Trading (or other qualified body such as a local trading standards department) can seek a voluntary assurance that the creditor desist from using such agreements or if necessary apply for a court injunction restraining the creditor from continuing use the offending agreement or terms (**Pt 8** of the **Enterprise Act 2002**). It is important to note that these orders only apply to the creditor's future conduct and do not provide for payment of compensation to individual debtors for past breaches. The OFT has issued a guidance document, 'Unfair Relationships' OFT854, May 2008, on how they intend to use their powers under Part 8 to secure voluntary assurances and court orders in this area.[1]

Already a steady jurisprudence is building up on unfairness – see *Shaw v Nine Regions* [2009] EWHC 3514 (QB), 18/12/2009, *MBNA Europe Bank Ltd v Lynne Thorius* (Lawtel

---

1   This can be seen on the OFT website: http://www.oft.gov.ac.uk.

4/1/2010), *Upendra Rasiklal Patel v Vithalbhai Bikabhai Patel* [2009] EWHC 3264 (QB) and *Tew v Bank of Scotland (Shared Appreciation Mortgages) No 1 Plc* [2010] EWHC 203 (Ch) 22/1/2010.

NEW DISPUTE RESOLUTION REGIME

Vulnerable debtors are extremely reluctant to use the courts even if they are aware of their rights, which in many cases they are not, and so many of the protections provided by the **CCA 1974** were theoretical rather than real. A key plank of the **CCA 2006** is to provide a less formal and cheaper method of dispute resolution. This is done by extending the jurisdiction of the Financial Ombudsman Service set up under the **Financial Services and Markets Act 2000**[2] (**ss 59–61** and **Sched 2** of the **CCA 2006**). The scheme is free for the individual debtor to use and is financed by fees and levies on the consumer credit industry. The FOS can award up to £1,000,000 in compensation, including damages for distress and inconvenience caused by the actions of the creditor. The awards are enforceable as court judgments. If a debtor is unhappy with how he has been dealt with by the creditor in relation to any matter connected with the credit agreement, the debtor, after first exhausting the creditor's internal complaints procedure, which he is required to have under the scheme, may take the matter to the FOS. Only if a complaint to the creditor fails to resolve matters can the complaint be taken to the FOS. If unhappy with the award of the FOS, the debtor can go the courts, but the creditor is bound by the ruling, subject to any judicial review challenge, for example that the FOS has exceeded its jurisdiction or acted unfairly. The defendant can contend that the complaint raises a novel point of law with significant consequences, and if the FOS agrees that it would be more suitably dealt with as a test case, it can be pursued in the courts, but the defendant creditor must agree to pay the costs of the complainant even if the complainant is unsuccessful. The courts accord the FOS a very wide discretion, and providing the decision is fair and reasonable in all the circumstances, the FOS is not bound to follow the strict letter of the law, subject only to their decision being set aside on the grounds that it was perverse or irrational (*R (on the application of Heather Moor & Edgecomb Ltd) v Financial Ombudsman Service* (2008)). Issues 68, 75 & 81 of the *Ombudsman News* feature a useful cross-section of decisions of the FOS: http://www.financial-ombudsman.org.uk/publications/technical_notes/consumer_credit_resource.html

IRRESPONSIBLE LENDING

One way of course of avoiding problems and disputes is to ensure that borrowers act prudently in the first instance and that creditors do not create debt problems building up by irresponsible lending. Among the reforms introduced by the **Consumer Credit Act**

---

2   See the website of the FOS for more detail: www.financial-ombudsman.org.uk.

2006 was a new provision, **s 25 (2B) of the Act**, which made it explicit that among the business practices which the OFT may consider to be deceitful or oppressive or otherwise unfair or improper, for the purposes of considering fitness to hold a consumer credit licence, are practices that appear to the OFT to involve irresponsible lending. The OFT has now published guidance in *Irresponsible Lending – OFT Guidance for Creditors* (OFT 1107, March 2010); among the general criteria set out are:

❖ not use misleading or oppressive behaviour when advertising, selling, or seeking to enforce a credit agreement;
❖ make a reasonable assessment of whether a borrower can afford to meet repayments in a sustainable manner;
❖ explain the key features of the credit agreement to enable the borrower to make an informed choice;
❖ monitor the borrower's repayment record during the course of the agreement, offering assistance where borrowers appear to be experiencing difficulty; and
❖ treat borrowers fairly and with forbearance if they experience difficulties (para 2:2).

Lenders engaging in irresponsible lending and encouraging debtors to take on unsuitable and unsustainable commitments may find they lose their licences. This is reinforced by Article 8.1 of the new **EU Consumer Credit Directive, 2008/48/EC ('CCD')**, which requires the creditor to assess the consumer's creditworthiness on the basis of 'sufficient information', which will include access on a non-discriminatory basis to databases across the European Union (**Article 9 CCD**).

It can also be noted that further reforms introduced by the **EU Consumer Credit Directive 2008/48/EC** require prospective creditors to assess the 'creditworthiness' of prospective debtors and to provide an 'adequate explanation of the nature of the credit agreement being entered into (implemented by **s 55A** and **s 55B CCA 1974**).

QUESTION 23

[Assume the **Consumer Credit Act 2006** is fully in force.]

John acquired a car on hire purchase terms from Fleece You Finance. It provided for an initial payment of £2,000 and 24 monthly instalment payments of £500 each. After making the first monthly instalment payment, John fell into arrears with his next instalment. Fleece You Finance served a default notice which expired without John paying off the arrears and, thus, Fleece You Finance terminated the agreement. This was three weeks ago, and Fleece You Finance has today discovered that John had been involved in an accident with the car which has been repaired by Menders

Ltd where he took it for repair. Fleece You Finance now wishes to recover possession of the car.

▶ Advise Fleece You Finance.

(i)   What difference, if any, would it make to your advice if John had made his first six monthly instalment payments before falling into arrears?

(ii)   What further advice would you give upon learning that, while Fleece You Finance was seeking your initial advice, John visited Menders Ltd, paid the repair bill and took the car to Auctioneers Ltd who, on John's instructions, sold it in an auction to a buyer whom it has so far proved impossible to trace?

Answer Plan

The issues raised are:

❖   Did Fleece You Finance have the right to terminate the agreement?
❖   Was the agreement temporarily unenforceable by the creditor for failure to issue a relevant arrears notice and/or default notice?
❖   If so, can it recover possession of the goods without going to court?
❖   (Related to the latter question) are the goods protected goods?
❖   Does Menders Ltd have the right to enforce its improver's lien against Fleece You Finance?
❖   In relation to rider (ii), is Fleece You Finance entitled to recover the car from the purchaser at auction, that is, assuming he can be traced?
❖   Can Fleece You Finance maintain an action against the auctioneer?

This question is written in more or less chronological order and that is the order of the issues just identified. It makes sense to deal with them in that order, taking care to deal first with the first issue, since, if the answer to that is definitely 'no', many of the other issues do not arise.

ANSWER

First, we shall examine whether Fleece You Finance had the right to terminate the agreement as it has purported to do.

Fleece You Finance has served a default notice, which presumably asked for the arrears to be paid off. As John was not currently in arrears to the amount of at least two instalments at the time the default notice was issued there does not appear to be any complication caused by a failure to issue an arrears notice under (**s 86B CCA 1974** – if one had been required and not issued, no enforcement procedures could have been taken until a proper arrears notice had been issued (**s86D CCA 1974**). It is **s 87** of the **Consumer Credit Act 1974** that states the requirement for a default notice prior to the creditor being entitled to terminate the agreement. **Section 87** does not, however, confer a right of termination. Fleece You Finance will have had the right to terminate the agreement if either the agreement specifically stated that in the circumstances (late payment of one instalment), it was entitled to do so, or else the agreement stated that prompt payment of sums falling due under the agreement was 'of the essence' of the agreement (*Lombard North Central v Butterworth* (1987)). Otherwise, Fleece You Finance had no such right arising merely from one late instalment (*Financings v Baldock* (1963)).

Assuming that Fleece You Finance did have the right to terminate the agreement, it appears to have satisfied the **s 87** requirement. At least that is so, provided that the default notice complied with the requirements of **s 88** (as amended by **s 14** of the **CCA 2006**), including giving at least 14 days' notice. On the assumption that it has complied with the default notice requirement, it is in principle entitled to recover possession of the car. There are, however, qualifications to that proposition. First, it cannot, otherwise than by court action, recover possession 'from the debtor' if the goods are protected goods. On the facts given, the car is not protected goods since the amount so far paid under the agreement by John comes to only £2,500, which is less than one-third of the total price of £14,000. If, to adopt the hypothesis in rider (i) in the question, John had paid six of the instalments before falling into arrears, then the goods would be within the definition of protected goods in **s 90**. In those circumstances, Fleece You Finance would be prohibited from helping itself to the goods either from John or from the garage to whom he had taken it for repair; the phrase in **s 90** preventing recovery of the car 'from the debtor' extends to prevent recovery from the garage where John had taken it for repair (*Benlinck v Cromwell* (1971)). Helping itself to the car in contravention of **s 90** would involve Fleece You Finance being liable to repay to John every payment he had made under the agreement. Even if the goods were not protected goods, there is still one other problem about Fleece You Finance being able to recover the car by helping itself: it may be unable to do so without trespassing on the garage's premises. If Fleece You Finance were to do this, then it would be liable for breach of statutory duty: **s 92**. All of that, however, only prevents Fleece You Finance from helping itself to the car. Fleece You Finance can still bring court proceedings to recover the car. There would possibly be two people trying to resist such proceedings.

Firstly, John might seek to resist the proceedings by applying for a time order under **s 129** – if he has been served with an arrears notice under **s 9** of the **CCA 2006** he can make his own proposals for payments under such an order but must give the creditor 14 days' notice of these proposals with the aim of securing a mediated settlement or an agreed submission to an order issued on those terms by the court (**s 16** of the **CCA 2006**). Depending upon the evidence of John's means, and there being a realistic chance of the rescheduled payments being met (*Southern and District Finance v Barnes* (1995)), the court might grant such an order, thereby allowing John a further chance at paying off his debt in such instalment pattern as the court decides. Secondly, even if John does not resist the proceedings, Menders Ltd, the garage, may wish to claim that it has a lien over the car for the cost of the repairs that it carried out. This is an improver's lien. Of course, John is primarily liable to pay the repair bill since it was he who incurred it. In the absence of him doing so, Menders Ltd may wish to claim that its lien is enforceable against Fleece You Finance, the lien being the right to retain possession of the goods until the repair bill is paid. The lien is likely to be enforceable in law against Fleece You Finance, and that is so even if Menders knew that John was buying the car on hire purchase terms, and it is still so even if the hire purchase agreement expressly forbade John from creating a lien (*Albemarle Supply Co v Hind* (1928)). The lien being enforceable against Fleece You Finance means that it is not entitled to recover the car without first paying off the repair bill. In those circumstances, once it had paid the bill, it would of course have a right to indemnity from John under the doctrine of subrogation. There are two circumstances where the lien would not be enforceable against Fleece You Finance. The first is if the agreement expressly forbade John from creating a lien (or expressly denied him authority to do so) and Menders Ltd knew that fact when the car was brought in for repair. The second is if, when John took the car in for repair, the agreement with Fleece You Finance had already been terminated. In that case, Fleece You Finance would be entitled to the car free of the lien and that is so even if Menders Ltd was unaware that the agreement existed or, if it knew of it, was unaware that it had been terminated (*Bowmakers v Wycombe Motors* (1946)). It seems from the wording of the question that the agreement probably had not been terminated, that is, the default notice had not expired at the time John took the car in for repair. The relevant time is the expiry of the default notice, not when it was served, because, on the wording of **ss 87** and **88(2)**, Fleece You Finance was not entitled to terminate the agreement until that moment. It appears that John did take his car in for repair before the expiry of the default notice.

What is the position if the agreement neither made prompt payment by John 'of the essence' nor expressly conferred a right to terminate in the event of a lateness in payment? In those circumstances, Fleece You Finance would have no right to recover possession of the goods, either from John or from Menders Ltd, unless of course the agreement expressly forbade the creation of a lien. In that case, the creation of the lien might well amount to a repudiation of the contract by John, in which case, Fleece You Finance might well be entitled to terminate the agreement. Whether it could recover possession without a court action would depend upon the factors already spelt out about that. Whether it could recover the car free of the lien would depend upon whether Menders Ltd knew of the restriction in the contract.

Having already dealt with rider (i) (in relation to protected goods), attention will now be turned to rider (ii). In this scenario, should the car ever be traced, **s 90** will be no restriction upon Fleece You Finance recovering the car, since it only prevents recovery 'from the debtor' and does not apply where the debtor has effectively said goodbye to the goods. There may, of course, be some other, more fundamental, restriction upon Fleece You Finance recovering possession of the goods. It may be that whoever now has possession of the car has actually acquired title to it. This is because **Pt III** of the **Hire Purchase Act 1964** will confer Fleece You Finance's title upon the first private (that is, non-trade) purchaser, provided he bought in good faith, which means without actual notice of the prior hire purchase agreement (*Barker v Bell* (1971)). The auctioneers will not have been a private purchaser and, in any case, probably were not purchasers at all, but were simply agents of John in his selling the car. The person who bought the car in the auction presumably bought in good faith and thus, if he were a private (that is, non-trade) purchaser, will now have good title to the car (*GE Capital Bank Ltd v Rushton* (2005)). Assuming that that is the case or, alternatively, that the car is never traced, there are two possible defendants for Fleece You Finance to consider proceeding against. First of all, John has quite clearly now done an act which is wholly repugnant to the contract. If the contract has not already been validly terminated, Fleece You Finance should consider serving another default notice and thus bringing about its termination and then proceeding against John for the outstanding balance of the price. On any view, the amount of damages to which Fleece You Finance is entitled is the outstanding balance, minus any (statutory) rebate for early payment.

Fleece You Finance should also consider bringing a claim for conversion against the auctioneers. Selling someone's car without the owner's authority is undoubtedly conversion, and it is no defence to say that you were unaware that it was their car (*Union Transport Finance v British Car Auctions* (1978)); there would be no liability if the car were withdrawn from the auction without reaching its reserve and the auctioneer had acted in good faith (*Marcq v Christie, Manson and Woods* (2003)). It is an example of strict liability. To be able to bring an action in conversion, Fleece You Finance needs to be able to show that, at the time of conversion (that is, the sale of the car in the auction), it had an immediate right to possession. At common law, it undoubtedly did, since either the agreement was already terminated by virtue of the late payment (default notice and its expiry) or, if not, John's putting the car into the auction, being an act wholly repugnant to the agreement, was an act entitling Fleece You Finance immediately to terminate the agreement and thereby entitling it to immediate possession (*Union Transport Finance v British Car Auctions*). However, the latter will not be effective in Fleece You Finance's case because, however repugnant John's acts are to the agreement, they do not entitle the creditor to terminate *immediately*. First, a default notice must be served. Thus, in the present case, we can say that Fleece You Finance will be able to proceed against the auctioneers in conversion only if Fleece You Finance had an immediate right to possession. Moreover, it will have had an immediate right to possession only if (as discussed earlier) it had a right to terminate the agreement as a result of the lateness of John's payment. If it did, then, on the facts given, the default notice had already expired before the car was sold at auction, and thus it would be able to maintain an action for conversion against the auctioneers.

FINANCIAL OMBUDSMAN SERVICE – CONSUMER CREDIT JURISDICTION

One of the problems with the regime set up by the **Consumer Credit Act 1974** has been the reluctance of consumer debtors to use it, which in part is due to the fact that individual disputes have to be resolved by legal action. One of the purposes of the **Consumer Credit Act 2006** is to provide a less formal and cheaper method of dispute resolution (**ss 59–61** and **Sched 2** of the **CCA 2006**). The **2006 Act** does this by extending to consumer credit disputes the jurisdiction of the Financial Ombudsman Service set up by the **Financial Services and Markets Act 2000**.[3] The Scheme is free for the individual debtor to use and is financed by fees and levies on the consumer credit industry. The FOS can award up to £100,000 in compensation, including damages for distress and inconvenience caused by the actions of the creditor. The awards are enforceable as court judgments. If unhappy with how he has been dealt with by the creditor in relation to any acceleration payments issues, the debtor, after first exhausting the company's internal complaints procedure which they are required to have under the scheme, may take the matter to the FOS. Only if a complaint to the creditor fails to resolve matters can the complaint be taken to the FOS. If unhappy with the award of the FOS, the debtor can go on to the courts, but the creditor is bound by the ruling, subject to any judicial review challenge, for example that the FOS has exceeded its jurisdiction or acted unfairly. The defendant can request that the complaint raises a novel point of law with significant consequences, and if the FOS agrees that it would be more suitably dealt with as a test case, it can be pursued in the courts but the defendant must agree to pay the costs of the complainant even if they are unsuccessful.

FIRST CLASS ANSWER

The first class answer will need to separate out and deal clearly with the three dimensions of the question – the consumer default issues such as the need, where

---

3   See the website of FOS for more detail: www.financial-ombudsman.org.uk.

relevant, for arrears notices under **s 86B–F CCA 1974**, default notices (**ss 87–89 CCA 1974**) and the options open to both the debtor and creditor; secondly, the title issue raised by the unauthorised sale and the impact of **Pt III** of the **Hire Purchase Act 1964** and the repairer's lien issue. This is quite a difficult question because it is not confined to one area and the good candidate will realise the importance of and discuss each of the discrete areas. The awareness of the conversion cases, such as *Union Transport Finance v British Car Auctions* (1978), in particular will mark out a comprehensive in-depth answer.

Common Pitfalls ✗

The first common pitfall is failure to appreciate the 'protected goods' issue and the consequences of the goods being protected – and often simple arithmetic errors in assessing whether one-third of the total hire-purchase price has been paid. It must also be appreciated that in most cases, by accepting the debtor's repudiation by breaching the credit contract or refusing to pay any more instalments, it is the creditor who is terminating the agreement by accepting the debtor's repudiation.

Secondly, failure to consider the scope and availability of time orders under **ss 129–131 CCA 1974** and that time orders are discretionary and both the interests of the debtor and creditor are relevant, so that if there is no realistic option of the debtor repaying even over an extended period, one will not be made.

Thirdly, ignoring the non-credit dimensions of the question – in particular the title implications of what happens in a case such as this – in particular the application of **Pt III Hire Purchase Act 1964** in effect protecting a good faith consumer purchaser but not trader in this context, and what options there are to sue in the tort of conversion against third parties, such as auctioneers or garages who deal with the finance company's car. Equally, the poor candidate will overlook the point about a garage repairer's lien.

QUESTION 24

Consider what the most likely significant impacts will be on current UK domestic consumer credit law by the implementation of the **EU Consumer Credit Directive 2008/48/EC of 23 April 2008**?

Answer Plan

This is a question that requires the candidate to take an overview of the **EU Consumer Credit Directive 20008/48/EC ('CCD')** and assess the main changes it will require in UK domestic law. The candidate will not be required to go into all the intricate detail of implementation but to focus on significant changes required and the relationship of the new law to the pre-existing domestic regime. Among the main points to consider:

❖ the CCD is only a partial harmonisation of consumer credit law, eg it does not deal with provisions relating to unfair credit transactions or regulated hire agreements;

❖ however, where it does apply it follows the maximum harmonisation approach, not the traditional minimum harmonisation approach;

❖ the UK Government has retained much of the existing domestic law, particularly in areas where the CCD does not apply, eg to small business credit contracts and to hire agreements;

❖ outline the main areas of reform in relation to pre-contractual informational requirements;

❖ the information requirements in agreements, in particular the *Standard European Credit Information Sheet*;

❖ new unilateral right of withdrawal form credit agreements;

❖ new provisions in relation to credit intermediaries.

ANSWER

The **EU Consumer Credit Directive 2008/48/EC of 23 April 2008** ('CCD') is a partial harmonisation of European consumer credit law in EU Member States, eg it does not apply to provisions relating to unfair credit transactions, deal with damages for breach of consumer credit contracts or apply to certain categories of agreements, eg consumer hire agreements. However, where it does apply the approach adopted is that of maximum harmonisation, leaving Member States with no element of discretion, unlike the traditional minimum harmonisation approach where Member States could adopt stricter rules for their own nationals provided that credit agreements that complied with a directive provided by nationals of other EU Member states were acceptable (**Article 22 CCD**). As is common with most EU consumer law protection, the protections cannot be waived or excluded and cannot be avoided by a choice of law clause nominating the law of a non-EU country (**Article 22(2)–(4) CCD**). One major area that is untouched is the regulation of creditors (**Article 20 CCD**) – so although creditors must be properly supervised, the UK can retain the current licensing system operated by the Office of Fair Trading.

The UK has largely adopted a 'bolt-on approach' with the regime being created by the **CCA 1974 and 2006** being largely retained and with the new rights being added on or interwoven into current provisions. This has complicated an already complex legal regime even more, and the UK Government has extended the time for compliance with the new hybrid regime to 1 February 2011, though the provisions should have been applicable from 12 May 2010 (**Article 27 CCD**). The CCD does not apply to hire agreements (**Article 2(d) CCD**) but the UK will retain the provisions regulating hire agreements in the **CCA 1974**. The CCD only applies to agreements with '*a natural person, who in transactions covered by this Directive, is acting for purposes which are outside his trade, business or profession*' (**Article 3(a) CCD**); however, UK law will retain existing protections for small business debtors and in some cases extend the new protections to these debtors even though not required to do so by the **CCD**. A good example of the marrying of a UK provision with a provision required by the **CCD** is the connected lender liability provision in **s 75 CCA 1974** – the UK managed to secure the right to retain such a connected-lender liability provision (**Article 15(3) CCD**) but to comply with linked liability provision in **Article 15(2) CCD** – adopting the approach commonly used in civil law in EU countries that you can only sue a creditor when an attempt to recover compensation from the supplier has failed. An additional alternative linked liability action is provided for in **s 75A CCA 1974** – which will apply where the main provision in **s 75 CCA 1974** does not apply but nevertheless the agreement falls within the scope of the CCD. So the linked liability provision will not apply where the cash price of the item is under £30,000 and so, within the scope of the main **s 75 CCA 1974**, and not where the amount of credit advanced exceeds £60,260 (75,000 euros), the upper limit in sterling of the application of the Directive. Small business debtors will be able to take advantage of this additional form of protection, though this is not required by the CCD. In some cases new definitional categories will exist alongside pre-existing similar domestic categories, eg '*credit intermediaries*' (**Article 3(f) CCD**), '*credit brokers*' (**s 145(2) CCA 1974**), '*linked credit agreements*' (**Article 3(n) CCD**) and '*linked transactions*' (**s19 CCA 1974**). In some cases domestic rights will cease to apply where new EU rights are introduced, eg the new unilateral right of withdrawal (**Article 14 CCD** implemented in **s 66A CCA 1974**) will largely supplant the existing cancellation right in **s 67 CCA 1974**, but the cancellation regime will continue to apply to those cases not falling within **s 66A CCA 1974**.

Many of the changes will be of detail and the UK consumer will not see significant changes in the essence of protection.

The main changes will be:

- ❖ standard information to be included in advertisements (**Article 4 CCD**);
- ❖ toughened pre-contractual information (**Articles 5 & 6 CDD**);

❖ an obligation to assess the creditworthiness of the consumer (**Article 8 CCD**);

❖ standardised information in relation to credit agreements and in particular the introduction of Standard European Credit Information (**Articles 10–12 & Annex II CDD**);

❖ a unilateral right of withdrawal from a credit agreement (**Article 14 CCD**);

❖ a right to sue a creditor where action against a supplier has failed to produce compensation where the goods or services supplied are not in conformity or only partially in conformity with the contract (**Article 15(2) CCD**);

❖ standardised method for assessing early repayment rebate (**Article 16 CCD**);

❖ new standardised calculation of the annual percentage rate of charge (**Article 19 and Annex I CCD**);

❖ new disclosure requirements in relation to receipts of commissions and whether tied to a particular creditor or independent imposed on credit intermediaries (**Article 21 CCD**);

❖ Member States to provide '*adequate and effective*' out-of-court dispute resolution procedures (UK already complies with the consumer credit jurisdiction of the Financial Ombudsman Service (FOS)) and encourage those bodies to cooperate in order to resolve cross-border disputes (**Article 24 CCD**).

Given that many consumers do not take advantage of or understand informational requirements in credit advertisements, agreements or copies of agreements, in many ways the chief advantage which will flow from the **CCD** is the ability of the creditors to take advantage of more cross-border opportunities for the provision of credit, eg aware that in advertisements the illustration of a '*representative example*' (eg that he can reasonably expect to supply at least 51% of debtors on those terms) will be the same throughout the EU, making pan-European advertising campaigns easier – see **Regs 1, 4 and 5 Consumer Credit (Advertisement) Regulations 2010/1012**).

From a debtor perspective it should make entering credit agreements with creditors in other EU countries easier. In practical terms the main improvements in relation to consumers will firstly be the stronger disclosure receipts of commissions and the nature of their relationship with the prospective creditor imposed on credit intermediaries – particularly in the sub-prime market, where brokers are often used (see **s 160A CCA 1974** implementing **Article 21 CCD**). Secondly, the reforms increase the movement of consumer credit law towards a 'know-your-customer' approach that is common in such areas as the selling of investments and insurance. **Section 55A–C** implementing **Article 6 CCD** considerably tightens the pre-contractual requirements regime already in existence in **s 55 CCA 1974** and **Consumer Credit (Disclosure of Information) Regulations 2004**. New pre-contract disclosure requirements are also introduced by the **Consumer Credit (Disclosure of Information) Regulations 2010**. **Section 55A CCA 1974** introduces a requirement for an 'adequate explanation' of the prospective transaction (including some potential disadvantages – **s 55A(2)(c) CCA 1974**) – *'the features of the agreement which may operate in a manner which would have a significant adverse effect on the debtor in a way which the debtor is unlikely to foresee.'* **Section 55B** will require the creditor to undertake an assessment of the debtor's creditworthiness and this, linked to more joined-up access to databases as a whole throughout the EU, may mean fewer 'no questions asked' loans and recklessness in ignoring overextension by a prospective debtor.

Another major improvement is a movement to a unilateral 14-day withdrawal period (**Article 14 CCD** implemented by **s66A CCA 1974**). This is a welcome move from the byzantinely complicated cancellation provisions in **ss 67–74 CCA** – tied in to the often irrelevant fact that the agreement was signed off trade premises and the need for 'antecedent negotiations' to be conducted in the presence of the debtor, so ruling out telephonic communications. It will also bring consumer credit law more into line with other withdrawal rights.

CONCLUSION

Given that the UK had one of the most sophisticated consumer credit regimes in the EU, the changes being brought in by the CCD will not have a radical impact on the levels of protection. However, key changes in the pre contract regime and the new right of withdrawal are welcome changes for consumers. For creditors, the third major set of legal reforms in six years means an unwelcome increase in compliance costs and the 'bolt-on approach' adopted by the UK increases the complexity of an already complex regime.[4]

---

4 Two useful websites providing information on consumer credit and the reform consumer credit law are the Department for Business, Innovation and Skills website (http://www.bis.gov.uk/policies/consumer-issues/consumer-credit-and-debt/consumer-credit-regulation) and the Office of Fair Trading website (http://www.bis.gov.uk/policies/consumer-issues/consumer-credit-and-debt/consumer-credit-regulation).

Connected Lender Liability

[Assume the EU Consumer Credit Directive 2008/48/EC, 23 April 2008 has been fully implemented in the UK.]

INTRODUCTION

This chapter covers the liability of the creditor for breaches of contract or misrepresentation by the dealer/supplier. The **Consumer Credit Act 2006** does not amend either **s 56** or **s 75** dealing with connected lender liability and deemed agency. The **EU Consumer Credit Directive 2008/48/EC** ('CCD') does not amend the deemed agency provision in **s 56**, leaves intact the connected lender liability provision in **s 75** (**Art. 15(3) CCD**), but has required the introduction of an additional liability against creditors in relation to 'linked credit transactions' ('linked liability') in **Article 15(2) CCD**.

Checklist ✔

The following topics should be prepared in advance of tackling the questions:

- definitions in the **Consumer Credit Act 1974** and, in particular, that of debtor–creditor–supplier agreements;
- **s 56** of the **Consumer Credit Act**;
- **s 75** of the **Consumer Credit Act**;
- **s 75A** of the **Consumer Credit Act**;
- **Article 15** of the **EU Consumer Credit Directive 2008/48/EC (CCD)**.

QUESTION 25

John and his wife, Susan, have always lived in England. John has a credit card agreement, made in 1990. Susan is a second cardholder on John's account. Two months ago, while on holiday in France, Susan used the card in Fashions à la Mode to pay for a two-piece suit; the jacket was priced at 135 euros and the skirt at 60 euros, that is, the equivalent at the then rate of exchange of £90 and £40, respectively. The pound subsequently weakened and, by the time the transaction reached John's account a month ago, the debit amounted to a total of over £150, Susan's jacket thus costing in fact over £103 and the skirt over £46. Susan has since then contracted dermatitis from the jacket as she has proved allergic to some dressing in the collar. Also, the suit, which bore a label stating (in both English and French) that it was suitable for dry cleaning, has reacted badly to being given normal dry cleaning and both items have shrunk to half their original size.

John and Susan have learned that Fashions à la Mode has become insolvent and gone out of business. Advise Susan what remedy, if any, she might have against John's credit card company.

Answer Plan

The issues raised involve s 56 and, especially, s 75 of the **Consumer Credit Act 1974**. The issues raised are as follows:

- ❖ Is John's credit card agreement one which is regulated by the **Consumer Credit Act**?
- ❖ Can a second cardholder take advantage of ss 56 and 75?
- ❖ Are there 'arrangements' between the creditor and the supplier?
- ❖ Do these sections apply when the card is used abroad?
- ❖ If they do, does English law apply?
- ❖ If the above questions are all answered in the affirmative:
  - (a) are the requirements for liability under s 75 established?
  - (b) are the requirements for liability for misrepresentation, relying on s 56, established?

ANSWER

If Susan's transaction with Fashions à la Mode is governed by English law, she might be able to show that she was the victim of an actionable misrepresentation and also a breach of contract by Fashions à la Mode. Whether she can show either of those will be considered a little later. Assuming she can do so, to have a valid claim against the credit card company, Susan will need to rely upon either **s 56** or **s 75** of the **Consumer Credit Act 1974**. This requires, *inter alia*, John's credit card agreement to be a regulated consumer credit agreement. It will not be a regulated agreement if it is exempt (for example, if, like a traditional American Express card, it requires each periodic account to be settled in a single payment).

CAN A SECOND CARDHOLDER TAKE ADVANTAGE OF SS 56 AND 75?

The question refers to the transaction reaching 'John's' account. Thus, Susan presumably is not jointly liable with John. It would seem at first sight, therefore, that Susan cannot rely on either of the sections in question, since **s 56** refers to negotiations with 'the debtor' being conducted by the negotiator (here, Fashions à la Mode) as agent of the creditor, and **s 75** applies where 'the debtor' has a claim against the supplier. Not being jointly liable with John, Susan is not in ordinary parlance a 'debtor'. However, the definition of debtor in **s 189** is of 'an individual receiving credit under a consumer credit agreement . . .'. Therefore, Susan arguably is a debtor since she does not have to pay immediately for the goods purchased and that is a financial accommodation; thus, she receives 'credit' which is defined by **s 9** as including a cash loan and 'any other form of financial accommodation'. This interpretation is as yet uncertain, since there is no reported case on the issue, and it is also arguable that since it is John who is going to have to pay the account, it is he (and not Susan) who receives a financial accommodation, although Susan would argue that they both received such a financial accommodation. If she is not a 'debtor' within the meaning of the Act, she will have no claim against the credit card company.

'ARRANGEMENTS'

There must be 'arrangements' between the credit card company and Fashions à la Mode for there to be liability by virtue of **ss 56** and **75**. Neither section applies unless the credit card agreement is a 'debtor–creditor–supplier' agreement. If it is such an agreement, that will be because it falls within **s 12(b)** of the Act and it will not fall within **s 12(b)** unless it was made under pre-existing *arrangements*, or in contemplation of future *arrangements*, between the credit card company and Fashions à la Mode. Given that John's credit card company is an English one and Fashions à la Mode was a French retailer, it is quite likely that John's credit card company was not the merchant acquirer, that is, was not the person who introduced Fashions à la Mode to the VISA or other payment collection system to which they both belong. It is also quite likely that Fashions à la Mode received payment *indirectly* from John's credit card company. Some banks and credit card companies have claimed that in these circumstances, there are no 'arrangements' between the credit card company and the supplier. This, however, seems a 'try on' by the credit card companies in question, since 'arrangements' is clearly a wide word and does not require direct contractual relations between the creditor and supplier. It has now been decided that there will be 'arrangements' in this context in both the case of three-party and four-party credit agreements, so albeit that dealings will be indirect through an intermediary 'merchant acquirer' there will be 'arrangements' between John's credit card company and Fashions à la Mode (see *Office of Fair Trading v Lloyds*

TSB plc (2006)). The term 'arrangements' is to be given a broad construction and its meaning was not to be cut down by **s 187(1)**.

USE OF CARD ABROAD

Does the **Consumer Credit Act** apply to cards used abroad? It has been decided that the Act does apply to regulated agreements made in England (as John's appears to have been) where the card is used to purchase goods abroad (*Office of Fair Trading v Lloyds TSB plc* (2007)). A credit card agreement contains what amounts to a standing offer, that is, an offer to supply credit on the terms of the credit card agreement. That offer is accepted *pro tanto* each time an authorised cardholder uses the card to finance a transaction. The standing offer is made in an agreement (the credit card agreement) made in England. When accepted, even by being used abroad, the account is expected to be settled (by John) in England and in sterling. Therefore, it is submitted that English law applies not only to the credit card agreement, but also to the individual contract (pursuant to that credit card agreement) to finance Susan's purchase. Of course, there is yet a further contract, namely, the contract made between Susan and Fashions à la Mode. That contract (being a business-to-consumer contract) is probably governed by the law of the place of habitual residence of the consumer (Susan), namely, English law. Even if it was governed by French law, that would not prevent English law applying to the credit card agreement and to the finance contract made each time the card is used (*Office of Fair Trading v Lloyds TSB plc* (2007)). The difficulties that the credit card company might have in enforcing its right to a statutory indemnity under **s 75(2)** against a foreign supplier did not lead to a more restrictive interpretation of **s 75(1)**.[1]

SECTION 75

Are the requirements for **s 75** liability established? It has already been argued that, firstly, English law applies; secondly, the agreement is a debtor–creditor–supplier agreement within **s 12(b)**; thirdly, that Susan is a 'debtor' within the meaning of the Act. Is the transaction within the financial limits in **s 75(2)**? It will be, provided Fashions à la Mode attached to the item in question a cash price exceeding £100. The significant figure here is not the amount subsequently debited from John's account, but the cash price attached to the item by Fashions à la Mode (that is, when Susan made her purchase). Neither the jacket nor the skirt had a cash price of over £100 attached. The only way that Susan could bring herself within **s 75** is by arguing that the two-piece suit was sold as a single item, which might be difficult since the skirt and jacket were separately priced. Assuming Susan's argument succeeds here, she still

---

1   In relation to use of cards abroad, see 'Consumer Credit Agreements – Credit Cards – Territorial Application – Foreign Transactions', Harvey (2006) JPIL [3] C121–26.

has to show that she has a claim against Fashions à la Mode, for **s 75** does not create a new claim, but merely enables the debtor to bring a claim against the credit card company which the debtor already has a right to bring against the supplier. In an English court, if French law is not proved, it will be assumed to be the same as English law. In any case, as stated earlier, English law will apply when the buyer is a consumer habitually resident in England. According to English law, Susan would very likely have a valid claim against Fashions à la Mode, firstly for breach of the conditions as to satisfactory quality and fitness for purpose in **s 14** of the **Sale of Goods Act 1979** and, secondly, for misrepresentation. For her dermatitis, provided that Susan did not contract this condition because she was unusually sensitive (see *Griffiths v Peter Conway* (1939) and *Slater v Fining* (1997)), she would have a valid claim under both conditions in **s 14**. Equally, both conditions would seem to be broken in circumstances where a description attached to the clothes stated that they were suitable for dry cleaning when they were liable to considerable shrinkage under normal dry cleaning (see the definition of satisfactory quality in **s 14(2)** and **(2A)–(2F)** of the **Sale of Goods Act 1979**). Thus, subject to the many difficulties already outlined, Susan may be able to bring that claim against John's credit card company under **s 75**.

MISREPRESENTATION

It is possible, assuming, as stated above, that English law applies or that the French law on misrepresentation is not proved to be different from English law, that Susan has a claim against Fashions à la Mode for misrepresentation – that is, provided that before she bought the clothes she had read, and been, at least partially, influenced by, the label indicating that they were suitable for dry cleaning. If so, Susan could rely on **s 75** to bring that claim against the credit card company – again, subject to the difficulties already outlined. Alternatively, Susan may be able to rely on a claim for that same misrepresentation by the credit card company, that is, via its agent, Fashions à la Mode. This would involve relying on **s 56(1)(c)** to establish that agency. **Section 56** is subject to many of the same difficulties as **s 75**. However, it is not subject to the requirement that the cash price attached to the item in question was over £100 and the courts have interpreted it quite widely and in favour of the consumer (*Forthright Finance v Ingate* (1997)). However **s 56** is not without limits, and did not apply in *Black Horse Ltd v Christopher Langford* (2007), where a car dealer sold a car to an intermediary broker who in turn sold it to the creditor before it was supplied to the consumer by the creditor on hire purchase; **s 56(1)(b)** did not apply because it requires the goods to be sold directly to the creditor by the supplier before forming a hire-purchase or conditional sale agreement between the creditor and the consumer. Liability under both **s 56** and **s 75** is non-excludable (**s 173(1)**). Liability under both **s 56** and **s 75** is non-excludable (**s 173(1)**).

CONCLUSIONS

There are many difficulties, including uncertainty as to the law in one or two respects, in the way of Susan establishing liability on the part of the credit card company. It may be that she can succeed. Although not asked for by the question set, Susan might be well advised to consider the alternative of an action (that is, in respect of her dermatitis) for product liability under **Pt I** of the **Consumer Protection Act 1987**; this would be a claim against the manufacturer or, if the clothes were imported into the European Union, whoever first imported them into the EU (not the UK if a different person).

NOTE

Some of the issues raised in this question were discussed in an article in the *Student Law Review Yearbook* of 1992. Some of them were also discussed in the book *Credit, Debit and Cheque Cards* by Graham Stephenson, published by Professional Publishing in 1993. Mr Stephenson appears not to agree with the views expressed in this answer about the position of the second authorised cardholder. On authorised users, see 'Credit Cards, Card Users and Account Holders', SA Jones (1988) *Journal of Business Law* 457–76. The operation of **s 75** is well illustrated and discussed in the *Office of Fair Trading v Lloyds TSB* (2007). For a useful overview of the some of the 'common misconceptions' with how **s 75** operates see *'common misunderstandings about claims made under section 75 of the Consumer Credit Act'* (Issue 86 *Ombudsman News*, June/July 2010: http://www.financial-ombudsman.org.uk/publications/ombudsman-news/86/86-consumer-credit.htm).

Aim Higher ★

The key to a first class answer in a problem is to carefully discuss all the material issues that arise, and here clearly separating out the possibilities of liability under **s 75** and **s 56**. It will be important to discuss any 'grey areas – in this question the position of the liability made by authorised users of the credit card other than the account holder. Discussion of key authorities such as *Office of Fair Trading v Lloyds TSB* (2007) and, where relevant, any shortcomings or problems with a decision as far as it relates to the facts of the problem.

Common Pitfalls ✗

The first main pitfall to be avoided is that merely because the contract of sale or supply is concluded abroad, **s 75** does not apply when it does. A second pitfall is overlooking the alternative 'deemed agency' liability in **s 56**, particularly where the contract price of an item is less than £100, and not confusing the application of the two separate forms of connected lender liability. A third pitfall is ignoring the detailed requirements of **s 75**, such as it not applying where the cash price of an item is under £100 or exceeding £30,000; wrongly applying **s 75** to debit cards and charge cards and failing to realise the creditor is liable for the same amount of damages as the supplier, not merely the amount of the credit advanced.

QUESTION 26

(a) Despite the connected lender liability provision of **s 75** of the **Consumer Credit Act** being regarded by the credit industry as a 'flawed provision', successive UK governments have refused to amend **s 75** and the new **EU Consumer Credit Directive 2008/48/EC** permits the UK to retain the provision.

▶ Discuss.

(b) Betty decided to have a new kitchen installed. At Kitch Kitchens Ltd, she contracted to have the work done according to an agreed specification. She needed to borrow money to finance the new kitchen and, at Kitch Kitchens Ltd, she also signed a proposal form for a loan from Flash Finance. This was a loan of £5,000 to be paid direct to Kitch Kitchens and to be repaid by Betty by monthly instalments spread over five years. All documentation and other formalities required under the provisions of the **Consumer Credit Act** were observed in the making of the loan agreement. It is now three months since the new kitchen was installed and Betty has found that the new waste disposal unit is defective, the new cupboards are falling off the walls and the turbo-charged oven will never work properly, since it needs an outlet to the outside. Therefore, it must be installed immediately in front of an outside wall, and Betty's kitchen has no outside wall.

It is going to cost £3,000 for Betty to get a substitute oven and to have the other matters put right. Kitch Kitchens Ltd is insolvent and has gone into liquidation.

(i)   Advise Betty;

AND

(ii)   Would your advice differ it the kitchen had a cash price of £50,000 and Betty had borrowed the money from Flash Finance?

Answer Plan

This is a typical two-part question, where (a) requires some critical discussion of an area of law and (b) requires an application of those same rules of law to two specific situations. As with all such questions, it is wise to spend a roughly similar amount of time on each part. When dealing with a question, such as in (b), which demands an application of the rules in **s 75**, it must be established that there is legal liability on the part of the supplier and that the basic requirements for **s 75** and **s 75A** have been satisfied. Those two issues are dealt with in that order followed by the consequences for Betty. It is also important in answering not to overlook the second sub-part of question (b), which involved new law introduced by the **EU Consumer Credit Directive 2008/48/EC** and implemented in the UK by **s 75A Consumer Credit Act 1974.**

ANSWER

(A)

The origin of **s 75** is to be found in the Crowther Report, which laid the policy foundations for the **Consumer Credit Act 1974**. That report described the close business link sometimes to be found between a supplier (of goods or services) and a finance house. Those links would arise from the fact that a supplier would need to be able to offer credit to his customers. Thus, a finance company would be quite keen to have a supplier hold a stock of that finance company's proposal forms and to have the supplier suggest that a customer wanting credit should fill out the form. The arrangement often to be found between the finance company and the supplier includes the understanding that the finance company will make finance available to such of the supplier's customers who apply for it and who satisfy the finance company's usual creditworthiness criteria. The Crowther Committee described such suppliers and finance houses as being in a 'joint venture for mutual profit'. The Committee pointed out that the existence of this link and the ready supply of credit to customers of the supplier meant that sometimes a supplier was kept in business for longer than would occur without such support. The Committee recommended that there should be 'connected lender' liability, that is, that the finance company should share liability towards the customer for breach of contract or misrepresentation by the supplier. It is important to note that **s 75** applies both to three-party arrangements, where there is a consumer–supplier–credit card company, and also to the increasingly prevalent four-party arrangements, where there is a consumer–supplier–merchant acquirer–credit card company. In this four-party situation the merchant acquirer, usually a bank, recruits suppliers to the network and processes vouchers from customers and deals with the credit card company, subject to commission and interchange fee arrangements, so there need be no direct link between the credit card company and the supplier for **s 75** joint liability to apply (*Office of Fair Trading v Lloyds TSB* (2007)).

In all of this, the credit industry argues that there is one clear flaw in the policy and there are several others, which are flaws either in the policy or else in its implementation in **s 75**. Consumer groups, on the other hand, have strenuously argued for the retention of **s 75** as one of the most effective consumer protection measures in the **1974 Act**.

The first and obvious flaw is that although it is no doubt beneficial for the credit customer to have the liability of his supplier towards him effectively guaranteed by the creditor, there is actually no reason why the credit customer should have this guarantee and the cash, charge card or debit card customer should not. Thus, the customer who has saved up for his purchase and then paid cash has no remedy for the defective goods or services once the supplier has become insolvent, but the credit customer is given such a remedy. Not only does this not encourage thrift and saving up prior to purchase, but it then positively favours the credit customer. When an unbonded travel agent becomes insolvent, it is the cash customer who is penalised and the credit customer who is saved. Yet, the latter is no more deserving than the former.

The second flaw is the fact that there is no limit on **s 75** liability. The creditor who supplies only a relatively small amount of credit under a regulated agreement can be held liable under **s 75** for unlimited damages. Thus, an oven costing £500 might be paid for by use of a regulated credit card and, because it is defective, might burn down the house causing, say, £100,000 worth of damage. The creditor, who is not in the business of supplying ovens, has nevertheless to pick up the £100,000 bill. It is true that **s 75** gives the creditor a right of indemnity against the supplier. However, where the supplier is insolvent, this is of little use, though the credit card company may have a claim against the insolvent supplier's insurers under any relevant third-party liability policy by virtue of the **Third Parties (Rights Against Insurers) Act 1930**[2] (see *First*

---

2   This will shortly be replaced by the Third Parties (Rights Against Insurers) Act 2010 but the position would be the same under the new Act in this respect.

National Tricity Finance v Ellis (2004)). Many creditors have the opinion that if it is right for there to be a **s 75**-type liability, it should be confined to the amount of credit advanced in relation to the transaction in question.

A further flaw in **s 75** is in relation to **subs (3)**. This sub-section was intended to prevent creditors being made liable for relatively trivial claims. As drafted, however, it does not work to rule out claims according to their size, but rather according to the cash price attached to the item in question. Thus, there is in **s 75(3)** a lower figure of £100, the result of which is that if the cash price of the item in question is £100 or less, no **s 75** claim can be made. That is so even if the item in question causes a vast amount of damage.

Thus, the defective toaster which burns down the house will not attract **s 75** liability, since its cash price will not have exceeded £100. **Section 75(3)** seems to be encouraging creditors to give credit for a lot of small items, but not to give a lot of credit for any one item – unless the item costs more than £30,000. The sense of doing this is difficult to see. This is especially so where, in the case of a misrepresentation by the supplier, the debtor may be able to avoid this limitation in **s 75** by the simple device of relying upon the deemed agency provision in **s 56**. **Section 56** has no equivalent limitation.

There is a further flaw in the implementation of the policy. It is that, quite apart from the limitation in **s 75(3)**, **s 75** does not always work to protect the debtor in circumstances where the supplier is effectively in a joint venture for mutual profit. This is because there are other ways in which the creditor can help to finance the supplier or the supplier's customers without incurring liability under **s 75**. One of these ways is simply to lend money direct to the supplier. This might, on the one hand, avoid **s 75** and, on the other, still leave the creditor reasonably well protected against the risk of the supplier's insolvency by virtue of charges over the supplier's assets granted to the creditor. Another way of arranging the finance is for the finance company to enter into an arrangement with the supplier whereby it is the latter who himself makes the credit agreement with the debtor, but where subsequently the supplier assigns the benefit of the credit agreement to the finance company. Thus, the latter becomes entitled to the receivables (that is, the debtor's repayments) under the credit agreement, but avoids being liable to the debtor. This is because an assignee takes only the benefits of the contract and not the burdens. Of course, where a debtor has a claim under the credit agreement against the supplier, that claim could be used as a set-off against money owed by the debtor (to the assignee, that is, the finance company) and this would then, by a roundabout way, make the finance company 'liable' (that is, by way of set-off) for the supplier's default towards the debtor. That 'liability' would, however, be limited to the amount of credit (and interest) due under the credit agreement.

Thus, there are serious flaws in **s 75**. It should also be pointed out that there were other 'difficulties' in **s 75**, which are not least the cross-border implications (for example, those arising out of the use of regulated credit card agreements abroad) and the doubt over the position of the second credit cardholder *vis-à-vis* **s 75**.[3]

The cross-border issue has now been resolved by the House of Lords decision in *Office of Fair Trading v Lloyds TSB* (2007), ruling that **s 75** liability does apply where a credit card covered by a regulated agreement is used outside the UK.

The **Consumer Credit Act 2006** which introduced significant reforms to the 1974 regime did not amend or change **s 75**, which suggests the Government at least is happy with its operation. Some of the issues discussed here in relation to **s 75** were discussed at a European level as a result of the European Commission's proposal for a revised **Directive on Consumer Credit**. Draft proposals were published in 2002. These proposals suggested a type of connected lender liability (such as that which **s 75** imposes) which: (a) would not extend to credit cards other than store cards; (b) would, apparently, not include claims for consequential loss; and (c) would require the removal of the lower and upper price limits to the application of **s 75** liability. However, a second modified version produced in 2005 dropped any reference to harmonising national rules on connected lender liability. Ultimately **Article 15(3)** of the **EU Consumer Credit Directive 2008/48/EC** permitted the UK to retain the 'joint and several' liability provision in **s 75**, which the UK has done. Thus despite strong lobbying by the credit industry, it seems that they will continue to face 'joint and several' liability under **s 75** for the foreseeable future.

(B)(i)

It seems reasonably clear that Betty has a good claim in law against Kitch Kitchens for breach of implied (or express) terms of the contract of supply. This appears to have been a contract for the provision of services or work and materials, with some goods being incidentally supplied. Even so, there are still implied terms as to satisfactory quality and fitness for purpose (**s 4** of the **Supply of Goods and Services Act 1982**). In the case of the waste disposal unit, it appears that there is a breach of the term as to satisfactory quality and, in the case of the oven, a breach of the term as to fitness for purpose, since she must have indicated to Kitch Kitchens the particular purpose (installing it in her kitchen) for which she wanted the oven. So far as the cupboards are concerned, it appears that there has been a breach of the term in **s 13** of the same Act, that the work will be carried out with reasonable care and skill (see *Jones v Callagher t/a Gallery Kitchens and Bathrooms*

---

3   For general criticism of the policy behind s 75, see an article by Dobson at (1978) 128 NLJ 703 and 'Credit cards and section 75: time for a change in the law?', Andrew Campbell (1996) 11 JIBL 527–32.

(2004)). The problem in this case is that it is of no use to Betty that she has a good claim in law against Kitch Kitchens Ltd, because the latter is insolvent.

The issue is what remedies Betty may have against Flash Finance by virtue of the **Consumer Credit Act**. **Section 75** provides that in certain circumstances, the debtor (here, Betty) may bring a claim against the creditor (here, Flash Finance) for breach of contract or misrepresentation by the supplier (here, Kitch Kitchens Ltd). For **s 75** to apply, the credit contract must be a regulated debtor–creditor–supplier agreement within **s 12(b)** or **(c)**. It seems highly likely that the loan agreement satisfies this requirement and falls within **s 12(b)**. It does not fall within **s 12(c)** since it appears to be an agreement for restricted-use credit, because the loan was to be paid not to Betty, but direct to Kitch Kitchens. The agreement will fall within **s 12(b)**, however, only if it was made under 'arrangements' between Kitch Kitchens and Flash Finance. Since it appears that Kitch Kitchens had a stock of Flash Finance loan proposal forms, it would seem quite likely that there were such arrangements. If there were a commission paid by Flash Finance to Kitch Kitchens (or indeed vice versa), that would be conclusive. Assuming such arrangements exist, Betty has a like claim against Flash Finance as she has against Kitch Kitchens. According to a Scottish case (*United Dominions Trust v Taylor* (1980)), a like claim means that in circumstances where the debtor has a right to rescind the supply contract, the 'like' claim under **s 75** is to rescind the loan contract. This case is controversial in the way it reached the result. That, however, is perhaps unimportant in the case of the problem here, since it appears that this being a contract for services (and not a sale of goods contract) the debtor, Betty, will not be seeking to recover all her money paid to Kitch Kitchens, but will wish to make simply a money claim, that is, for damages. There might be some problems if she wanted to reject the physical components of the kitchen in that she may be taken to have 'accepted' them, especially if they have been altered in the fitting, though the fact that three months had elapsed would not seem to amount to 'acceptance of the goods' (see *Jones v Callagher t/a Gallery Kitchens and Bathrooms* (2004)). That claim being a valid legal claim against Kitch Kitchens, Betty is entitled to succeed with it against Flash Finance.

In this sort of situation, it is quite common for the finance company still to expect the debtor to maintain monthly payments under the loan agreement while the other claim is still being contested and, if the debtor ceases to maintain those payments, the finance company will keep sending reminders; and of course there will be default interest, which the finance company will show on each successive statement, though the pressure is less with the bringing into force of **s 13** of the **CCA 2006** which stipulates that only simple interest can be charged on default sums under regulated consumer credit agreements and not compound interest, which of course involves charging interest on interest. This operates as a clear pressure upon the debtor, who may doubt the likelihood of success with her claim under **s 75**. Cautious advice to Betty is therefore to maintain her loan repayments while also pursuing her claim against Flash Finance.

(B)(ii)

Most European Union states did not have the equivalent connected lender liability provisions that the UK had but rather a substituted liability in relation to contracts financed by a credit company where the consumer had failed to get redress from the supplier. If action to get redress from the supplier had failed, action for redress could be taken against the creditor but the debtor always had to take reasonable steps against the supplier first. **Article 15(2)** of the **EU Consumer Credit Directive 2008/48 (CCD)** provides for this type of liability. The UK has provided for such an action in those cases falling outside the connected lender liability provision in **s 75 CCA 1974** but within the scope of the **CCD**. This is done in **s 75A** of the **CCA 1974**. This can be described as the '*linked liability*' provision and would kick in if Betty had failed to get redress from Kitch Kitchens. There are four situations where the section can apply:

❖ the supplier cannot be traced;
❖ the debtor has contacted the supplier but the supplier has not responded;
❖ the supplier is insolvent;
❖ the debtor has taken reasonable steps, which need not include litigation, to pursue the claim against the supplier but has not obtained satisfaction of his claim – satisfaction includes accepting a replacement product or service or other compensation from the supplier in settlement of the claim.

However, this provision will only apply where the cash value of the goods or services is in excess of £30,000 and under £60,260 (the upper limit of the Directive converted from euros to sterling at date of UK's adoption of the Directive) Betty is covered here as the cash value of the kitchen is £50,000. Neither has Betty seemingly acquired the kitchen '*wholly or predominantly*' for business purposes carried on by her – if she had, the protection would not have applied (**s 75A(6) CCA 1974**).

The sole issue that might cause problems is whether the provision of a loan for the acquisition of the kitchen and its fitting is a '*linked credit agreement*'. A '*linked credit agreement*' means a regulated consumer credit agreement that serves '*exclusively*' to finance an agreement for the supply of specific goods or the provision of a specific service and where:

(a) the creditor uses the service of the supplier in connection with the preparation or making of the credit agreement; OR
(b) the specific goods or provision of a specific service are explicitly specified in the credit agreement (**s 75A(5) CCA 1974**).

The question says she signed the Flash Finance loan form at Ktich Kitchen's premises, which suggests that condition (a) is satisfied and probably condition (b) as well. If this is the case and she has failed to secure compensation from Kitch Kitchens, and on the facts she seems to have taken reasonable steps to do so, she can then pursue her claim for £3,000 against Flash Finance under **s 75A CCA 1974**.

General Principles of Agency

8

INTRODUCTION

The doctrine of privity in contract law normally prevents a person acquiring rights under a contract unless he is a party to it. The long-established exception to that rule is the concept of agency. The most important feature of the relationship created by an agency agreement is that where a contract is concluded by an agent on behalf of a principal, the agent's acts are treated as if they were the acts of the principal and the principal becomes a party to the contract through the agreement. Examiners often set questions dealing with the general concept of agency contracts, either in the form of whole-essay questions or part-essay questions.

A contract of agency is governed by the general law of contract and is subject to the same rules as other contracts. However, unlike other types of contract, there are special terms which are implied into agency contracts, such as the fiduciary relationship between the principal and the agent as a result of which a number of duties are cast on the agent and, similarly, the agent has rights as against the principal. In addition, in relation to one type of agent – the 'commercial agent' – the relationship will be at least partially governed by the **Commercial Agents (Council Directive) Regulations 1993**. These Regulations, deriving from a European Directive, are particularly important in relation to the rights of the agent on termination of the agreement. They apply only to self-employed agents engaged to arrange contracts for the sale or purchase of goods.

The questions in this chapter concentrate on the general principles of agency contracts, and those in Chapter 9 deal with the scope of an agent's authority to bind the principal.

Students should be familiar with the following areas:

❖ general concept of agency and its relationship to the doctrine of privity;
❖ rights and duties of an agent *vis-à-vis* the principal;
❖ ratification – when can it be used and what are its effects;

❖ termination of an agency contract;
❖ the **Commercial Agents (Council Directive) Regulations 1993**.

QUESTION 27

The duties owed by agents to their principals may or may not be dictated by the express terms of the contracts between them.

▶ **Explain the duties of an agent in the context of this statement.**

Answer Plan

As with any other contract, the express terms of a contract of agency primarily determine the obligations of the parties to it. However, by the very nature of the relationship, the agent stands in a position of trust *vis-à-vis* the principal. A fiduciary relationship therefore exists between them and other important duties are implied into the contract, based on the notion of good faith, save insofar as these are not excluded or modified by the express terms of the contract.

In relation to commercial agents falling within the **Commercial Agents (Council Directive) Regulations 1993**, there is a duty to act 'dutifully and in good faith' which cannot be modified by the contract between principal and agent. Even where an agent acts gratuitously (and therefore there is no question of contractual obligations arising), the agent still owes fiduciary duties and the lack of consideration *per se* is no bar to these arising, and the possibility of a general liability in tort arises.

The following points need to be considered:

❖ express contractual duties determined by the terms of the contract;
❖ fiduciary duties which, if not expressly provided for in the contract, are either implied or enforceable *per se*;
❖ in the case of a gratuitous agent, a general duty of care in tort.

ANSWER

Any contract between a principal and an agent may expressly impose duties on the agent and, in the absence of any relevant express duties, the obligations of the agent are regulated by a number of duties as a matter of law. Even in the absence of a contract, an agent who acts gratuitously owes fiduciary duties to the principal in the law of tort.

Where there is an agency contract, the terms of that contract will generally dictate the internal obligations between the principal and the agent. In relation to commercial agents falling within the **Commercial Agents (Council Directive) Regulations 1993**, however, there is a non-derogable duty on the agent to look after the principal's interests and to act dutifully and in good faith. Subject to this, an agent's duties will include the following.

OBEDIENCE

An agent must obey the principal's lawful instructions and must not exceed his authority. This applies to both paid and gratuitous agents. Where the agent's instructions are ambiguous, however, he will not be liable if he acts on a reasonable interpretation of them (*Weigall v Runciman* (1916); *The Tzelepi* (1991)), although a duty will be imposed on the agent to seek clarification of the instructions.

A paid agent must act according to the terms of the contract and is liable for loss caused either by a failure to act or acts in excess of the authority. In *Turpin v Bilton* (1843), for example, an agent who was instructed to insure his principal's ship but failed to do so was liable in damages to his principal when the ship was lost.

A gratuitous agent is generally under no duty to act so that, albeit liable for exceeding his authority, he cannot be liable for a complete failure to act. There is generally no liability in tort for negligent omissions. However, some academic authorities maintain that liability could arise if the agent does not warn the principal that he has not or does not intend to perform the agency.[1] On this basis, a gratuitous agent acting in *Turpin* above would still have been liable to the principal.

CARE AND SKILL

All agents owe a duty of care to their principals to exercise reasonable care and skill in the execution of their authority. A paid agent is expected to exercise care and skill which is usual and proper in the type of business or work for which the agent is employed. An unpaid agent's duty of care arises in tort, and his actions are judged against the skill actually possessed. Whether or not an agent has fulfilled this duty is a question of fact in each case. Any attempt by an agent to exclude or limit liability for failure to exercise care and skill is subject to the **Unfair Contract Terms Act 1977**.

---

1 *Hedley Byrne & Co Ltd v Heller & Partners Ltd* (1964) suggests that liability will be imposed for loss caused by a failure to warn the principal where the agent had voluntarily assumed such a responsibility, although the point remains undecided in English law.

The standard of care required is whatever is reasonable in the circumstances of each case. Where the agent holds himself out as being a member of a profession, the standard of care and skill expected of him is that of a reasonably competent member of that profession, irrespective of the degree of skill he may personally possess. In deciding what care is reasonable, the court will take into account whether or not the agent is paid.

In *Chaudry v Prabhakar* (1988), P, who had recently passed her driving test, asked a friend, A, to buy a car on her behalf, stipulating that the car must not have been involved in an accident. A, who was not a mechanic and acted gratuitously, bought a one-year-old car for P. When P discovered that the car had been badly damaged in an accident, P sued A. The Court of Appeal, taking into account that A acted gratuitously, held that, on the facts, A had failed to exercise reasonable skill and was liable to P.

PERSONAL PERFORMANCE

As a general rule, an agent must personally perform the task because, in every case, the principal places trust in the agent: 'confidence in the particular person employed is at the root of the contract of agency', *per* Thesiger LJ in *De Bussche v Alt* (1878). This is often expressed in the Latin maxim *delegatus non potest delegare*. There are exceptions to the rule, but if the agent delegates duties without authority to do so, the agent is liable to the principal for breach of duty. The principal is not bound by an unauthorised sub-agent's acts unless the agent had apparent authority to delegate and the principal is thereby estopped from denying the want of authority. There are some exceptions to this rule.

Firstly, where the agent is expressly authorised to delegate. In *De Bussche v Alt*, for example, an agent employed to sell a ship at a specified price at one of a number of specified places was unable to do so and obtained the principal's authority to appoint a sub-agent who subsequently sold the ship according to the principal's instructions. This was held to be a permissible delegation by the agent of his authority. Secondly, where the agent has implied authority to do so in the circumstances because of a custom in a particular trade or profession. For example, a solicitor practising outside London generally has authority to appoint a London-based solicitor to conduct litigation on his behalf in London courts (*Solley v Wood* (1852)). Thirdly, where the principal is aware, at the time of making the contract of agency, that the agent intends to delegate part or all of his authority and the principal does not raise objections. Fourthly, where the circumstances necessitate delegation, for example, where a company is appointed as an agent, it must delegate performance to its employees since it must act through human agents. Finally, where the task delegated does not require the exercise of discretion, for example signing documents or sending notices. In *Allam v Europa Poster Services* (1968), for example, it was held that an agent who was instructed to revoke certain licences could delegate to his solicitor the task of actually sending the notices of revocation. Estate agents provide a common example where authority cannot normally be delegated. Selling the principal's property is not a purely ministerial act and, should they delegate their task to sub-agents without authority, they are not entitled to commission on a sale effected by the sub-agents.

NO CONFLICT OF INTEREST

This fiduciary duty of good faith is paramount and applies whether or not the agent receives payment. The duty is very strict and applies even where it can be proved that there was no actual conflict of interest. It is enough that there is the possibility of conflict. In *Boardman v Phipps* (1966), for example, where the duty was strictly applied, a solicitor, while acting as agent, acquired information relating to the value of certain shares. Acting in good faith, he used this information for his own benefit after the principal had declined to use it for his. The House of Lords held that the agent was accountable to his principal for the profit made, because the information that he had acquired and used for his own benefit belonged to his principal.

More generally, this duty is reflected in the principles that an agent should not purchase the principal's property nor act for both parties in a transaction. Where, for instance, an agent is instructed to buy property on behalf of the principal and the agent sells his own property to the principal, the agreement reached will be a breach of the duty owed to his principal. This is true even if it is a custom of a particular market (for example, the London tallow market) that agents in that market could sell their own goods to the principal (*Robinson v Mollett* (1875)). In such a situation, the potential for conflict is clear, since a seller's interest is to get the best price, whereas the buyer's is to pay as little as possible. Even if the agent acts fairly and pays a reasonable price, he will be in breach of duty unless there is full disclosure to the principal and the principal consents to the transaction.[2]

NOT TO MAKE A SECRET PROFIT

An agent must not make a secret profit over and above the agreed commission. Again, this rule is strictly applied and it is irrelevant that the agent acted in good faith or that the principal suffered no loss (see *Boardman v Phipps*). If a secret profit is made and discovered, it may be claimed by the principal. The duty applies equally to unpaid agents. In *Turnbull v Garden* (1869), for example, an agent was employed without payment to

---

2   Where an agent deals with the principal in breach of his duty, the principal may rescind the contract. His right to rescission subsists until the breach is actually discovered. (In *Oliver v Court* (1820), the principal was able to rescind 13 years after the transaction.)

purchase clothes for his principal's son. He was allowed a trade discount on the transaction by the seller, but sought to charge his principal the full price. The court held that the agent had to account to his principal for the discount that he had received.[3]

NOT TO TAKE A BRIBE

A bribe is a particular form of secret profit and arises where a payment between a third party and an agent is kept secret from the principal. If an agent takes a bribe, the principal is entitled to claim the amount of the bribe as money had and received (*Logicrose v Southend United Football Club* (1988)) or to damages against either the agent or the third party. The principal can also refuse to pay commission to the agent on that transaction (or recover any commission already paid) and summarily dismiss the agent, and can set aside the transaction with the third party. The principal's remedies are cumulative save that, in *Mahesan v Malaysia Government Officers' Co-operative Housing Society Ltd* (1979), the Privy Council held that the principal must choose between recovering the bribe or an action for damages (to prevent the principal receiving a windfall profit). If, however, property constituting or representing the bribe has increased in value, the principal can claim the full value (*Attorney General of Hong Kong v Reid* (1994)).

Furthermore, both parties to the bribe may be liable to prosecution under **s 1** of the **Prevention of Corruption Act 1916** if proof of corrupt motive can be shown (this is not required for the principal's civil remedies).

TO ACCOUNT

An agent must keep his principal's property strictly separate from his own and is treated in equity as though he was a trustee of the property. On the termination of the agency, an agent must account for all such property.[4] For example, in *Lupton v White* (1808), it was held that where an agent fails to keep the principal's property separate, the principal is entitled to a charge on the entire mixed property unless the agent is able to establish who owns what.

An agent is also required to keep proper accounts and present these to his principal.

....

3   See also *Hippisley v Knee Bros* (1905), where the court found that although the agent, acting in good faith, was in breach of duty, he was allowed to keep his commission on the transaction. Similarly, in *Boardman v Phipps* (1966), the agents were allowed some reimbursement for their expenses.

4   In recent years, sellers of goods have increasingly sought to rely on reservation of title clauses in their contracts of sale by making the buyer the seller's 'agent'. In practice, courts are reluctant to require such buyers to act as true agents in the sense of owing fiduciary duties, preferring that the agent should be a debtor to the principal.

Common Pitfalls ✗

Students need to focus on the question asked. Those who use this question as an excuse to write all they know about the fiduciary duties of agents will not score well.

QUESTION 28

(a) When is an agent entitled to claim commission?

(b) Bonnie engages Kavita to sell Bonnie's 'Dystern' industrial carpet-cleaning service. The terms of the contract specify that Kavita may only give 14 days' credit to purchasers, and provide for Kavita to be paid 2% commission on all sales arranged by her. Kavita negotiates contracts with Edward and Andrew, incurring considerable travelling and subsistence expenses in order to do so. In her negotiations, Kavita discloses her agency to Edward, but not to Andrew. In addition, Kavita agrees that Andrew can have 30 days' credit. Kavita communicates her dealings to Bonnie and Bonnie agrees to allow Andrew 30 days' credit. Contracts are entered into between Bonnie and Edward, and Kavita and Andrew, Bonnie subsequently confirming the latter contract directly with Andrew. Subsequently, a dispute arises between Kavita and Bonnie, and Bonnie refuses to supply the Dystern service to Edward and Andrew. She also refuses to have any further dealings with Kavita. Discuss the legal position of the parties involved.

Answer Plan

The first part of the question concerns the right of an agent to claim commission. The conditions for such payment at common law are as follows:

❖ the agent is acting with the principal's authority;
❖ the contract expressly or impliedly provides for commission to be paid;
❖ the event has happened on which payment was made conditional;
❖ the acts of the agent were the effective cause of that event happening.

The provisions of the **Commercial Agents (Council Directive) Regulations 1993** in relation to the payment of commission to commercial agents will also need to be noted.

The second part of the question deals with an agent's right to claim remuneration and expenses necessarily incurred in the course of her agency. The question also involves a discussion of an agent's rights and liabilities under a contract which she makes on behalf of an undisclosed principal. Finally, we need to consider whether an undisclosed principal may ratify a contract.

ANSWER

(A)

The general rule is that an agent is only entitled to commission if that has been agreed with the principal. There are, however, instances where the court will imply a term giving the agent a right to be paid for his services even if there is no express agreement.

If the contract is silent as to *when* commission is payable, the normal intention of the parties is that the agent can claim commission when the contract of sale is concluded, particularly where the agent is acting in the course of a profession or business. As regards commercial agents falling within the **Commercial Agents (Council Directive) Regulations 1993**, the time for payment of commission is dealt with by **reg 10**. In the absence of any more favourable agreement, commission will be payable when either the principal or the third party has 'executed the transaction', and at the latest when the third party has executed his part of the transaction (or should have done if the principal had executed his part as he should have). At common law, it is only rarely, however, that a court will interfere where to do so varies or is contrary to the express terms of the agency contract. For example, in *Kofi Sunkersete Obu v Strauss & Co Ltd* (1951), the contract provided for the agent to receive £50 per month as expenses but that the scale of commission was solely at the company's discretion. The Privy Council in that case was not prepared to intervene to determine the rate and basis of the commission that the agent claimed he had earned.

The principal's duty to pay commission only arises where the agent has earned it. If the agent acts contrary to instructions, therefore, under common law, no right to commission will arise. For example, in *Marsh v Jelf* (1862), an auctioneer was employed to sell property by auction and was held not to be entitled to commission when he sold the property by private contract. If the agent is in breach of instructions under the contract of agency, but a contract of sale has been concluded between the principal and a third party, the agent may still be entitled to commission if her breach was done honestly and in good faith (but she does forfeit her commission if she acted in bad faith).[5] As regards a commercial agent payable by commission, the right will only be lost if a contract concluded between the principal and a third party is not executed for a reason for which the principal is not to blame (for example frustration, or where the third party withdraws) (**reg 11** of the **Commercial Agents (Council Directive) Regulations 1993**). The Regulations make no provision for the right to commission to be lost as a result of the agent acting contrary to instructions, even where this is in bad faith. The agent will of course be in breach of the duty of good faith, and if this has resulted in loss to the principal, compensation could be sought, but commission cannot be withheld on this basis.

An agent will only earn her commission when she has been the direct or effective cause of the event upon which the principal has agreed to pay commission. The relevant phrase in the **Commercial Agents (Council Directive) Regulations** is where a contract 'has been concluded as a result of [the agent's] action' (**reg 7**). It is to be assumed that this will be interpreted in the same way as 'effective cause'. The question of causation is ultimately a question of fact in the absence of judicial definition of 'effective cause'. If some event breaks the chain of causation between the agent and the event on which payment of commission depends, then the agent will not be entitled to commission. Thus, in *Coles v Enoch* (1939), A was employed to find a tenant for P's property. T overheard a conversation between A and an interested party and, although A only gave T a general description of the location, T found the property himself and made an offer directly to P which was accepted. The court held that A was not entitled to commission since his actions had not been the direct cause of T's agreement with P.

A commercial agent may also be able to claim commission in relation to contracts between the principal and a customer previously introduced by the agent, even though the agent has not taken any action in relation to the later contracts (**reg 7(1)(b)** of the **Commercial Agents (Council Directive) Regulations 1993**).

In some cases, an agent will be entitled to commission where the principal wilfully breaks his contract with a third party whom the agent has introduced and whom the principal has accepted. In *Alpha Trading Ltd v Dunnshaw-Patten Ltd* (1981), a principal was introduced to a buyer for a quantity of cement. The principal accepted the introduction and contracted with the buyer accordingly. In order to take advantage of a rising market, the principal decided not to perform the contract of sale (preferring

---

5 See also *Hippisley v Knee Bros* (1905), where the court found that although the agent, acting in good faith, was in breach of duty, he was allowed to keep his commission on the transaction. Similarly, in *Boardman v Phipps* (1966), the agents were allowed some reimbursement for their expenses.

instead to pay damages for breach of contract). The agent claimed damages for lost commission. The Court of Appeal held that the agent was entitled to commission because it was an implied term of the agency contract that the principal would not deprive the agent of his commission by breaking the contract with the third party. As noted above, this common law principle also operates under **reg 11** of the **Commercial Agents (Council Directive) Regulations 1993**. If a contract is not performed for a reason for which the principal is to blame, the commercial agent is still entitled to commission.

Where a person is appointed 'sole agent', he is entitled to be paid even if the sale is not effected by him but by some other agent.[6]

(B)

KAVITA'S POSITION *VIS-À-VIS* BONNIE

Kavita's position here depends on applying the rules relating to an agent's rights against her principal. These are: the right to be remunerated; the right to be indemnified for expenses properly incurred; and the right to a lien over items of the principal's property in her possession.

Because the contracts negotiated by Kavita are for the supply of a service rather than the sale of goods, the **Commercial Agents (Council Directive) Regulations 1993** will not apply to this situation. The precise conditions to the right of remuneration will therefore depend on the terms of the agency contract but, in essence, the agent must have acted within the scope of her authority and her acts must have been the effective cause of the event she was employed to bring about. Whether or not the agent's acts were the 'effective cause' will be a question of fact in each case.

In the case of the contract with Edward, Kavita has fulfilled the criteria for payment and is entitled to her commission.

Unless excluded from doing so by her contract with Bonnie (of which there is no evidence), Kavita can also claim her expenses from Bonnie in relation to the contract with Edward, since these have been properly incurred in the performance of the agency. The right to indemnity covers all expenses and liabilities necessarily incurred by the agent while acting within her actual authority. Furthermore, should Kavita be in lawful possession of property or documents of title belonging to Bonnie, she

---

6   This takes the form of damages for breach of the term that he should be the 'sole' agent.

may protect her rights by exercising a lien[7] over them for unpaid commission and expenses.

The position in relation to the contract with Andrew is more problematic. Kavita exceeded her authority by giving Andrew 30 days' credit. Where an agent acts outside her authority, she is generally not entitled to commission, even though her principal may be bound by the transaction. Although Bonnie purported to ratify the contract, at law, an undisclosed principal cannot do so (*Keighley Maxsted & Co v Durant* (1901)). In that case, the agent entered into a contract for the purchase of wheat at a price in excess of the limit on behalf of himself and his principal. The agent did not disclose to the seller of the wheat his intention to contract on the principal's behalf as well as his own. Later, the principal purported to ratify the agent's act. The House of Lords unanimously held that an undisclosed principal cannot ratify. It seems therefore that whatever the position as between Andrew and Bonnie or Andrew and Kavita, Kavita is not entitled to commission on the contract made with Andrew.

As for Kavita's expenses, in order to render Bonnie liable to indemnify her, she must have acted within the scope of Kavita's authority. For the same reasons as above, Kavita will not be entitled to claim for her expenses because she has acted in breach of her instructions.

KAVITA'S POSITION *VIS-À-VIS* EDWARD AND ANDREW

Where an agent acts with authority and names or sufficiently identifies the principal in such a way that it is clear to the third party that the agent is acting as such, the contract is made between the principal and the third party, and the agent drops out of the transaction entirely. This is Kavita's position with regard to Edward – she incurs neither rights nor liabilities on the contract made between Edward and Bonnie.

In relation to Andrew, Bonnie's purported ratification of Kavita's actions is without legal effect, because a principal can only ratify if he was identified at the time the contract was made (*Keighley Maxsted & Co v Durant* (1901)). Thus, the position is exactly the same as it was when the contract was made – Andrew thought the contract was made with Kavita and, therefore, Kavita is contractually liable to Andrew. No question of breach of warranty of authority arises here, because Kavita was, at law, the principal when the contract was entered into. It is clear that an agent is personally liable on a contract where it has been negotiated on behalf of an undisclosed principal. If the agent is unable to supply the Dystern service under the contract made personally with Andrew, Kavita will be liable to pay damages for breach of that contract.

7   Agents normally exercise a particular lien, that is, the agent is entitled to retain the principal's property until debts relating to that property are discharged (cf a general lien exercised by certain types of agent, for example bankers and solicitors).

BONNIE'S POSITION *VIS-À-VIS* EDWARD AND ANDREW

Once again, the position in relation to Edward is straightforward. Kavita acted within her authority and identified Bonnie as her principal; the contract was therefore solely between Bonnie and Edward. Thus, if Bonnie refuses to supply the Dystern service to Edward, she is in breach of this contract and Edward has a right of action against Bonnie alone. In relation to Andrew, Bonnie is able to rely on the rule in *Keighley Maxsted & Co v Durant* (1901) that an undisclosed principal cannot ratify.

> ## Aim Higher ★
>
> Students should explain the position at common law before the position was changed by the **Commercial Agents (Council Directive) Regulations 1993**. The effect of these regulations needs to be explained.

QUESTION 29

(a) Outline the situations in which an agent will incur personal liability on a contract they make on behalf of their principal.

(b) Homer Ltd engages Bart to act for it in the sale of cast iron manufactured by Homer Ltd. The contract provides that Homer Ltd shall pay Bart '... 3% commission on the value of all sales of cast iron pursuant to this agreement ...' and that '... no sales shall be made through the intermediation of any other agent so long as this present agreement shall last'. Bart negotiates a sale to Krusty Ltd and has delivered to Homer Ltd a letter from Ned Ltd expressing its intention to place an order with Homer Ltd (through Bart) in the near future. In addition, Skinner Ltd places an order directly with Homer Ltd, having entered into preliminary negotiations with Bart some six months ago, negotiations which ended because, at the time, the specifications of the cast iron available from Homer Ltd did not meet Skinner Ltd's requirements. Subsequently, Ned Ltd makes a formal offer to purchase cast iron, which Homer Ltd rejects because it fears that the cast iron may be used to manufacture weapons. After this sequence of events, Homer Ltd cancels the contract with Bart by giving notice in accordance with the terms of the contract, and refuses to pay commission which Bart claims is owed to him. Bart claims commission on the sales to Krusty Ltd and Skinner Ltd, and damages in respect of Homer Ltd's refusal to sell to Ned Ltd.

❯ Discuss the legal position.

Answer Plan

The first part of this question asks you to *outline* the relevant situations. Since there are two parts to the question, the amount of detail required will be restricted to the time available to answering both parts.

The second part of the question concerns the right of an agent to claim commission. The conditions for such payment at common law are as follows:

- ❖   the agent is acting with the principal's authority;
- ❖   the contract expressly or impliedly provides for commission to be paid;
- ❖   the event has happened on which payment was made conditional;
- ❖   the acts of the agent were the effective cause of that event happening.

The provisions of the **Commercial Agents (Council Directive) Regulations 1993** in relation to the payment of commission to commercial agents will also need to be noted.

ANSWER

(A)

An agent will be personally liable on a contract in the following circumstances:

- ❖   *Where the agent intends to be a party to the contract*
  This might either be because the contract expressly states that the agent is a party or, on the proper construction of the contract, the agent will be held personally liable on it. In order to escape liability, the contract must make clear that the agent signs only in a representative capacity, for instance by signing *'per pro'* or 'A as agent for P'. Using descriptive words such as 'director' or 'agent' after a signature may well be insufficient. In *The Swan* (1968), a one-man company, JD Rodger Ltd, hired a boat belonging to JD Rodger himself, who was a director of the company. The company gave instructions through JD Rodger for repairs to be carried out. It was held that in all the circumstances, although the order for the work had been signed simply as 'Director', JD Rodger, the agent, was personally liable. It was natural for the ship repairers to assume that the shipowner would accept personal liability.
- ❖   *Where the agent does not disclose the existence of the principal*
  Here, the agent is both liable on and able to enforce the contract against the third party since the third party, at the time of the contract, believes that the agent is

the principal.[8] Merely failing to name the principal does not result in personal liability. An agent's liability ends when the principal fully performs the contract or, having discovered the principal's existence, the third party chooses to enforce the contract against the principal and not the agent.

❖ *In some circumstances where the agent signs a cheque or other bill of exchange*
A person who signs a bill of exchange becomes a party to it if his name appears on it, and he therefore incurs liability on it unless the representative nature of the signature is made perfectly clear. Again, merely adding words such as 'agent' or 'director' is insufficient to avoid personal liability. However, in *Bondina Ltd v Rollaway Shower Blinds Ltd* (1986), the Court of Appeal held that, provided a cheque is printed with the company's name and account number, the company and not the person signing is liable on the cheque, even if the representative nature of the signature is not stated.[9]

❖ *Where an agent executes a contract by deed*
The agent and not the principal may enforce it. This rule does not, however, apply to a deed executed under a power of attorney, that is, where the agent is appointed by deed (**s 7** of the **Power of Attorney Act 1971**).

❖ *Where trade usage makes the agent liable*
It is also clear that if there is a custom or trade usage (for example, in the tallow trade: *Thornton v Fehr* (1935)) that agents are personally liable or entitled under the contract, the courts will give effect to it, provided that it is consistent with the express terms of the contract and the surrounding circumstances.

❖ *Where the principal does not exist*
This situation does not usually arise as the result of the literal non-existence of the principal, but as a result of their legal non-existence, almost always involving an agent acting on behalf of a yet-to-be-incorporated company. The common law approach was demonstrated by *Kelner v Baxter* (1866), where it was held that the promoters were personally liable on the contract. This has been given statutory force by **s 51** of the **Companies Act 2006**, where the agent will be personally liable,

---

8   Where the agent acts on behalf of a foreign principal, it used to be the rule that only the agent was liable on and able to enforce the contract but, since *Teheran Europe Co Ltd v ST Belton* (1968), it has been recognised that the court will now consider all the facts to decide if the contract has created privity between the principal and the third party, and the foreign nationality of the principal will be only one factor to be taken into account.

9   It should be noted, however, that in modern practice, cheques are rarely negotiated (being used largely as an alternative to cash) and usually include details of the company's name and account number on the face of the document. Thus, the party seeking to enforce it is usually the party to whom the cheque is given and that party will have sufficient notice that the intention is that it is the company, and not the person signing, who should be liable on the cheque. Since bills other than cheques are more likely to be negotiated and therefore less likely to include printed details of account numbers etc, a person signing them will incur liability unless some other intention is clearly expressed.

subject to a term in the contract to the contrary. More generally in these situations, the agent will be liable for breach of warranty of authority under the principle in *Collen v Wright* (1857).

(B)

On the assumption that Homer Ltd's termination of Bart's contract is justified, this question involves an agent's right to receive commission (more generally discussed in part (a)). Since Bart is a self-employed agent engaged under a continuing authority to sell goods for Homer, he is a 'commercial agent' within the **Commercial Agents (Council Directive) Regulations 1993**. The common law position will therefore be modified by the provisions of these Regulations.

KRUSTY LTD

In relation to the contract placed by Krusty Ltd, it is clear that (as required by the Regulations) the transaction was concluded as a result of Bart's action or, in common law terms, his actions were the effective cause of the sale and therefore Bart is entitled to 3% of the sale price as commission. The contract is quite specific as to the commission payable, and Bart's role in effecting the sale is unequivocal.

NED LTD

Here, the issue is not one of commission, since no contract was concluded on which commission would be payable, but one of whether the principal has the right to take actions which prevent the agent from earning his commission. In the absence of an express term in the agency contract, might the courts be prepared to imply such a term in the circumstances of this question? Decided cases show that they are reluctant to do so. This situation is not one which is dealt with by the Regulations.

In the leading case of *Luxor (Eastbourne) Ltd v Cooper* (1941), agents were instructed to sell two cinemas and commission of £10,000 was payable on completion of a sale. The agents introduced a prospective purchaser who was willing and able to proceed with the purchase, but the owners of the cinemas refused to sell to him. The agents alleged the existence of an implied term preventing the owners interfering with an agent's ability to earn his commission. The House of Lords held that no such term could be implied. It was not necessary to achieve business efficacy in the contract and, given the size of the commission in relation to the work involved,[10] the agents were held to have taken the risk that the owners might not proceed with any sale arranged by the

10   £10,000 was, in 1941, the equivalent of the remuneration for a year's work by the Lord Chancellor.

agents. However, a contrary view was taken by the court in *Alpha Trading Ltd v Dunnshaw-Patten Ltd* (1981) (see Question 29).

The commission claimed by Bart is probably of a different order from that claimed by the agent in *Luxor*. Nor was there a deliberate breach of an existing contract or, on the facts, any evidence of a pecuniary motive behind Homer Ltd's refusal to proceed as there was in *Alpha Trading*. Thus, both cases can be distinguished on the facts. It would appear to be a situation in which general principles are most likely to apply – unless there is an express term stopping Homer Ltd from doing anything that prevents Bart earning his commission, Homer Ltd is able to do so. An action by Bart for damages is thus likely to fail.

SKINNER LTD

The issue involved in this third situation is whether the sale of cast iron to Skinner Ltd has been concluded as a result of Bart's actions (as required by the Regulations). If it has, then Bart is entitled to receive commission.

It is assumed that English courts, in tackling this issue, will adopt the common law approach of asking whether the agent's actions were the 'effective cause' of the contract. 'Effective cause' has not been judicially defined. It concerns the question of causation which depends on the facts of each case. Although Bart was responsible for the initial contact and negotiations with Skinner Ltd, there is arguably no direct connection between these and the subsequent sale because, at the time of the initial negotiations, Homer Ltd did not have cast iron that matched Skinner Ltd's requirements. On this basis, Bart cannot be said to be the effective cause of the sale and he would therefore not be entitled to commission (*Coles v Enoch* (1939)).

The term of the contract '. . . no sales shall be made through the intermediation of any other agent so long as this present agreement shall last' appears to amount to a 'sole agency'. A sole agency agreement is a variant of a standard agency agreement because it prevents the principal selling goods through other agents. However, a 'sole agency' agreement does not prevent the principal himself from selling goods. If, therefore, after the termination of the agency contract, Homer Ltd and Skinner Ltd enter into new negotiations, whereby Homer Ltd concludes the contract with Skinner Ltd for goods now matching Skinner Ltd's requirements, the effective cause of the sale is not the introduction by Bart (although to some degree it remains), but Homer Ltd itself. Thus, Bart is not entitled to commission on this transaction. This is not affected by anything in the Regulations.

Relationship with Third Parties

9

INTRODUCTION

This chapter is concerned with the scope of an agent's authority and when a principal will be liable, or be able to sue, on a contract made by the agent without authority. The different types of authority must be understood, in particular, apparent authority (sometimes known as 'ostensible' authority) and usual authority. Furthermore, students must pay sufficient attention to the important concept of the doctrine of the undisclosed principal. *The general rule is that an undisclosed principal can sue and be sued on the contract made by the agent on his behalf, if it was within the scope of the agent's actual authority.* The justification for the doctrine of the undisclosed principal has been the subject of much discussion by academic writers. It is generally accepted that, although it runs against the fundamental principles of privity of contract (that is, there must be agreement between the parties), the doctrine is justified on grounds of commercial convenience.

QUESTION 30

Lord Diplock *Freeman & Lockyer v Buckhurst Park Properties* [1964] 2 QB 480, at p 503 said:

> . . . apparent authority . . . is a legal relationship between the principal and the contractor created by a representation made by the principal to the contractor, intended to be and in fact acted upon by the contractor, that the agent has authority to enter on behalf of the principal into a contract of a kind within the scope of the apparent authority so as to render the principal liable to perform any obligations imposed upon him by such a contract.

▶ Discuss.

Answer Plan

A third party hardly ever relies on an agent's 'actual' authority. This is because 'actual' authority is the authority which the principal specifically places on the agent. This does, of course, carry some implied authorities, but a third party can only know what those implied authorities are if he knows what the express authority is. Since a third party does not normally know what the principal has expressly authorised the agent to do or the extent of that authority, the third party needs to rely on the perception as to the authority of the agent. This is where apparent authority kicks in.

ANSWER

Apparent authority is often called agency by estoppel. If a principal puts his agent in a position where it is reasonable for a third party to assume the agent has authority, the principal cannot go back on his representation of authority. Apparent authority is 'the authority as it appears to others', *per* Lord Denning in *Hely-Hutchinson v Brayhead*. In this case, the chairman had no express authority to enter into the indemnity agreement on behalf of the principal company. No authority could be implied from the fact that he was chairman. But, by allowing the chairman to act as de facto managing director, the chairman had authority implied from the conduct of the parties and the circumstances of case (implied actual authority). Thus, whenever an agent acts within the scope of his apparent authority, the principal is bound as if he actually authorised the transaction. This is true even if an agent's agreement with his principal has ended.[1]

Apparent authority cannot be created out of nothing. The requirements are embodied in Lord Diplock's statement in *Freeman & Lockyer v Buckhurst Park Properties*. In this case, the company's board of directors had the power to appoint a managing director. They did appoint a managing director but did not do so under the procedures as required under the company's articles of association. They nevertheless allowed the managing director to enter into a contract with a third party firm of architects to apply for planning permission to develop large piece of land. The question for the court was whether managing director had the apparent authority to bind the principal company. The House of Lords held that the managing director did have apparent authority and the principal company was bound to the contract with the architects.

---

1   In *Summers v Solomon*, the principal owned a jeweller's shop. He employed a manager to run it for him and regularly paid for jewellery ordered by the manager from a third party to sell in the shop. The manager left the principal's employment, ordered jewellery in the principal's name and absconded. The third party sued for the price of the unpaid jewellery. The court held that the principal was liable to pay for the jewellery. The agent had no actual authority to purchase jewellery from the third party once his employment had been terminated. But, because of previous course of dealings, the third party was entitled to rely on the apparent authority of the manager and the third party was not given actual notice of the termination of the agency agreement.

The board of directors knew the managing director was employing architects and permitted him to do so, and thus, by conduct, represented that the managing director had the authority to enter into the contracts of the type managing directors would normally have authority so to do on behalf of the company.

Apparent authority thus acts as an estoppel, that is, the principal is estopped from denying that his agent had the authority to do what he did.

There are two distinct requirements arising from Lord Diplock's statement.

(1) THERE MUST BE A REPRESENTATION OF AUTHORITY MADE BY THE PRINCIPAL TO THE THIRD PARTY

The representation can be made in several ways: expressly (orally or in writing); impliedly (for example, through previous course of dealings); or by placing an agent in a specific position which carries usual authority.[2]

The representation must be made by the principal.[3] It is not sufficient for an agent to say he has authority. In *AG for Ceylon v Silva*, Crown agents falsely told the buyers they had authority to sell steel plates which were Crown property. The Privy Council held that the Crown was not bound by the sale, because the agent had no actual authority and the principal did not represent that the agent had apparent authority.

Lord Diplock in *Freeman & Lockyer* said that the representation needs to be made by a principal who had actual authority. There is some difficulty with this. A company can only operate through agents. It cannot by itself do any act, and it cannot make representations. In *Freeman & Lockyer*, the principal was a company. If companies can only act via agents, then the representation of authority has to come from one of its agents. Thus, if one agent (A1) represents that another agent (A2) has authority, Lord Diplock is essentially saying that A1 must have 'actual' authority in order to invoke apparent authority. On the other hand, if A1 represents A1 has authority, the principal is not bound. In *Armagas v Mundogas*, the vice president of a company said he had authority to agree the deal for the sale and leaseback of a ship. The third party knew the agent did not have actual authority because it was unusual. The third party

....

2   It also seems clear from the facts of *Freeman & Lockyer* that representation can include representation by omission, that is, where the principal failed to intervene when he knew that his agent was acting in a particular way is deemed to constitute representation to the third parties that the actions are authorised.

3   The principal cannot therefore be an undisclosed principal. Such an idea is logically inconsistent with the requirement of a representation by a principal.

nevertheless sought to enforce the agreement against the principal on grounds that the vice president had the apparent authority to enter into the contract. The House of Lords held that the company was not bound because the principal company made no such representation. It was not usual in the company's business that vice presidents agree to the sale and leaseback of ships, and the third party knew this.

The position is not without difficulty. There is nothing to prevent a principal from authorising an agent to make representations about the agent's own authority to act on behalf of the principal. Thus, it is possible for A1 (who has actual authority) to tell A2 that A2 has authority to make representations that A2 has authority. In this situation, the representation is made by the principal. In *First Energy v Hungarian International Bank*, a senior bank manager did not have actual authority to agree credit facilities. The third party knew this but asked the bank manager for credit facilities nevertheless. After several meetings, the bank manager wrote to the third party saying he had obtained approval from head office to go ahead. The Court of Appeal held that the bank was bound by the agreement.

Although the agent did not have apparent authority to enter into the transaction, it was reasonable for the third party to believe the agent had apparent authority to communicate that the transaction had been approved. This is because it would be unreasonable to expect a third party in this situation to check to see whether the bank's head office had in fact given approval to the transaction. Bank managers usually have authority to sign and send letters on behalf of a bank. But, if a third party knows that it is not usual, he cannot rely on apparent authority to bind the principal.

In *British Bank of the Middle East v Sun Life*, a branch manager of an insurance company had no usual authority to authorise policy pay-outs. It was well known that only the head office could do this. The House of Lords held that the third party cannot rely on the apparent authority of the branch manager.

It seems, therefore, that if an agent represents that he has authority, the principal is not bound unless it was reasonable in the circumstances for the third party to believe that the agent had authority to make representations about their own authority on behalf of the principal.

First Energy should perhaps be treated as an exceptional case, decided on its own facts. Although the bank manager did not have actual authority to make the decision, his position as senior bank manager armed him with apparent authority to communicate his principal head office's decision to a third party. In *Armagas*, the vice president was not in a position that would lead a reasonable third party to believe that the vice president had such authority.

(2) THE THIRD PARTY MUST HAVE RELIED ON THE REPRESENTATION

Apparent authority cannot help a third party unless he relied on the principal's express or implied representation that the agent had authority. So, if the third party knew or ought to have known the agent did not have actual authority, he cannot bind the principal on grounds of apparent authority.[4] In *Overbrooke Estates v Glencombe Properties*, the auction sales catalogue stated that the auctioneer did not have the seller's authority to make representations about the sale property. Before the sale, the auctioneer told the buyer that the local authority had no plans regarding the property. The buyer bought the property and found that the auctioneer's statement was untrue – the local authority was intending to include the property in a slum clearance programme. The court found that the buyer knew (or ought to have known) of the terms in the sales catalogue, so the buyer knew the auctioneer did not have the seller's actual authority to make representations. Therefore, the buyer could not have relied on the apparent authority of the agent.

Can silence amount to a representation that the agent had apparent authority? The answer must necessarily be no. However, in *Spiro v Lantern*, the wife contracted to sell her husband's house. She did not have actual authority and the third party buyer thought he was dealing with the wife as principal.[5] After the contract had been entered into, the husband said nothing to the third party and did nothing to discourage the third party from incurring expenses trying to conclude the purchase of the house. The husband refused to sell and the third party brought action asking for specific performance. The Court of Appeal held that the husband was estopped from denying that his wife had authority to sell the house on his behalf. The husband was under a duty to inform the third party of the non-existence of authority.

Not only must the principal have made the representation, the third party must have relied on that representation. Reliance is normally evidenced by the third party entering into the contract.[6] Note however, in *Spiro*, both the principal's representation and the third party's reliance occurred after the contract was concluded.

Some argue that the third party's reliance must have resulted in detriment to third party. There are cases either way. Lord Diplock in *Freeman & Lockyer v Buckhurst Park Properties*

---

4   In *Armagas v Mundogas* (1986), the third party knew the vice president did not have authority.
5   The third party cannot therefore argue apparent authority.
6   That is, based on the principal's representation that the agent had authority, the third party entered into the contract.

considered a change of position as sufficient. In *Farquharson Bros v King*, the House of Lords held that not only must the third party rely on the representation, the third party needed to suffer detriment. The strict requirements of estoppel means there does need to be detriment, but the modern approach to apparent authority seems to be that the only detriment that needs to be shown is the entering into contract.[7]

Apparent authority is a form of estoppel. The rationale for the doctrine of estoppel of course is that it is unfair for someone to back out of his promise. It would be unconscionable for someone to make promise, have that promise relied on and then go back on that promise. Thus, if a principal represents that his agent has his authority, it is unconscionable for the principal to go back on his representation. Of course, a principal's representation to a third party can be artificial, especially where the representation amounts to no more than putting someone in a position that carries usual authority for an agent of that type. Lord Diplock's statement is true in that apparent authority is a legal relationship between the principal and the third party, but it is not 'real' authority. The principal cannot sue a third party unless he ratifies his agent's unauthorised act. Apparent authority does not of itself allow a principal to enforce a contract against a third party.[8] Apparent authority merely creates the appearance of authority which, for policy reasons, the law recognises as giving the agent power to affect the legal relations of his principal.[9]

Aim Higher ★

Students must not simply put down the names of cases without explaining what those cases decided. The examination aims to test understanding of the issues and not the ability to memorise case names.

QUESTION 31

Furnitor Ltd appoints Sandra to act as its agent in the sale and purchase of furniture for sale through its shops in England. Sandra is instructed to obtain the consent of the company's board of directors before making any purchase above £15,000. Sandra has undertaken various actions.

7   *The Tatra* (1990).
8   The concept exists primarily to protect the third party. It does not create an agency relationship between the principal and his agent. Thus the relationship does not create any rights for the principal.
9   Apparent authority arguably arises by operation of law, because the concept relies on the perception of authority by a third party.

(i)   Beds-R-Us bed manufacturer contacts Sandra offering to sell a consignment of beds. Beds-R-Us is in financial difficulties and, therefore, offers the beds for £20,000, which represents a substantial discount on the normal price, but Beds-R-Us requires an immediate decision. Sandra says, 'I need to check with the company's board for such a large transaction, but they usually back my opinion on such matters, especially in an emergency like this.' Sandra, therefore, agrees to buy on behalf of Furnitor Ltd. The next day, Beds-R-Us receives a better offer for the beds from another furniture retailer. Beds-R-Us telephones Sandra and says it is withdrawing from the deal. That afternoon, the board of directors of Furnitor decides it wishes to go ahead with the purchase from Beds-R-Us.

(ii) Sandra is offered by Warners Ltd wardrobes for £10,000, which is the normal price. During negotiations, the sales manager of Warners says to Sandra, 'Once this deal goes through, you'll be on the top of the list for a Christmas hamper which contains a voucher for a one-week all expenses paid caravan holiday'. Sandra agrees to buy the wardrobes, but manages to persuade Warners to agree to a price of £9,500. Later, she receives a Christmas hamper containing the holiday voucher from Warners. When asked about this by the board of directors, Sandra strongly denies that she was influenced by the promise of a Christmas hamper. Sandra points out that Warners wardrobes have always been popular with customers.

(III) Sandra contracts to buy table lamps from a manufacturer in Estonia for £5,000. The lamps do not conform to safety standards and cannot be sold in England.

▶ Advise Furnitor.

Answer Plan

This question concerns the extent to which a principal can be bound by contracts which the agent has made without authority. Part (i) involves the principal's attempt to ratify its agent's act. The general requirements of ratification need to be stated. Beds-R-Us is aware that Sandra has no authority to accept its offer. Since ratification requires an agent to purport to act for the principal, there is no agreement for the board of directors to ratify. In Part (ii), Sandra may be in breach of her fiduciary duties not to make a secret profit nor take a bribe. An agent is required to perform with honesty and good faith for the benefit of the principal. The consequences of such a breach need to be discussed. Part (iii) requires a discussion of the Estonian manufacturer's possible breaches of the **Sale of Goods Act 1979**, namely, under s 14.

ANSWER

Furnitor wants to know whether they are bound by the transactions carried out by Sandra. In order for Furnitor to be bound, Sandra, as their agent, must have had some form of authority from Furnitor to enter into the transactions. If Sandra had no authority, then Furnitor cannot be bound to the contracts made with the third parties. We will look at individual situations to see if Furnitor are bound.

(I) BEDS-R-US

An agent has actual authority when what is done has in fact been previously authorised either expressly or impliedly by the principal. Furnitor instructs Sandra to obtain the consent of the company's board of directors before making any purchases above £15,000. There is nothing vague or ambiguous about these instructions (*Weigall v Runciman* (1916)). So Sandra does not have actual authority to conclude the contract to purchase beds for £20,000. Although this was what Sandra explained to Beds-R-Us, Sandra agreed to buy the beds anyway, in the belief that the board would approve the transaction. Indeed, she is correct, because the board of directors in fact does wish to go ahead with the deal.

Although a principal may ratify an agent's unauthorised act, there are limitations to this rule. The right to ratify depends on whether the agent purported to act on behalf of the principal at the time of agreeing to the transaction (*Keighley, Maxsted v Durant* (1901)). Beds-R-Us knew Sandra did not have authority, because Sandra specifically told Beds-R-Us this. Even though Sandra believed that the Furnitor board would approve the transaction, when she agreed to purchase the beds from Beds-R-Us, Sandra did not purport to act on behalf of Furnitor. Thus, there was no unauthorised transaction which Furnitor's board of directors could ratify. This is unlike the situation in *Bolton Partners v Lambert* (1889), where the managing director of a company accepted the offer to purchase a property on behalf of the company without its authority. When the third party wanted to withdraw from the contract, the court held that it was too late, because when the company ratified the agent's unauthorised act, ratification related back to the time when the unauthorised act was concluded. It was thus too late for the third party to withdraw. Here, Sandra did not conclude the unauthorised act on behalf of Furnitor. She specifically told Beds-R-Us that she did not have the company's authority. Thus, there is no concluded transaction which Furnitor's directors could ratify. The effect of ratification is that an unauthorised contract made by an agent becomes an authorised one from when it was made. Here, Furnitor cannot ratify because there was no unauthorised contract to which they were a party. Thus, there is no binding contract with Beds-R-Us and Beds-R-Us can withdraw their offer at any time up to the point of acceptance (*Payne v Cave* (1789); *Byrne v Van Tienhoven* (1880)).

Furnitor has no action against Sandra, since she had followed her instructions and had acted within the limits of her purchasing power on behalf of Furnitor. She has not acted in excess of her actual authority.

(II) WARNERS LTD

Sandra has express authority to purchase furniture. So, *prima facie*, Furnitor is bound by contract to purchase wardrobes with Warners. But as Furnitor's agent, Sandra owes a fiduciary duty and is in a position of trust and confidence. So equity will intervene and place fiduciary duties on an agent to protect the principal from an abuse of trust. A major consequence of this is that an agent must not put herself in a situation where there might be a conflict of interest and duty. The fiduciary duty of good faith has been applied very strictly (*Boardman v Phipps* (1966)) and it appears that Sandra is in breach of this paramount duty. Furthermore, Sandra must not make a secret profit nor take a bribe. She cannot accept commission from a third party.

It seems clear that Warners is aware that Sandra is an agent. Nevertheless, they offer her a Christmas hamper containing a holiday voucher. This constitutes a bribe. It is conclusively presumed against Warners that their motive was corrupt and that Sandra was affected and influenced by the offer of the hamper and holiday. It is irrelevant that Sandra managed to persuade Warners to reduce the price to £9,500. In this situation, Sandra may be summarily dismissed, even if appointed for a fixed period. We are not told what Sandra's remuneration package was, but certainly Sandra would lose her right to commission on this transaction. If Sandra has already consumed the contents of the hamper and used the holiday voucher, Furnitor could claim damages from Sandra and Warners for any loss they suffer as a result of the bribe. Furnitor can, if they wish to do so, set aside the transaction with Warners (*Logicrose v Southend UFC* (1988)). Furthermore, Sandra and Warners may incur criminal liability under the **Prevention of Corruption Acts**.

It is not clear whether Sandra is a commercial agent within the **Commercial Agents (Council Directive) Regulations 1993**. The Regulations would apply if she is a self-employed intermediary with continuing authority to negotiate the sale and/or purchase of goods (**reg 2**). If Sandra is a commercial agent, she is certainly in breach of her duties to look after the interests of Furnitor and to act 'dutifully and in good faith' (**reg 3**). Although the Regulations state that an agent is entitled to commission where a transaction is concluded as a result of an agent's action (**reg 7**), the Regulations are silent as to whether an agent loses the right to commission if the agent acts contrary to instructions – even if the agent acts in bad faith. Certainly, Sandra is in breach of her duty of good faith under **reg 3** and, if this resulted in loss to Furnitor, compensation could be sought, but it seems that her commission on this transaction cannot be withheld. Although an agent has the right to an indemnity or compensation on termination of the agency agreement (**reg 17**), if Furnitor terminates Sandra's agency contract as a result of her taking a bribe, **reg 18** will preclude her from making such a claim.

(III) ESTONIAN MANUFACTURER

Sandra has actual authority to purchase furniture on behalf of Furnitor, so Furnitor is bound in contract with the Estonian manufacturer. However, the table lamps cannot be sold in England. Furnitor has two possible actions: first against the Estonian manufacturer and, secondly, against Sandra.

Assuming the sales contract is governed by English law, the **Sale of Goods Act 1979** requires goods sold by a seller in the course of business to be of satisfactory quality (**s 14(2)**) and fit for their purpose (**s 14(3)**). Since Furnitor resells the goods in the course of their business, the sales contract is not a consumer transaction (*R and B Customs Brokers v United Dominion Trust* (1988); *Feldaroll Foundry v Hermes Leasing* (2004)). This means that the court has a discretion where it is just to do so to treat the implied terms under **s 14** as giving the buyer a right to warranty damages only (**s 15A**).

By **s 14(2)**, goods are required to be of satisfactory quality. We are told that the table lamps do not conform to safety standards. If these standards were applicable worldwide, it is likely that the Estonian manufacturer would be in breach of **s 14(2)**, since no reasonable person would regard table lamps to be of satisfactory quality if they are not safe and do not meet a general level of safety.

It may be, however, that although the table lamps supplied by the Estonian manufacturer are in general satisfactory but merely do not meet the standards for resale in England, then whether or not Furnitor has an action against the manufacturer would depend on whether there is a breach of **s 14(3)**. Certainly, if the Estonian manufacturer knows that Sandra is contracting on behalf of an English company and that the goods are to be delivered to England, this will be sufficient to impliedly make it known to the Estonian manufacturer that the goods are required to be fit for resale in England. However, there will be no breach of **s 14(3)** if either the buyer does not rely on the skill and judgement of the seller, or it is unreasonable to rely on the seller to supply suitable goods. In *ST Belton v Teheran Europe* (1968), air compressors were sold to a Persian buyer. The Persian buyer complained that the goods were unfit for their purpose because the air compressors did not meet the safety regulations and could not be resold in Persia. The court held that there was no breach of **s 14(3)**, since it was unreasonable for the buyer to rely on the seller's knowledge of the safety regulations in Persia. Following this case, therefore, it may be that Furnitor has no action against the Estonian manufacturer. If the court finds otherwise, and Furnitor has an action for breach of **s 14(3)**. this would normally entitle Furnitor to reject the entire consignment of lamps and claim damages under the *Hadley v Baxendale* (1854) principles. However, as discussed, since Furnitor are business buyers, the court has a direction under **s 15A** to make an award of damages only.

Furnitor's second possible action would be against Sandra. Although she has carried out her instructions in purchasing furniture within her credit limit, she is under a duty to act with due care and skill. If she is being paid for special skills as a purchasing agent, a greater degree of care and skill is expected of her. If she has failed in purchasing suitable furniture and this results in loss to Furnitor, she is in breach of her agency contract, entitling Furnitor to claim an indemnity from her for their loss either under the common law or under the **Commercial Agents (Council Directive) Regulations 1993**.

QUESTION 32

On 1 April, Gregory, an art dealer in London, appoints Esther as his agent in Liverpool and that same day, he sends a letter to Finestuff Ltd, a company dealing in paintings in Liverpool, confirming Esther's appointment and her authority to buy and sell pictures on his behalf. In fact, Esther is under an express instruction not to deal with any pictures alleged to have been painted by Warholle, because of the risk of forgery. On 10 May, Esther, purporting to act on behalf of Gregory, contracts with Finestuff to buy from it *The Damsel in Distress*, a genuine Warholle painting, for £17,000. On 12 May, Esther visits the office of Posh Galleries and, without mentioning Gregory, contracts to sell it *The Damsel in Distress* for £23,000. Esther intends to keep the profit from this transaction for herself. On 16 May, Finestuff discovers what Esther is trying to do, and tells Gregory that it intends to withdraw from the contract and keep *The Damsel in Distress*. On 17 May, Gregory purports to ratify Esther's actions of 10 and 12 May.

▶ **Consider the rights and liabilities of all parties.**

Answer Plan

Part of this problem is concerned with authority and, in particular, apparent authority. This relates to the effect of Esther's actions on 10 and 12 May, and whether they can be regarded as falling within the scope of her authority so as to bind Gregory. The approach to the issue of apparent authority should be the same as is outlined in the answer plan for Question 4.

The second issue that should be looked at is Esther's attempt to make a secret profit out of her position as Gregory's agent. The duty of the agent to act in good faith and account for any secret profit (for example *De Bussche v Alt* (1878)) needs to be noted here. Esther may also be said to have broken another duty of an agent in her failure to follow instructions.

Finally, there is Gregory's attempt to ratify what Esther has done. The general requirements of ratification should be stated, that is:

- ❖ the agent must purport to act for the principal (*Keighley Maxsted & Co v Durant* (1901));
- ❖ the principal must be in existence at the time of the contract (*Kelner v Baxter* (1866)); and
- ❖ the principal must have capacity at the time of contract and at the time of ratification (*Grover and Grover v Matthews* (1910)).

These should be applied to the problem, and you should also note the effects of ratification, in particular its retrospective nature (*Bolton Partners v Lambert* (1889)).

The answer could well conclude with a summary of the position of each of the parties.

ANSWER

This question raises issues relating to the extent of an agent's authority, the duties of an agent and the power of a principal to ratify an agent's unauthorised acts. These will be looked at in turn in discussing the rights and liabilities of all the parties.

In making the contracts of 10 and 12 May, Esther is acting outside the actual authority given to her by Gregory, in that she has been forbidden to deal in pictures by Warholle. This does not necessarily mean, however, that her actions cannot bind Gregory. This is because she may have 'apparent' authority (also known as 'ostensible' authority or 'agency by estoppel'). The requirements for this, as set out by Slade J in *Rama Corp Ltd v Proved Tin and General Investment* (1952), are: (a) that there is a representation of authority by the principal to the third party;[10] (b) that the third party relies on that

---

10   In *Armagas v Mundogas* (1986), the House of Lords emphasised that for apparent authority to exist, the representation must come from the principal, not from the agent. In this case, the vice president of a company had indicated that he had authority to agree a deal for the sale and charter-back of a ship. His plan was to make a secret profit out of the transactions. When his deceit came to light, the third party argued that the shipowners were bound by the agent's apparent authority. The House of Lords disagreed, holding that there was no representation of authority from the principal as opposed to the agent, and that therefore apparent authority could not arise.

representation; and (c) that the third party alters his position in reliance on the representation. This approach was followed by the Court of Appeal in *Freeman and Lockyer v Buckhurst Park Properties (Mangal) Ltd* (1964), which made it clear that the representation could be by conduct, rather than by a statement. Here, however, as far as Finestuff is concerned, there was a clear and apparently unequivocal representation as to Esther's authority in Gregory's letter of 1 April. Provided that Finestuff could show that it was important to it that Esther was Gregory's agent – in other words, that it was relying on Gregory's representation – then the apparent authority would seem to operate. This would mean that if, on 10 May, Finestuff had sought the £17,000 from Gregory, it would have had every chance of success. This does not mean, however, that Gregory can necessarily enforce the contract against Finestuff. The doctrine of apparent authority has developed to protect third parties. It is unlikely that the courts would allow it to be used against a third party in a situation such as this. That is why it will become important to look later at Gregory's power to ratify Esther's actions.

In relation to the contract with Posh Galleries, the position is different. We are not told of any letter being sent to it about Esther's authority. Moreover, Esther apparently purports to contract on her own behalf. Even if she had been acting for Gregory, so that Gregory was an undisclosed principal, this would not affect the position. There can be no apparent authority without a representation from the principal to the third party, and it is difficult to see how this could occur if the third party is unaware of the existence of the principal. The possibility of Gregory's ratifying what Esther has done will be considered later.

Turning to Esther, what is her position? Her actions have involved breaches of two of the duties which an agent owes to a principal. Firstly, she has disobeyed an instruction not to deal with Warholle pictures.[11] She will be liable for any loss flowing from this. This rule has been applied strictly, even in cases where there was some doubt as to whether, even if the agent had carried out his instructions, the principal would have avoided the loss. An example of this is *Fraser v Furman* (1967), where the agent failed to take out an insurance policy on the principal's behalf, but argued that even if he had taken it out, the insurer would have been able to avoid paying out because of a minor omission on the part of the principal. The Court of Appeal refused to get involved in that argument, and held the agent liable.

Secondly, Esther is in the process of breaching one of her fiduciary duties, that is, the duty not to make a secret profit out of her position as agent. If she does, she will be liable to account to the principal for the profit. This is what happened in *De Bussche v*

---

11   This assumes that Esther has a contractual relationship with Gregory.

Alt (1878), where an agent, engaged to sell a ship, bought it himself at the minimum price specified by the principal and shortly afterwards sold it at a substantial profit. This profit had to be handed over to the principal. Here, if Esther completed her transactions as she planned, the £6,000 profit on the resale of the picture would have to be handed over to Gregory. There is no suggestion in the facts that Esther has taken any bribe. This type of secret profit is dealt with even more severely, with the principal being entitled to dismiss the agent, and sue both the agent and the third party for any losses resulting (*Logicrose v Southend United Football Club* (1988)), but it does not appear to be relevant on these facts.

Although Esther has been acting beyond her instructions, and has been trying to make a profit for herself, Gregory has now apparently recognised that the contracts which Esther has negotiated in relation to *The Damsel in Distress* amount to a good bargain. He is therefore trying to take the benefit of them himself by ratifying Esther's actions of 10 and 12 March. Can he do this?

The power of a principal to ratify the unauthorised acts of an agent is well established. There are, however, certain limitations. First, the agent must have purported to act for a principal. This was established in *Keighley Maxsted & Co v Durant* (1901). The agent was authorised by the principal to buy wheat for their joint account at a certain price. He made a contract with the third party (Durant) at a higher price. He intended this to be for the joint account, but did not tell Durant this. The next day, the principal ratified what the agent had done, but subsequently refused to take delivery. An action by Durant against the principal failed because the agent had not purported to act for the principal, and ratification was therefore impossible.[12] Provided that the agent says that the contract is on behalf of a principal, however, it does not matter that in fact the agent is acting on his own account. In *Re Tiedemann and Ledermann Freres* (1899), it was held that in these circumstances, the principal could still ratify.

The second limitation on the power to ratify is that the principal must have been in existence at the time of the contract between the agent and the third party. This problem arises where contracts are made on behalf of companies which have not yet been incorporated. In *Kelner v Baxter* (1866), the promoters of a company which had not yet been incorporated made a contract to buy stock for it. When the company was incorporated, there was an attempt to ratify this contract. It was held that this was ineffective, and the promoters remained personally liable.

---

12   The lower courts disagreed on the result, but this was the unanimous decision of an eight-person House of Lords.

The third requirement is that the principal must have been able to make the contract at the time of the contract and at the time of ratification. The first part of this will be a problem where, for example, a minor attempts to ratify a contract which the minor would not have had capacity to make. The second part will also apply where at the time of ratification the contract would simply not have been possible. In *Grover and Grover v Matthews* (1910), for example, there was an attempt to ratify a contract of fire insurance after a fire had destroyed the property that was the subject of the insurance. It was held that ratification was impossible, because at that stage, the principal would not have been able to make the insurance contract.

How does all this apply to the facts of the problem and to Gregory's attempts to ratify Esther's actions? The second two requirements appear not to create a problem, so we must concentrate on the first – that is, that the agent must purport to act for a principal. In relation to the contract made on 10 May, this is no problem. Esther clearly says that she is acting for Gregory, and we have seen that the fact that she is in reality acting for her own benefit is irrelevant (*Re Tiedemann and Ledermann Freres*). When Esther makes the contract with Posh Galleries on 12 May, however, she makes no mention of Gregory or any other principal. This contract cannot therefore be ratified by Gregory. So, it seems that Gregory can take over the contract to buy *The Damsel in Distress*, but not the contract to sell. What about Finestuff's attempt to withdraw, which comes before the ratification? This does not matter, because ratification is retrospective; it was so held in *Bolton Partners v Lambert* (1889), where it was said that the contract, once ratified, had to be treated as if it had been made with proper authority from the start. Similarly, in *Re Tiedemann and Ledermann Freres*, the third party had tried to withdraw on the basis of the false pretence about whom he was contracting with (which is similar to the situation here), but was prevented from doing so by the subsequent ratification of the contract.

Where does all this leave the various parties?

Gregory has a contract to buy *The Damsel in Distress* at £17,000, but no contract for resale. He may also be able to take action against Esther for her various breaches of duty.

Esther has a contract with Posh Galleries to sell it *The Damsel in Distress*. She will have difficulties fulfilling this contract, since *The Damsel in Distress* now belongs to Gregory. She is also likely to face action by Gregory, as noted above.

Finestuff is obliged to sell *The Damsel in Distress* at £17,000 to Gregory, and seems to have no possibility of any action against anyone else. Gregory's ratification of Esther's actions prevents it from pursuing her. Posh Galleries has a contract to purchase *The*

Damsel in Distress from Esther which, as we have noted, Esther will have difficulty fulfilling. It will be able to sue her for breach of contract. Finally, the best outcome for all concerned, apart from Finestuff, might be for Gregory to get together with Posh Galleries, and see if they can come to a similar arrangement to that negotiated by Esther.

QUESTION 33

Sally, who owned a shop named 'Sally Fruits and Flowers', sold the business earlier this year to Bigpot, which appointed Sally as manager and renamed the business 'Sally Flower Specialists'. A sign was put up stating 'Under new management, part of the Bigpot group'. Sally knows that Bigpot does not sell fruit at any of its business outlets.

Sally, however, continues to sell at the shop fruit grown in her own garden. Eddie, who bought some strawberries from her, is claiming that the fruit was infected, causing him severe stomach pains which prevented him from working for two weeks. Eddie is an architect and lost the opportunity to bid for a lucrative contract during that period. He is threatening to sue Bigpot.

Arthur, Sally's former landlord, accepts five bouquets of flowers in part-settlement of Sally's unpaid rent.

Sally is persuaded by Charlotte on one occasion to sell some fairy cakes which she has baked. Charlotte gives Sally £10 for doing this.

▶ Advise Bigpot.

Answer Plan

Part of this question is concerned with the types of authority, in particular usual or apparent authority, and the extent to which a principal can be bound by contracts that the agent has made without authority. This relates to Sally selling fruit and the fact that it is unclear whether Bigpot had given her any instructions in this respect. If Eddie does not have a claim against Bigpot, Sally may be personally liable (*The Swan* (1968)). The amount of damages Eddie may recover will also need to be discussed.

As for Arthur, Sally has used her position as manager to satisfy a personal debt. If Bigpot sues Arthur for the value of the five bouquets of flowers, set-off may offer a partial defence to such a claim. This will depend on whether Bigpot is held to be a disclosed or undisclosed principal.

In accepting £10 from Charlotte, Sally is in breach of one of her fiduciary duties, that is, the duty not to make a secret profit out of her position as agent. The consequences of such a breach need to be discussed.

ANSWER

This question concerns the issue of an agent's authority and, in particular, the extent to which a principal can be bound by contracts which the agent has made without authority.

As far as selling fruit is concerned, Bigpot did not give any express instructions to Sally. The general rule is that where an agent is expressly appointed, the scope of his authority depends on the construction of the agreement. If the terms of the agreement are ambiguous, the court will generally construe them in a way which is most favourable to the agent as long as the agent construes his instructions reasonably (*Weigall v Runciman* (1916)). Therefore, it could be argued that Sally was entitled to continue to sell fruit. The more likely view, however, is that Sally should have known that Bigpot would not permit the selling of fruit, partly because of the renaming of the business to 'Sally Flower Specialists' with no mention of 'fruit', and partly because Sally knew that Bigpot did not sell fruit at any of its outlets. Furthermore, it would be reasonable to expect Sally, faced with an ambiguity in her agency agreement, to seek clarification from Bigpot (*European Asian Bank v Punjab & Sind Bank (No 2)* (1983)). Therefore, not only did Sally have no actual express authority to sell fruit, but it could be said that Sally should have known of the restriction not to sell fruit.

However, if it is usual for a flower shop manager such as Sally to have certain authority, then Bigpot will be liable to a third party even if Sally knows that she is prohibited or restricted from acting in the way she did unless the third party had notice of the limitation (see *Watteau v Fenwick* (1893)). This doctrine of usual authority, however, may only be relied on by a third party where the agent makes a contract within the scope of the usual authority of an agent in that position. Bigpot may rely on the fact that a business named 'Sally Flower Specialists' does not imply that anything other than flowers would be sold in that shop, and a manager of such a shop would not have the authority to sell fruit. Bigpot may thus escape liability on this basis.

The other possibility is that Eddie could argue for the existence of apparent authority (also known as 'ostensible' authority or 'agency by estoppel'). From the decisions in *Rama Corp v Proved Tin and General Investment Ltd* (1952) and *Freeman and Lockyer v Buckhurst Park Properties (Mangal) Ltd* (1964), the factors that must be present to create apparent authority include a representation that the agent has authority, which must be made by the principal. Such a representation must have been relied on by the third party claiming apparent authority.

The essence of a principal's representation is that the agent is authorised to act on his behalf. It is an authority which 'apparently' exists, having regard to the conduct of the parties. The principal's representation need not depend on previous course of dealings, as in *Summers v Solomon* (1857), but could it be argued that simply by employing Sally as the manager, Bigpot is representing that Sally has authority to do all the things that a flower shop manager would normally do, including selling fruit? The answer on the facts is likely to be in the negative, on the ground that a third party such as Eddie would not expect the manager of a well-known flower shop chain to have the authority to sell anything but flowers. Since the sign that was put up clearly states that 'Sally Flower Specialists' is part of the Bigpot group, it is unreasonable for Eddie to believe that he is dealing with a manager who possesses the necessary authority to sell fruit.

Eddie does not seem to be on strong ground against Bigpot. This does not mean, however, that Eddie has no claim at all. Sally may be personally liable to Eddie if the intention was that Sally should be personally liable. The intention is to be gathered from the nature and terms of the contract and the surrounding circumstances. An objective test is applied so that if Sally sells strawberries to Eddie in circumstances that make it reasonable to assume that Sally was contracting personally, Eddie will have an action against Sally.

In *The Swan* (1968), the defendant owned a boat called *The Swan* which was hired to a company of which he was a director. The company instructed the plaintiff to repair the ship on company notepaper which was signed by the defendant as director of the company. The company could not pay, and the question was whether the defendant was personally liable on the contract to repair the ship. The court held that the defendant contracted as agent for the company, but since it was reasonable for the repairer, who knew that the defendant owned the boat, to assume that the owner would accept personal liability for such repair, the defendant was personally liable on the contract. Applying this case to the question, if Sally sold the strawberries in such a way that Eddie reasonably assumed that Sally was selling in her personal capacity, then Sally will be personally liable to Eddie in damages.

If, as is more likely, Sally is held not to have contracted personally but to have contracted as an agent, Sally cannot be made personally liable on the contract. However, since Sally had no authority to sell fruit, Sally will be liable to Eddie who has contracted with her on the faith of her representation of authority. The nature of her liability depends on whether Sally had knowledge that she had no authority to sell fruit,[13] or whether she merely acted negligently or in good faith and under the honest but mistaken belief that she was contracting with Bigpot's authority. The latter is the more likely, rendering Sally liable to Eddie for breach of the implied warranty of authority.

The amount of damages recoverable depends on the nature of the wrong committed. Essentially, the measure of damages will be either the loss that flowed directly as a natural or probable consequence, or the loss that was foreseeable by the parties as a probable consequence, of the breach of warranty. It seems, therefore, that Eddie will be able to sue Sally for damages. Whether or not Eddie can recover for the lost opportunity to bid for the 'lucrative' contract will depend on whether this opportunity was made known to Sally at the time the contract was made. This seems unlikely, in which event, Eddie will not be able to recover damages on the basis that the damage was too remote (*Victoria Laundry (Windsor) Ltd v Newman Industries Ltd* (1949)).

As far as Arthur is concerned, can Bigpot recover from Arthur the price for the bouquets of flowers? The right of a third party to set off a liability against a principal will only apply where the principal has induced the third party to believe that the agent is acting as a principal and not as an agent, that is, where the principal is undisclosed. Did Arthur know of the existence of Bigpot? Clearly, Arthur knew that Sally had owned the business, but the question is really whether Arthur had *actual* notice[14] of the existence of Bigpot. This will depend on whether Arthur noticed the sign which had been put up – that the business was now part of the Bigpot group. If Arthur had actual notice, then Arthur has no right of set-off and Bigpot is entitled to recover the price of the bouquets of flowers from Arthur.

As far as accepting £10 for selling Charlotte's fairy cakes is concerned, Sally is in breach of one of her fiduciary duties, that is, the duty not to make a secret profit out of her position as agent.[15] Unless Sally has revealed all the circumstances to

---

13 In which event, Sally acted fraudulently and will be liable in the tort of deceit (*Polhill v Walter* (1832)). This will be the case if Sally knew Bigpot's policy of restricting the types of goods sold at its outlets.

14 It is clear from *Greer v Downs Supply Co* (1927) that in respect of the existence of an undisclosed principal, the kind of notice that is required in order to be effective is actual notice, and constructive notice will be insufficient to affect the position of the third party.

15 The facts do not suggest that the £10 was a bribe. This type of secret profit is dealt with more severely, with the principal being entitled to summarily dismiss the agent and sue both the agent and the third party for any losses resulting. If an agent takes a bribe, the principal is entitled to claim the amount of the bribe as money had and received (*Logicrose v Southend United Football Club* (1988)).

Bigpot and Bigpot has consented to her retaining the profit, she will be liable to account to Bigpot for the profit. If an agent takes a bribe, the principal is entitled to claim the amount of the bribe as money had and received (*Regier v Campbell-Stuart* (1939)).[16]

QUESTION 34

Jacob, the owner of a shop selling antique British goods, has several red telephone boxes for sale. Jacob is an eccentric and is well known for his dislike of Americans. Madison, an American, knows that Jacob is unlikely to sell a telephone box to him and therefore asks his friend, Sonya, to visit Jacob's shop and to purchase one of the telephone boxes on his behalf, promising to buy it from Sonya for 10% more than she paid for it. Sonya takes Jacob out for lunch (the bill for which came to £30) and buys from him a telephone box for £300. She also agrees to buy an old chimney pot for £100. Madison is delighted with the telephone box and also wants to take up Sonya's offer to sell the chimney pot for £120. Jacob learns of Sonya's association with Madison and purports to cancel both agreements.

▶ Consider the rights and liabilities of all parties.

Answer Plan

Part of this question is concerned with the problem of 'who is an agent?' It is not always easy to recognise an agent. It is the effect in *law* of the conduct of the parties that must be considered in order to determine whether the agency relationship has come into existence. This question requires you to analyse the nature of the relationship between Madison and Sonya, and to consider whether Sonya is acting as an agent or buying in her own name and reselling to Madison. If it is the latter, then the agreement is not one of agency (*Lamb v Goring Brick Co* (1932); *AMB Imballaggi Plastici SRL v Pacflex Ltd* (1999)).

If Sonya is an agent, she has acted on behalf of Madison in such a way that the agency is wholly undisclosed. Many of the cases dealing with the effects of undisclosed agency are old, but will need to be discussed. There is a general right for the undisclosed principal to intervene on and enforce the contract made on his behalf, but there are restrictions on that right, as in *Said v Butt* (1920).

---

16   Sally holds the £10 on constructive trust (*Boardman v Phipps* (1966)). See also Question 27 on the duties owed by an agent.

ANSWER

This question raises issues relating to the nature of the relationship between a principal and his agent, the concept of the undisclosed principal and the right of an agent to be remunerated and indemnified for expenses in the performance of an agency agreement. These will be looked at in turn in discussing the rights and liabilities of Madison, Sonya and Jacob.

Madison asks Sonya to buy a telephone box which Sonya does not own or possess at the time of the contract. It is a difficult question of fact whether this agreement between them involves Sonya as the 'seller' of goods acting for Madison as the 'buyer', or as an agent acting for Madison as the 'principal'.

If Sonya is held to be buying and reselling on her own account, then she is not a true agent in law (*Lamb v Goring Brick Company* (1932); *AMB Imballaggi Plastici SRL v Pacflex Ltd* (1999)). Accordingly, Jacob would be in breach of his agreement if he were to refuse subsequently to sell the telephone box to her. If the opposite is true, that is, Sonya is procuring the telephone box for Madison as Madison's true agent and Sonya is authorised to create privity between Madison as principal and Jacob as the third party, Madison may intervene and enforce the contract made on his behalf, subject to certain restrictions which will be discussed.

On the facts, it is likely that Sonya is acting as an agent. A particularly important factor in favour of this is the fact that Sonya's remuneration in carrying out Madison's instructions has been fixed at 10% of the purchase price. Further, Sonya's duty to buy a telephone box on Madison's behalf is not absolute, in the sense that she will not be liable to Madison if she does not obtain the telephone box: her duty is to use her care and skill as an agent to endeavour to obtain what Madison wants (*Anglo-African Shipping Co of New York Inc v J Mortner Ltd* (1962)).

The essence of an agency agreement is the agent's power to affect the principal's legal position *vis-à-vis* third parties. Sonya has been authorised by Madison to buy a telephone box, but does not reveal the fact of agency to Jacob at all and purports to be acting on her own behalf. The general rule is that there is no need for an agent to identify his principal. Provided that an agent has his principal's actual authority for his actions, the undisclosed principal may enforce a contract made by his agent with a third party.[17] This rule may appear harsh, since its effect on this question is that Jacob deals with Sonya in ignorance of the presence of an American being interested in the contract. The doctrine does, however, carry certain restrictions to protect the position

17   Similarly, the third party may enforce the contract made by an agent against his principal.

of the third party and, in some cases, the undisclosed principal is entirely prohibited from intervening on the contract.

In *Said v Butt* (1920), the principal was a theatre critic who had been banned from a particular theatre after a bad review. He wanted to obtain a ticket for the opening night of a new play and, knowing that the theatre manager would not let him have one, employed an agent to obtain one for him. When he arrived at the theatre, he was refused entry. He then sued for breach of contract. The court held that he was not entitled to enforce the contract, on the basis that if the identity of the person with whom the third party is contracting is material to the making of the contract, the failure to disclose the fact that the agent is acting on behalf of a principal will deprive the principal of the right to sue on the contract. Applying this case to the question here, it would appear that Madison will not be able to sue Jacob on the contract if Jacob refuses to sell the telephone box. Certainly, courts are likely to favour the interpretation of the situation which best protects the third party where third-party rights in goods are in issue.

However, there have been criticisms of the decision in *Said v Butt* on the basis that personal dislike of the undisclosed principal should not normally prevent him intervening on a contract. In *Dyster v Randall & Sons* (1926), the agent, without revealing the fact that he was acting on behalf of a principal, entered into a contract for the sale of land. The court held that the identity of the person contracting with the third party was not material and, therefore, a valid contract was made with the principal who could sue for specific performance. Again, in *Nash v Dix* (1898), although the third party would not have sold the property concerned to the undisclosed principal, the court held that the identity of the contracting party was immaterial. Since Jacob's objection to the contract for the sale of the telephone box is not based on a particular dislike of Madison, but on his dislike of Americans generally, this would not amount to personal reasons. Madison will be entitled to intervene on the contract and sue Jacob for specific performance.

As far as the chimney pot is concerned, Madison will be able to enforce the contract on the basis that Sonya was not acting as his agent at the time of her agreement to purchase it from Jacob (and is thus free to resell to whoever she wishes).[18]

We are also told that Sonya takes Jacob out for lunch, presumably to conduct her negotiations for the purchase of the goods. The general rule is that all agents are

---

18 Ratification does not apply here, since one of the requirements is that an agent must purport to act for the principal at the time the contract was made (*Keighley Maxsted & Co v Durant* (1901)). Clearly, Sonya did not disclose the agency at the time she agreed to buy the goods from Jacob.

entitled to be reimbursed expenses necessarily incurred in the course of performing their duties. This is so whether or not the agent is acting under a contract of agency. Sonya thus has the right to be indemnified for the expenses of lunch, such expenses having been incurred while acting within her actual authority to persuade Jacob to sell goods to her on Madison's behalf.

If Sonya has taken possession of the goods, she is entitled to protect her rights to remuneration and indemnity by retaining the telephone box and the chimney pot until the amounts outstanding relating to the goods are discharged.[19]

To summarise the positions of the parties: Jacob has a contract with Madison to sell him the telephone box and a contract with Sonya to sell her the chimney pot. If Jacob cancels either contract, he will be liable to damages to Madison and Sonya, respectively. Sonya is entitled to her 10% commission *vis-à-vis* the telephone box, has agreed to resell the chimney pot to Madison for a profit of £20 and has a lien over the goods in her possession until she is paid. Sonya is further entitled to be indemnified for the cost of lunch.

Aim Higher ★

Before discussing the issues identified, a good answer needs to consider the question of whether Sonya is in fact an agent or just a reseller.

QUESTION 35

In January, Martin appoints Janine as the manager of his restaurant. He tells her not to buy dairy products from a new company, Sellanything & Co, because he has heard that its products are of poor quality. In February, Barnaby, a representative of Sellanything & Co, visits the restaurant and as a result, Janine orders £100 worth of dairy products. Barnaby is unaware of Martin's instructions to Janine. When, later in the day, Martin discovers what Janine has done, they have an argument and Janine resigns. The following day, Janine goes to 8-10 Ltd, Martin's regular supplier of wines and spirits, and purchases three cases of gin on credit in Martin's name. She then absconds with the gin.

▶ Advise Martin as to his liability to Sellanything & Co and 8-10 Ltd.

19 Sonya is entitled to a particular lien, that is, she may retain Madison's property until debts relating to that property are discharged (cf a general lien exercised by certain types of agents, for example, bankers and solicitors).

Answer Plan

This question is concerned with the issue of an agent's authority, and in particular the extent to which a principal can be bound by contracts which the agent has made without authority.

The two contracts concerned here raise different points, though there is some possibility of overlap. In relation to the contract with Sellanything & Co, there is the possibility of Martin being liable on the basis of 'usual' authority, as in *Watteau v Fenwick* (1893). This will involve looking at what is the usual authority of a restaurant manager.

The contract with 8-10 Ltd, on the other hand, will only be binding on Martin if Janine can be said to have 'apparent' authority. This is sometimes referred to as 'ostensible' authority or 'agency by estoppel'. It involves the principal having made a representation of the agent's authority which is then acted on by the third party. *Freeman and Lockyer v Buckhurst Park Properties (Mangal) Ltd* (1964), which is one of the leading authorities on this area, will need discussion, though the case of *Summers v Solomon* (1857) is closer to the facts in the problem.

The overlap arises from the fact that it might also be possible to treat the contract with Sellanything as being binding on the basis of apparent authority, if it can be established that there was some representation of authority by Martin on which Sellanything & Co could rely.

ANSWER

An agent frequently has the power to make contracts which are binding on his principal. Problems arise, however, where the agent exceeds the authority given. In what circumstances can the principal still be liable? There are two main ways. First, if it is customary for an agent of a particular type to have certain authority, then restrictions on that authority will be ineffective unless the third party knows about them. This is also referred to as 'usual' authority, or sometimes 'implied' authority.[20] An example of this type of authority which will be discussed below is the case of *Watteau v Fenwick* (1893). The second type of extended authority that we will need to

---

20   Though it is probably preferable to restrict 'implied' authority to filling out the relationship between principal and agent, as in *Waugh v Clifford* (1982), rather than as indicating the extent to which the agent may bind the principal to a third party despite a clear breach of the authority given by the principal.

consider is 'apparent' authority, which arises where the principal has made some representation of the agent's authority on which the third party has relied. An example of this is the case of *Freeman and Lockyer v Buckhurst Park Properties (Mangal) Ltd* (1964). We will need to examine whether either type of authority will lead to Martin being bound to either of the two contracts made by Janine.

In relation to the contract with Sellanything & Co, the most obvious type of authority to consider is usual authority. In *Watteau v Fenwick* (1893), the defendants owned a beerhouse which was managed by a man named Humble.[21] Humble was under instructions not to buy cigars for the business from anyone other than the defendants. In breach of this instruction, Humble bought cigars on credit from the plaintiff. At the time of the contract, the plaintiff thought that Humble was the owner of the beerhouse. When he discovered the truth, however, he sought payment from the defendants. The defendants resisted on the basis that Humble had no authority to bind them to this contract. On the contrary, he was acting in breach of express instructions not to act in this way. The court nevertheless found the defendants liable. They said that it was within the usual authority of the manager of a beerhouse to be able to buy cigars from any source. The fact that Humble had been instructed not to do so was irrelevant, since the plaintiff was unaware of this restriction. He was entitled to rely on Humble's usual authority, and thus the defendants were obliged to pay for the cigars. The issue of what constitutes usual authority is a question of fact, which will have to be decided in each case. The decision in *Watteau v Fenwick* can, for example, be contrasted with the earlier case of *Daun v Simmins* (1879), where it was held that where a public house was 'tied' to a particular brewer, the third party should have realised that the freedom of the manager to purchase would be restricted.

Watteau v Fenwick has been the subject of considerable criticism, in that it applied this approach to a situation where the third party was unaware that he was dealing with an agent. This, however, does not detract from the general principle. Even if it only applies where the principal is disclosed, it is still a type of authority that can bind the principal even where the agent has exceeded his actual authority.

Applying this to the problem, we find that Janine, the manager of a restaurant, has, like Humble in *Watteau v Fenwick*, failed to follow an express limitation on the contracts she is entitled to make. It is not clear whether Barnaby knew that he was dealing with an agent. If he did not, it is possible that the court would refuse to apply *Watteau v Fenwick* on the basis that, despite what happened in the case itself, the concept of

21   Humble had in fact previously been the owner of the beerhouse.

usual authority should not be applied to situations involving an undisclosed principal. It seems more likely, however, that Barnaby would have realised that he was dealing with a manager rather than the owner of the restaurant. In that case, the next issue to decide concerns the limits of the usual authority of the manager of a restaurant.

As indicated above, this is a question of fact, not of law. In other words, it would be necessary to look at evidence as to what was normally accepted as being within the scope of the authority of someone like Janine. If it was found that such managers usually had authority to purchase goods from suppliers chosen at their own discretion, then Martin will be likely to be found liable for this contract. If the opposite is found, or if it is not possible to determine any particular usual authority for such managers, then Sellanything will probably have to pursue Janine rather than Martin. The only other possibility is if Sellanything could argue for the existence of apparent authority. Consideration of this point, however, will be left until after the discussion of the position as regards 8-10 Ltd.

In respect of the contract for the gin, there is no possibility of using usual authority, because Janine is no longer an agent when she makes the contract. The only possibility here will be for 8-10 to argue that Janine had apparent authority to make this contract (the phrases 'ostensible authority' and 'agency by estoppel' are also used to describe this concept). As defined by Diplock LJ in *Freeman and Lockyer v Buckhurst Park Properties (Mangal) Ltd* (1964), this requires a representation by the principal[22] intended to be acted on by the third party, and in fact acted on, that the agent does have authority to make the contract.[23] The representation need not be in the form of words: conduct will be sufficient. In *Freeman and Lockyer v Buckhurst*, a person had been allowed to act as managing director of a company by the other directors, although he had never been appointed as such in the manner required by the company's Articles of Association. It was held that the directors' actions in allowing him to act in this way amounted to a representation to the outside world that he had authority to do so. The company was therefore bound by his actions. The case which is closest to the facts of the problem, however, is *Summers v Solomon* (1857). Solomon owned a jeweller's shop and employed a manager to run it. Solomon regularly paid for jewellery that had been ordered by the manager from Summers. After the manager had left Solomon's employment, he ordered jewellery in Solomon's name from

---

22   It was confirmed in *Armagas v Mundogas* (1986) that the representation must be by the principal. A representation by the agent will not be sufficient. But cf *First Energy (UK) Ltd v Hungarian International Bank* (1993) (discussed in Question 36).

23   Note also *Rama Corp Ltd v Proved Tin and General Investment* (1952), where Slade J identified the need for: (i) a representation; (ii) reliance on the representation by the third party; (iii) an alteration of position resulting from such reliance.

Summers and then absconded with it. It was held that Solomon was bound to pay for the jewellery. His previous conduct in paying for the jewellery had amounted to a representation of the manager's authority. That representation had not been contradicted or withdrawn, and so Summers was still entitled to rely on it.

At first sight, this decision would seem clearly to mean that Martin will have to pay 8-10 for the gin. There are, however, two questions that need to be asked. We are told that 8-10 is Martin's regular supplier. What we do not know, however, is what the usual ordering procedures were. In particular, was it usual for goods to be ordered on credit? If so, did Janine follow the usual procedures in placing this order and immediately taking the goods away? If the answer to either of these questions is no, Martin may escape liability. If it was not usual for goods to be ordered on credit, then there is less in the way of a representation of authority for what Janine has done in this case. Secondly, if Janine has not followed the normal procedures, should 8-10 not have been put on notice that something unusual was happening, and therefore made some attempt to confirm that Janine was acting with authority? If, however, these issues are not resolved in Martin's favour, then it seems certain that he will be bound by Janine's apparent authority and will have to pay for the gin.

The final point to consider is whether the contract with Sellanything could fall under the heading of apparent authority as well. The problem here is that of finding a representation. We are told that Sellanything is a new company, and therefore there will have been no previous dealings. It might be argued, however, that simply by employing Janine as a manager, Martin is representing that she has authority to do all the things that a restaurant manager would normally do, including, perhaps, making contracts to buy dairy products. This was the kind of approach adopted in *United Bank of Kuwait v Hamoud; City Trust v Levy* (1988), where it was held that a firm that employed X as a solicitor was representing to the world that X had authority to engage in all transactions on the firm's behalf which came within the normal scope of a solicitor's responsibilities.[24] If this was followed here, it would be another argument for making Martin responsible for Janine's contract with Sellanything.

The advice to Martin in relation to these two contracts must be that he is on fairly weak ground. The doctrines of usual and apparent authority taken together mean that it is very likely that he will have to meet the obligations under the contracts with both Sellanything & Co and 8-10 Ltd. His only remedy then will be to try to trace Janine, and attempt to recover his losses from her.

....

24   Cf also *Gurtner v Beaton* (1993). This approach if used widely would, of course, render the concept of usual authority virtually redundant.

QUESTION 36

In January 2010, Lampard approached Barbara, New Business Manager of DingdongBank plc, seeking a loan of £200,000 to start up a business selling sportswear. Barbara told Lampard that approval was needed from Head Office for loans over £100,000. She sought approval for him, but Lampard's application was rejected.

In April 2010, Lampard, together with his wife, Rebecca, again approach Barbara, this time seeking a loan of £150,000 to set up an Internet business selling sportswear. On 10 May 2010, Lampard and Rebecca receive a letter from Barbara, addressed to them both, stating 'I am pleased to inform you that your loan can proceed' and asking them to call in to deal with the paperwork. In fact, the papers are made out in Lampard's name alone, since the loan is secured on property which is in his sole ownership. Rebecca resigns from her well-paid job as a lawyer so that she can devote her time to the new business.

Before the money is paid, however, Dingdong Bank informs Lampard that Barbara has agreed the loan without authorisation. Although they have in the recent past ratified some loans of more than £100,000 arranged by Barbara without authorisation, in this case they are not prepared to do so because of the risks involved in Internet businesses.

▶ **Advise Lampard and Rebecca.**

Answer Plan

There are two main issues to discuss in this question:

❖ Did Barbara have apparent authority to make the loan to Lampard?
❖ If she did not, what remedies might Lampard and Rebecca have against Barbara?

The first issue requires consideration of whether any representation has been made by Dingdong Bank plc to Lampard as to Barbara's authority, as required by *Freeman and Lockyer v Buckhurst Park Properties (Mangal) Ltd* (1964) and *Armagas v*

Mundogas (1986). The case of *First Energy (UK) Ltd v Hungarian International Bank Ltd* (1993) on the extent to which an agent can represent his own authority will also need to be considered.

As regards the second issue, since there is no basis for making Barbara liable on the loan contract, this will involve consideration of the remedies available against her in tort, or for breach of the implied warranty of authority. As far as Rebecca's reliance on the implied warranty is concerned, the effect of the decision in *Penn v Bristol and West Building Society* (1997) will need to be considered.

ANSWER

This question concerns the extent to which agents may bind their principals even when acting outside their actual authority. It also raises the question of what remedies a third party will have if the agent has acted without authority, and this has led to loss.

The best outcome for Lampard and Rebecca in this situation would be for it to be found that Dingdong Bank plc was obliged to make Lampard the loan for the business, despite the fact that Barbara had not sought approval for it. If that is not possible, however, they may well wish to seek a remedy against Barbara personally.

There is no doubt that Barbara has acted beyond her actual authority in arranging the loan to Lampard. She did not have authority to approve loans of over £100,000, and Lampard was aware of this as a result of their previous dealings. Although Dingdong Bank has ratified some loans of over £100,000 made recently by Barbara, there is no suggestion that her actual authority has changed. Dingdong Bank is not obliged to ratify any contract, and is quite entitled to 'pick and choose' which ones it is prepared to accept. The fact that it does not wish to become involved in Lampard's Internet business is therefore a decision which it is free to take.

Lampard may argue, however, that Barbara has bound Dingdong Bank to the loan agreement on the basis of apparent authority. The requirements for apparent authority were established by *Freeman and Lockyer v Buckhurst Park Properties (Mangal) Ltd* (1964). There must be a representation (by words or conduct) from the principal to the third party, which is relied on by the third party and which leads to an alteration of position by the third party. There is no doubt here that Lampard has relied on an assumption that Barbara had authority, and changed his position by entering into the loan contract. The more difficult question is whether the assumption has been created by any representation from Dingdong Bank to him. In some situations, it can be argued that by placing a person in a particular position (for example, New Business Manager) this in itself amounts to a representation of authority or, alternatively, that agents in such a position might be argued to have the 'usual' authority attaching to that position. That cannot apply here, however, since Lampard is aware of the limitation on Barbara's authority as a result of their dealings in January 2010. Nor can it be said that the ratification by Dingdong Bank of other loans of over £100,000 amounts to a representation, since there is no evidence that Lampard is aware of these.

Could it be argued that the letter that Barbara wrote to Lampard is a representation that she has authority to agree the loan? It may well have this implication, but the problem is that it emanates from Barbara, rather than from Dingdong Bank. In *Armagas v Mundogas* (1986), the House of Lords emphasised that, for apparent authority to exist, the representation must come from the principal, not from the agent. In this case, the vice president of a company had indicated that he had authority to agree a deal for the sale and charter-back of a ship. His plan was to make a secret profit out of the transactions. When his deceit came to light, the third party argued that the shipowners were bound by the agent's apparent authority. The House of Lords disagreed, holding that there was no representation of authority from the principal as opposed to the agent, and that therefore apparent authority could not arise.

This case would suggest that Lampard will not be able to rely on apparent authority, since he has only had dealings with Barbara, and there has been no direct representation from Dingdong Bank. The subsequent decision of the Court of Appeal in *First Energy (UK) Ltd v Hungarian International Bank Ltd* (1993) must, however, also be considered. The facts of this case bear some similarity to those of the problem. A branch manager of a bank had, in contravention of limitations on his actual authority, agreed arrangements with a third party for the provision of credit facilities to customers of the third party's business. The third party knew that the manager had no personal authority to enter into such arrangements on behalf of his principal, but assumed from a letter written by the manager that the appropriate approvals had been obtained. Although this appeared to amount to a representation by the agent, and therefore to fall foul of the decision in *Armagas v Mundogas*, the Court of Appeal felt able to distinguish the earlier case. It held that an agent who does not have apparent authority to enter into a particular transaction may nevertheless have apparent authority to communicate to a third party that such a transaction has been approved. Part of the reason for this was a feeling that it would be unreasonable to expect a third party to have to check in such situations whether the Board, or whatever other body within the principal company was appropriate, had in fact given approval to the transaction. It may well be, therefore, that it would be held here that Barbara did have apparent authority to communicate to Lampard that the necessary approval for his loan had been obtained. If that is the case, then Lampard will be able to insist that the loan goes ahead, or claim compensation if it does not.

What is the position, on the other hand, if the strict requirements as laid down in *Armagas v Mundogas* are held to apply in this situation, so that Barbara did not have apparent authority, even to the limited extent found to exist in *First Energy (UK) Ltd v Hungarian International Bank Ltd* (1993)? Lampard will then have to seek a remedy from Barbara herself. This is not a situation where Barbara would be liable for the loan contract itself. Lampard will rather be looking for compensation for any losses he may have suffered. There are two ways in which this might be possible. First, there is the possibility of an action in tort for deceit or negligent misstatement under the *Hedley Byrne v Heller* (1964) principle, as modified in *Caparo v Dickman* (1990). If Barbara is found to have made a statement as to the fact that the transaction had been authorised, which she knew was false, or which she made without proper care, this could give an action for damages.

Alternatively, and this is particularly applicable if Barbara's misrepresentation was innocent (that is, neither deliberately deceitful nor negligent), Lampard may be able to sue for breach of the implied warranty of authority which is held to be given by agents (see, for example, *Collen v Wright* (1857)). This may enable him to recover all losses which have resulted from the fact that Barbara was in fact acting without authority.[25] It is possible to obtain either expectation or reliance damages under this action.

Finally, what is Rebecca's position? She was not a party to the purported contract with Dingdong Bank, but this does not necessarily mean that she would have no action against Barbara. In reliance on Barbara's letter, she has given up her job, and can therefore claim to have suffered loss. It is clear that she could bring an action in deceit, if it is clear that Barbara's misrepresentation was made to her and she acted on it. Similarly, an action for negligent misstatement would also be possible, provided that Rebecca could be said to be owed a duty of care by Barbara under the principles of *Caparo v Dickman* (1990). This would not seem to be too difficult on the facts. Barbara's letter was addressed to both Lampard and Rebecca; Rebecca was therefore within the group whom Barbara could have expected to rely on the statements in the letter. The type of action she took (giving up her job) was reasonably foreseeable, and she could therefore claim for damages consequent upon this.

....

25 The existence of the warranty does not depend on the agent's awareness of the lack of authority. This was established in *Collen v Wright* (1857) and taken to its logical extreme in *Yonge v Toynbee* (1910). In the latter case, the warranty was held to operate against a solicitor who had continued to act for a client who, unknown to the solicitor, had become mentally incapacitated (which had the automatic effect of terminating the solicitor's authority). The fact that the solicitor had acted in good faith throughout was regarded as irrelevant.

What about a claim under the breach of the implied warranty of authority? It might be thought that this would not be applicable, since Barbara was not in the end someone whom Rebecca was purporting to bring into a contractual relationship with her principal. The decision in *Penn v Bristol and West Building Society* (1997), however, suggests that this may not be an obstacle. In this case, a solicitor agent's innocent misrepresentation of authority to a building society was held to give rise to liability for breach of the implied warranty, even though the building society's loss resulted not from attempting to contract with the solicitor's principal, but from lending money to someone who was entering into such a contract. It was held to be sufficient that the representation of authority had been made to the building society and that it had acted on it to its detriment. Applying that to the situation in the problem, the representation of authority was clearly made to Rebecca, and she has acted on it to her detriment by giving up her job. On this basis, Rebecca, like Lampard, could also seek damages for breach of the implied warranty from Barbara.

In conclusion, therefore, it seems that either Barbara will be found to have apparent authority, so that the loan agreement with Dingdong Bank will be enforceable or, if she did not have such authority, both Lampard and Rebecca will be able to recover compensation from her on the basis of an action in tort or for breach of the implied warranty of authority.

QUESTION 37

On 21 January 2010, Follies Ltd employed Sonny as the manager of its new bookshop in Portsmouth. The contract was for a fixed term of three years and stated that Sonny was to receive £15,000 per year and a 5% bonus if sales exceeded £50,000 in any one year. The contract forbade Sonny from selling books not supplied or ordered by Follies' head office.

Advise Follies in the following circumstances:

(a) Sonny sells a copy of *How to Pass Exams* by Hitchcock to Wendy, a student, who only agrees to buy it on Sonny's personal guarantee that Wendy will pass her exams if she follows the instructions in the book. She fails her exams.

(b) Sonny is out of stock of *Uncommon Law* by Cartwright and is told by Follies' head office that it would take four weeks before Sonny could expect fresh supplies of the book. Sonny approaches Weldys, who owns a bookshop, and obtains from Weldys 10 copies of *Uncommon Law* on credit.

(c) On 1 February 2011, Follies informs Sonny that the bookshop in Portsmouth is to be closed down due to a restructure of the company. The sales for the Portsmouth bookshop for 2010 were £55,000.

Answer Plan

This question concerns the issue of an agent's authority and, in particular, the extent to which a principal can be bound by contracts which the agent has made without authority. We have been asked to look at the agency contract from the principal's point of view.

We are concerned here with the two contracts which Sonny made with third parties. Although the contracts raise different points, there is some possibility of overlap. In relation to the contract with Wendy, Follies will only be bound if Sonny can be said to have had 'express' or 'usual' authority. This will involve looking at Sonny's express contractual obligations as well as his implied duties owed to his principal. As far as the contract with Weldys is concerned, Follies may be liable on the basis of 'usual' authority, as in *Watteau v Fenwick* (1893). We will need to look at what is the usual authority of a bookshop manager. The concept of 'apparent' authority will need to be discussed, as in *Summers v Solomon* (1857).

The final part of the question concerns Sonny's entitlement to claim remuneration where his employment contract is brought to an end earlier than the fixed term. Note that Sonny is not a 'commercial agent' because he is not self-employed.

ANSWER

The relationship between an agent and his principal is a contractual one and as such, it imposes upon both parties rights, duties and obligations. An agent frequently has the power to make contracts which are binding on his principal. Problems arise, however, where the agent exceeds the authority given when contracting with a third party. This question concerns two types of authority. Firstly, if it can be said that the nature and extent of Sonny's express contract with Follies Ltd includes the giving of a personal guarantee to customers, then Follies will be bound by the contract made with Wendy ('express' authority). Secondly, if it is customary for a bookshop manager such as Sonny to have certain authority, then restrictions on that authority will be ineffective unless the third party knows about them ('usual' authority). This is sometimes referred to as 'implied' authority.[26] We will need to examine whether either type of authority will lead to Follies being bound to either of the two contracts made by Sonny.

---

26   It is preferable to restrict the use of the type of authority here to 'usual' authority rather than using the phrase 'implied authority', since the latter should be regarded as merely filling out the relationship between principal and agent (see *Waugh v Clifford* (1982)).

(A) WENDY

In relation to the contract with Wendy, it does not appear that Follies had in any way incorporated into the employment contract with Sonny a term that Sonny should have the right to give personal guarantees to customers. Certainly, Sonny is contractually bound to sell books and Follies has invested Sonny with actual express authority to act on Follies' behalf. Although Sonny may have express authority to promote Follies' books to customers, the giving of a personal guarantee that, by using *How to Pass Exams*, a customer *will* pass exams seems likely to fall outside his express contract of agency.

It seems that Sonny's guarantee to Wendy is a personal one and will not bind Follies.

Furthermore, an agent has an implied duty, which is over and above his express contractual duties, to act in good faith in pursuance of the principal's interest. Sonny does not appear to be acting in the best interests of Follies. Even if Sonny expressly named Follies at the time of the contract with Wendy, Follies has the option of whether or not to ratify the guarantee.[27]

It seems unlikely that Follies will wish to ratify Sonny's guarantee even if Follies was named at the time of the contract, since this would clearly be to Follies' detriment. Accordingly, if Wendy decides to sue on the personal guarantee, Follies is entitled to hold Sonny personally liable. The guarantee that Sonny gave Wendy is a personal one and will not bind Follies.

(B) WELDYS

In respect of the contract for the purchase of 10 copies of *Uncommon Law* from Weldys, the most obvious type of authority to consider here is usual authority. In *Watteau v Fenwick* (1893), the defendants owned a public house and had appointed a man named Humble as its manager. The defendants forbade Humble from buying cigars for the business from anyone other than the defendants. In breach of this, Humble bought cigars on credit from the plaintiff. The plaintiff sought payment from the defendants, who resisted on the basis that Humble had no authority to bind them to this contract because Humble had acted in breach of express instructions not to buy cigars from anyone other than the defendants. The court nevertheless found the defendants liable to pay for the cigars. The court considered that it was within the usual authority of the manager of a public house to be able to buy cigars from any

---

27 If Follies decides to ratify Sonny's guarantee, Follies will have to adopt unequivocally all of Sonny's actions after his full disclosure (*Keighley Maxsted & Co v Durant* (1901)).

source. Since the plaintiff was unaware of Humble's restriction to do so, the plaintiff was entitled to rely on Humble's usual authority.[28]

Watteau v Fenwick has been the subject of considerable criticism on the basis that the approach was applied to a situation where the third party was unaware that he was dealing with an agent.[29] It has been argued that the principle should only apply where the principal is disclosed. Even so, the general principle is clear. 'Usual' authority can bind the principal even where the agent has exceeded his actual authority.

How does all this apply to the facts of the problem? Sonny has, like Humble in *Watteau v Fenwick*, failed to follow an express restriction on the contracts he is entitled to make. It is not known whether Weldys knew that he was dealing with an agent. If he did not, it is possible that the court would refuse to apply *Watteau v Fenwick* on the basis that the concept of usual authority should not be applied to a situation involving an undisclosed principal, despite the facts of that case itself. It seems more likely, however, that Weldys would have realised that Sonny was dealing as a manager rather than as the owner of the bookshop. In that case, the issue that needs to be discussed is what constitutes the usual authority of a bookshop manager. This is a question of fact which will have to be decided in each case. If it is normally accepted that bookshop managers have the authority to purchase books from suppliers chosen at their own discretion, then Follies will be likely to be found liable for this contract. If it is not possible to determine that bookshop managers have this usual authority, then Weldys will probably have to pursue Sonny for payment rather than Follies.

The only other possibility is if Weldys could argue for the existence of apparent authority (also known as 'ostensible' authority or 'agency by estoppel'). This requires a representation by the principal which is intended to be acted on by the third party, and is in fact acted on, that the agent does have authority to make the contract (*per* Diplock LJ in *Freeman and Lockyer v Buckhurst Park Properties (Mangal) Ltd* (1964)). In *Summers v Solomon* (1857), Solomon owned a jewellery shop and employed a manager to run it. Solomon regularly paid for jewellery ordered by the manager from Summers. After the manager left Solomon's employment, he ordered jewellery from Summers and then absconded with it. The court held that Solomon was bound to pay for the jewellery on the basis that his previous conduct in paying for the jewellery had amounted to a representation of the manager's authority. Summers was entitled to

....

28   If a third party knew or should have known of the restriction on the freedom of the manager to purchase from any source, it is unlikely that the third party may rely on the manager's 'usual' authority (*Daun v Simmins* (1879)).

29   At the time of the contract, the plaintiff thought that Humble was the owner of the public house.

rely on that representation since he was unaware that the manager's authority had been withdrawn.

Applying this to the contract with Weldys, the problem here is that of finding a representation. We are told that the Portsmouth bookshop is a new business and, therefore, there will have been no previous course of dealings. Could it be argued that simply by employing Sonny as the manager, Follies is representing that Sonny has authority to do all the things that a bookshop manager would normally do, including buying books from suppliers chosen at their own discretion? This approach was favoured by the court in *United Bank of Kuwait v Hamoud* (1988) and *Gurtner v Beaton* (1993). If followed here, it would make Follies liable for Sonny's contract with Weldys, and Follies will have to pay for the books.

(C) SONNY

The contract here is that Sonny is to receive £15,000 per year for three years and a 5% bonus payment if sales exceeded £50,000 in any one year. It would seem that Follies' decision to close down the Portsmouth bookshop amounts to a breach of the agency contract by Follies. It is unlikely that either of the contracts made with Wendy or Weldys will render Sonny guilty of misconduct entitling Follies to dismiss him. In the circumstances, Sonny will be entitled to claim remuneration from Follies for the full period of three years, since it has been expressed in the contract that Sonny was to be employed for that period.

The sales for 2010 exceeded £50,000 and it seems that Sonny will be entitled to his 5% bonus. Is Follies liable to pay compensation to Sonny for his removal of the opportunity to earn bonuses for 2011 and 2012? One test is whether or not the agency contract is one of service. Phillimore J in *Northey v Trevillion* (1902) indicated that if the contract is one of service, then the agency contract cannot be terminated without compensation to the agent. In *Turner v Goldsmith* (1891), the agent was employed for a period of five years on a commission basis by the principal to sell shirts. The principal's factory which manufactured the shirts accidentally burnt down. The court held that the principal was still liable to pay the agent a reasonable sum representing what the agent would have been likely to earn by way of commission. Since Sonny's contract contains an express term about the length of service and duration of the liability to pay bonuses, it seems that Sonny will also be entitled to recover a reasonable sum for loss of bonus which Follies' decision to close down the Portsmouth bookshop will prevent him from earning.

QUESTION 38

Rodney approaches his bank for advice on how best his affairs could be managed while he goes abroad for six months. The bank suggests that he give his brother

Edward, also a customer at the same branch, power of attorney for this period. Rodney, however, has never trusted his brother in business affairs and tells the bank this. He appoints his sister Sophia as his attorney, using the correct procedure, and instructs her in the strongest possible terms not to give any money to Edward in his absence. During Rodney's absence, however, Edward puts pressure on Sophia to lend him some money and she eventually draws two cheques on Rodney's account in favour of Edward, which the bank pays.

On his return, Rodney discovers the payments and wishes to recover the money from either Sophia or the bank. Advise him.

Answer Plan

The legal position in this situation involves the duties of Sophia as an agent and her failure to follow Rodney's instructions; the extent of her authority in relation to the drawing of the cheques and their payment by the bank; and the effect of the bank's knowledge of Rodney's distrust of his brother.

The bank will only be entitled to debit Rodney's account with the cheques if Sophia can be said to have 'apparent' authority. This is sometimes referred to as 'ostensible' authority or 'agency by estoppel'. It involves the principal having made a representation of the agent's authority which is then acted on by the third party. *Freeman and Lockyer v Buckhurst Park Properties (Mangal) Ltd* (1964), which is one of the leading authorities on this area, will need to be discussed.

ANSWER

The most basic duties of an agent owed to his principal include the duty to obey the principal's lawful instructions and the duty not to exceed his authority. Allied to this is the agent's duty to act with care and skill in following the principal's instructions. Even if Sophia is acting gratuitously, she owes a fiduciary duty to her principal in the law of tort in the absence of a contract (*Chaudry v Prabhakar* (1988)). Failure to follow instructions or failure to exercise care and skill renders the agent liable to the principal for any loss thereby caused. On the facts, it is clear that Sophia has not obeyed Rodney's instructions.

There is no question of Sophia having express authority to draw the cheques, because Rodney specifically told her not to give Edward any money. Apparent authority might exist, however, because Sophia has Rodney's power of attorney and it is probable that it expressly allows, or necessarily implies, a power to draw cheques. Apparent (or 'ostensible') authority does not depend on the agreement between the principal and the agent, but on the facts as they appear to third parties which operate to prevent the principal denying that the agent had authority to act. As Lord Denning said in *Hely-Hutchinson v Brayhead* (1968), apparent authority is the authority as it 'appears to others'. Specifically, it requires: (a) there to be a representation by the principal to the third party that the agent has his authority; (b) a reliance by the third party on that representation; and (c) an alteration of the third party's position as a result of the reliance (*Freeman and Lockyer v Buckhurst Park Properties (Mangal) Ltd* (1964)). The authorities are divided as to whether this last requirement also requires the third party to have acted to their detriment.

Should Rodney proceed against his bank rather than Sophia, the issue is whether Sophia had Rodney's authority to draw the two cheques. As an agent, Sophia's authority may be actual or apparent. Actual authority arises by virtue of the agreement between the principal and the agent, and requires either express authorisation (verbally or in writing) or implied authority (inferred from the circumstances).

As a power of attorney must be given in a deed, Sophia's authority is subject to the usual strict rules of construction which apply to deeds. Her authority will be limited to the purpose for which it was given. Even if the power of attorney is expressed in general terms, it will be limited to what is absolutely necessary to perform the authorised acts. In *Jacobs v Morris* (1902), for example, an agent was authorised to purchase goods for his principal and to draw and sign bills of exchange. The agent borrowed money on the security of some bills of exchange and appropriated the money. The agent was held to have exceeded his authority and his principal was not liable on the bills. Again, in *Midland Bank Ltd v Reckitt* (1933), a solicitor was given power of attorney to draw cheques on his principal's account and to apply the money for his principal's purposes. The power also contained a ratification clause by which the principal purported to ratify in advance anything the solicitor might do acting under the power of attorney. The solicitor drew some cheques on his principal's account and paid them into his own badly overdrawn account at the same bank. The House of Lords held that the deed must be construed strictly and the power could not be extended to cover the acts of the agent which were beyond the purposes set out in the deed.

The power of attorney is a clear representation by Rodney that Sophia had his authority and the bank has relied on it. The bank has also altered its position to its detriment by paying the cheques. Thus, it would appear that the bank was entitled to debit Rodney's account with the cheques unless the bank had knowledge that Sophia was acting in breach of her instructions.

Any limitation of an agent's apparent authority only affects a third party if that third party has actual notice of it. If a third party has actual notice, it must take the consequences of its actions and, if it is deemed to have constructive notice, it is not then inequitable for the principal to deny the agent's authority. In *Midland Bank Ltd v Reckitt*, for example, the bank was also held to have acted negligently. Applying this to the question, the bank is in breach of its duty of care in that, knowing of Rodney's distrust of Edward, the bank did not query the cheques before paying the monies. In *Barclays Bank v Quincecare Ltd* (1988), it was suggested that a bank would be negligent if it obeyed the mandate where the circumstances are such as to put on inquiry and provide reasonable grounds for suspecting that an attempt was being made to defraud the customer. The bank is certainly aware of Rodney's distrust of Edward and knows that Rodney was intending to be abroad for six months. Under these circumstances, the bank should have known of, or else it had a reckless disregard for, Sophia's lack of authority.

However, recent cases seem to suggest that where a principal, having placed his trust in the agent, puts him in a position to commit the fraud, the principal must bear the loss unless the circumstances are exceptional. The circumstances here do appear exceptional, because the degree of knowledge the bank possessed about Sophia's lack of authority should have required them to enquire about the two cheques drawn on the account. It seems, therefore, that Rodney will have a good claim against the bank in the tort of negligence, since the bank has ignored facts that would make a reasonable banker suspicious.[30]

QUESTION 39

> 'In the great mass of contracts it is a matter of indifference to either party whether there is an undisclosed principal or not. If he exists it is, to say the least, extremely convenient that he should be able to sue and be sued as a principal, and he is only allowed to do so on terms which exclude injustice.'
>
> (Lord Lindley in *Keighley Maxted & Co v Durant* (1901))

▶ Discuss.

---

30   If the bank is not able to rely on Sophia's apparent authority and the bank is held liable to repay Rodney, it may be able to bring an action against Sophia for breach of warranty of authority (*Collen v Wright* (1857)) or in the tort of deceit. Under the principle in *Collen v Wright*, the agent's liability does not arise under the agency contract, but under a separate contract between the agent and the third party, the essence of which is the agent's assertion of authority that he does not have.

Answer Plan

In most commercial contracts, it does not matter who the other contracting party is. So it does not matter to the third party at the time he contracts with an agent whether there is an undisclosed principal or not. This is the essence of Lord Lindley's statement, hence the general rule that the principal can intervene and enforce the contract. This is an exception to the doctrine of privity under the common law. The **Contracts (Rights of Third Parties) Act 1999** does not apply because an undisclosed principal is neither identified nor identifiable within the meaning of **s 1** of that **Act**.

ANSWER

The justification for the doctrine of the undisclosed principal has been the subject of much discussion. It is generally accepted that although it runs against the fundamental principles of privity of contract (that is, there must be agreement between the parties), the undisclosed principal rules are justified on grounds of commercial convenience. Generally, in commercial law, the assumption is that buyers and sellers are willing to buy/sell to anyone. Contracts are not personal and business people are not concerned about the identity of the other contracting party. As Lord Lloyd said in *Siu Yin Kwan v Eastern Insurance* (1994), an undisclosed principal can sue and be sued on a contract made by an agent on his behalf, if it was within the scope of the agent's actual authority, unless there are special circumstances.[31]

It is important to bear in mind that the initial contract is between the agent and the third party. The undisclosed principal intervenes in an existing contract. This contradicts the fundamental principal of contract law that there needs to be agreement between the parties. There are, therefore, limitations to the doctrine of the undisclosed principal. There needs to be, because it might be unfair to a third party who thought he was dealing only with the other party to then find out that that other party was in fact the agent of a principal.

(1) PERSONAL CONSIDERATIONS

The general rule is that an undisclosed principal cannot intervene if the agent's contract is of a personal nature, that is, where the third party relied on the skill,

---

31   *Greer v Downs Supply* (1927) is an example of such a special circumstance. The third party bought timber from an agent who was acting for an undisclosed principal. One reason for the purchase was because the agent owed the third party a debt on a previous transaction. The agent agreed to set off his previous debt against the purchase price. The Court of Appeal did not permit the undisclosed principal to intervene in this transaction because the third party intended to contract only with the agent. The agent specifically agreed that the third party could set off his previous debt against the purchase price. No other party can intervene.

solvency or other personal characteristics of the agent and which cannot be vicariously performed.[32]

Difficulty has been caused by cases where the third party is not relying on the agent's positive attribute but is objecting to the undisclosed principal's negative attribute. *Said v Butt* (1920) involved a theatre critic who wanted tickets to attend the first night of a play. He knew the theatre owners would not sell him a ticket because he had written an unfavourable review on a previous occasion. He asked a friend to obtain tickets for him. When the critic arrived at the theatre, the manager would not permit him entry. The critic sued the manager for breach of contract. The court held that there was no contract between the theatre and the critic, because the theatre had reserved the right to sell first-night tickets to selected persons and the critic was not a selected person. McCardie J said that the critic could not assert the right as an undisclosed principal because he knew the theatre was not willing to contract with him.

Said v Butt has been severely criticised. Whether an undisclosed principal should be allowed to intervene ought to depend on whether the third party felt the agent was the only person he wanted to deal with, that is, the agent has some positive attribute important to the third party. The *Said v Butt* decision is allowing a third party to argue that although the agent's identity does not matter, the undisclosed principal's personality is detrimental. The court in *Said v Butt* clearly felt that the first-night performance at the theatre was a special case. Whatever happened on the first night would more or less determine the success or failure of the play, so the theatre had special reasons to restrict the audience to people who could influence the outcome of first night in their favour. So the theatre would not wish to permit entry to antagonistic theatre critics.

The result in *Dyster v Randall* (1926) is preferred. A developer wanted to buy land from the owner, but he knew the owner mistrusted him. He therefore employed X to buy in X's name. The developer then said he intervened as an undisclosed principal. Specific performance was granted. The court held that there was a contract between the third party and the principal. Lawrence J agreed with some of what McCardie J said in *Said v Butt*. Perhaps the first night of a theatre performance was special. But in *Dyster*, the undisclosed principal could intervene because the third party did not rely on the personal

----

32 For example, if the third party and the agent enter into a contract whereby the agent is to paint the third party's portrait, the principal cannot intervene. This is because the third party is relying on the agent's positive attributes. These attributes need not be personal skills. It can be because of the agent's solvency or where the agent owes the third party money. We have already seen the case of *Greer v Downs Supply* (1927).

attributes of the agent. It was a simple agreement for the sale of land. The benefit of such agreements is assignable and the assignee can enforce specific performance.[33]

Courts favour this approach, particularly where commercial parties are involved.[34] The principle seems clear: an undisclosed principal can intervene even if the third party would not have dealt with the agent if he had known the agent was an agent of the principal. The decision in *Said v Butt* is out on a limb, that is, the limitation on the undisclosed principal's right to intervene should only relate to the agent's personal attributes and not to the principal's negative attributes.

(2) EXCLUSION BY TERMS OF CONTRACT

The doctrine of the undisclosed principal can be excluded by the terms of the contract. In *Humble v Hunter* (1848), an agent chartered out a ship. He signed the charterparty as 'owner'. His mother was in fact the owner. His mother then revealed herself as the undisclosed principal and wanted to enforce the contract. The court held that the undisclosed principal cannot intervene. The description of the agent as 'owner' in the charterparty contract was inconsistent with the terms of that contract. It was a term of the contract that the agent was contracting as the owner of property. He cannot then show that someone else is in fact the owner. The agent impliedly contracted that there is no principal behind him.

Humble v Hunter has been criticised and is unlikely to be followed. For example, in *Fred Drughorn v Rederiaktiebolaget Trans-Atlantic* (1919), the agent signed a charterparty as 'charterer'. The House of Lords held that the undisclosed principal can intervene in the contract. A charterparty is essentially a contract for the hire or use of a ship. It was a custom of the trade that charterers often contract as agents for undisclosed principals. *Humble v Hunter* was distinguished.

Only in exceptional cases will an undisclosed principal not be permitted to intervene on grounds that it is inconsistent with the terms of the contract. Possibly the only situation is if the agent signed as 'owner' or 'proprietor'.[35]

33   There was no direct misrepresentation in *Dyster*. If misrepresentation was involved, the undisclosed principal cannot intervene (*Archer v Stone* (1898)).

34   See also the case of *Nash v Dix* (1898), referred to by Lawrence J in *Dyster*.

35   In *Siu Yin Kwan v Eastern Insurance* (1994), an employer's liability insurance policy was taken out covering the crew on a ship. The agent's name was stated as the employer. In fact, the employers were the owners of the ship. The owners were negligent and the ship sank in a typhoon. Two crew members died. Because the owners were insolvent, the relatives of dead crew members sued the insurers. The question was whether or not they could do so. The answer depended on whether the owners could themselves have enforced the policy. The insurers argued that the insurance policy included a term that benefits under the policy could not be assigned, so the undisclosed principal cannot intervene. The Privy Council held that the undisclosed principal (who was the true employer) can intervene. It was of no consequence to the insurance company who the employers were because all the information required was the same and thus nothing material to risk. The relatives were entitled to recover against the insurers.

As Lord Lloyd said in *Siu Yin Kwan*, 'If courts are too ready to construe written contracts as contradicting the right of the undisclosed principal to intervene, it would go far to destroy the beneficial assumption in commercial cases . . .'.

(3) SET-OFFS

The general rule where the principal is undisclosed is that a third party can set off against the principal any defences accrued against the agent up to point the principal intervenes. On the other hand, if the third party did not consider the other contracting party's identity as relevant or did not believe he was dealing with an agent (that is, the third party thought there might be an undisclosed principal involved), the third party cannot set off the agent's debts against the principal.[36]

(4) MONEY PAID

Armstrong v Stokes suggests that if an undisclosed principal gives money to his agent to pay a third party but the agent fails to do so, the principal is absolved from liability to the third party.[37]

Armstrong v Stokes (1872) has been severely criticised and the Court of Appeal in *Irvine v Watson* (1880) suggested that *Armstrong* will probably not be followed.[38]

---

36 In *Cooke v Eshelby* (1887), the agents were cotton brokers. It was the practice of the Liverpool cotton market that brokers sometimes dealt on their own account and sometimes as agents. The agents sold cotton to a third party on behalf of an undisclosed principal. The third party did not enquire whether this transaction was on their own account or for an undisclosed principal. The third party had not paid when the undisclosed principal went into liquidation. The trustee in bankruptcy claimed the price from the third party. The third party argued that they should be allowed to set off what the agent owed them on a previous occasion. The House of Lords held that the third party had no right of set off. If it had really mattered to the third party that they dealt with the brokers on their own account (so they could set off previous debts), they should have enquired. The third party knew that the agents were either dealing on their own account or for an undisclosed principal. This was sufficient to put the third party on notice of the possible existence of a principal.

37 This case involved agents who were brokers. They dealt sometimes on their account and sometimes they acted for principals. The third party dealt with these agents many times. They never asked if the agents were acting for themselves or for principals. The agents bought shirts from the third party on behalf of an undisclosed principal. The shirts were delivered to the agents on credit. The principal paid the price of the shirts to the agent but the agent did not pay the third party. When the third party discovered the existence of a principal, the third party sued the principal for the unpaid shirts. The court held that the third party was not entitled to be paid. The principal had already made payment via its agents.

38 In *Irvine v Watson* (1880), a principal employed an agent to buy oil. The agent bought from a third party on payment terms 'cash on delivery'. The third party knew the agent was buying for a principal but the principal was unnamed. The third party delivered the oil to the agent without asking for cash payment. The principal was not aware that the agent had not yet paid the third party in accordance with the contract terms, and the principal paid the agent. The agent did not pass on the monies to the third party who now sued the principal for price. The Court of Appeal held that the principal must pay the third party.

In *Irvine v Watson*, the court said that the principal remained liable to the third party. Although the doctrine of the undisclosed principal exists for commercial convenience, it is important to protect the third party. In a situation where an agent fails to pass payment to the third party, either the principal or the third party will lose out. It is surely fairer to place the loss on the principal. It is submitted therefore that the better position is this: an undisclosed principal who pays his agent but whose agent does not pass the payment onto the third party, remains liable to the third party.

ELECTION

In an undisclosed principal situation, the initial contract is between the agent and the third party, which is why Lord Lloyd in *Siu Yin Kwan* said that an agent can sue and be sued on the contract. Once the undisclosed principal intervenes, the agent loses his rights of action against the third party. The agent nevertheless remains liable to the third party until the third party elects whether to hold the principal or the agent liable.

The third party cannot sue both, because the third party only makes one contract with one person, that is, there is only one obligation. So, the right to sue the agent and the right to sue the principal are alternatives. The third party may lose his right to sue one of them if he has 'elected' to hold the other liable. The third party cannot change his mind who to sue once he has elected.[39]

SUMMARY

As Lord Lindley's statement suggests, it is usually a matter of no importance to the contracting parties whether or not there is an undisclosed principal. The doctrine is justified on grounds of commercial convenience. Nevertheless, there needs to be some protection afforded to the third party so as to exclude injustice.

---

39 Commencing proceedings constitutes evidence of election, but this is not conclusive (*Clarkson, Booker v Andjel* (1964)).

Fob Contracts

10

INTRODUCTION

The central feature of an fob (free on board) contract is that the seller fulfils his obligations when he delivers goods conforming to the contract over the ship's rails. He must bear all the costs up to that point. Although he is not under a duty to insure the goods once he has delivered them, the seller is under a statutory duty to give notice to the buyer so that the buyer has an opportunity to insure. Examiners often set questions dealing with this duty under **s 32(3)** of the **Sale of Goods Act 1979**.

The primary duty of the fob buyer is to nominate an effective ship to carry the goods. Unless and until he does so, the seller is not obliged to deliver the goods. Examination questions often involve the buyer's inability to nominate an effective ship and the related problem of where there is a delay in the arrival of a ship which the buyer has nominated to carry the goods.

Questions on international sale of goods contracts invariably involve the financing arrangements between the parties, and the rules in relation to documentary credits are important. It should be remembered that the buyer in such transactions has two distinct rights of rejection: firstly, the right to reject documents arises when the documents are tendered; and, secondly, the right to reject the goods arises when they are landed and when, after examination, they are not found to be in conformity with the contract.

This chapter deals mainly with fob contracts, although it is usual to have parts of questions involving other types of international sale contracts (Question 40, for instance, deals with both an fob as well as a cif contract).

Chapter 11 deals mainly with cif contracts.

The following topics should be prepared in advance of tackling the questions:

❖ the duties of the parties to an fob contract;
❖ the requirements of proper shipping documents;
❖ the strict rules in relation to documentary finance.

QUESTION 40

VisualImpact plc, wholesalers based in London, enters into two separate contracts for the purchase of 5,000 (3,000 superior models and 2,000 standard models) video recorders cif London from Ricok (Japan) Ltd, and the purchase of 1,000 dolls' houses fob Amsterdam from Tinus. Both contracts called for September/October shipment and payment by irrevocable letter of credit at Gingko Bank on presentation of the shipping documents. The contract with Tinus contained a clause requiring the dolls' houses to be delivered in time to catch the Christmas trade.

An irrevocable letter of credit in favour of Ricok (Japan) Ltd was opened on 5 September and the bank paid on presentation of a received for shipment bill of lading, an insurance policy and an invoice. When the video recorders arrived in London, 2,000 standard models were immediately delivered to Precision Ltd, which had agreed to buy them from VisualImpact plc, and the superior models were transferred to VisualImpact's warehouse. Three weeks later, Precision returned all 2,000 video recorders on discovering that the electrical wiring was faulty.

A revocable letter of credit in favour of Tinus was opened on 27 August and the bank paid on presentation of the shipping documents, which included a bill of lading dated 31 October and a certificate of quality dated 1 November. The dolls' houses arrived in London on 28 November but, due to a shortage of staff at the docks, VisualImpact plc was not notified of this until 26 December.

Both contracts are governed by English law.
▶ **Advise VisualImpact plc as to its remedies.**

Answer Plan

Both parts of the question require you to discuss the opening of the documentary credit. Although the cases do not lay down a conclusive rule in the cases of either fob or of cif contracts, you will need to discuss the time at which documentary credit must be available to the seller.

The bank's position needs to be dealt with. Both Ricok and Tinus have presented the shipping documents to Gingko Bank, but neither set of shipping documents is in accordance with VisualImpact's instructions to the bank. The contractual nature of the bank's undertaking to VisualImpact and the bank's entitlement to reimbursement will need to be discussed.

It is not uncommon to find international sale questions involving certain provisions of the **Sale of Goods Act 1979**. In this question, you will need to discuss the buyer's remedy where there has been a breach of **s 14(2)** and **(3)** but where he may have accepted the goods under **s 35**.

The final part of the question involves stipulations as to time of delivery in fob contracts.

ANSWER

The general rule is that documentary credit must be opened in accordance with the contract of sale. The contracts with Ricok and Tinus do not provide a date for the opening of the credit. They do, however, stipulate a period for the shipment of the goods. It is clear from *Pavia & Co SpA v Thurmann-Nielsen* (1952) that in these circumstances, the documentary credit must be opened at the very latest on the first day on which shipment may take place. The reason for this is that the seller is not bound to tell the buyer the precise date when is he going to ship, but whenever he does ship the goods, the seller must be able to draw on the credit.[1]

As far as Ricok is concerned, the documentary credit was not opened until 5 September. Following the *Pavia* case, Ricok is not obliged to ship the goods and may terminate the contract and claim damages.[2] However, we are told that Ricok presents the shipping documents to the bank for payment. Thus, Ricok must have shipped the goods, although the credit was not opened until 5 September, and may be taken to have waived the breach or at least agreed to a variation of the contract.[3]

1   This principle applies to both cif and fob contracts. It has been argued that, since an fob buyer had the option as to the time of shipment, the documentary credit need only be opened at a reasonable time before the date nominated by the buyer in the shipping instructions. Lord Diplock in *Ian Stach Ltd v Baker Bosley Ltd* (1958) thought that such a rule would lead to uncertainties and concluded that the *prima facie* rule is that the credit must be opened, at the latest, on the first day of the shipping period.

2   The measure of damages, it seems, is not limited by the market price rule in s 50(3) of the Sale of Goods Act 1979, but may extend to the seller's lost profits, provided that they are not too remote under the rule in *Hadley v Baxendale* (1854); *Trans Trust SPRL v Danubian Trading Co Ltd* (1952).

3   The difference between a waiver and an agreement to a variation is that the former entitles the seller to reinstate the requirement on giving the buyer reasonable notice, and the latter will prevent the seller unilaterally to reverting to the original position. The significance of the distinction does not arise in this question.

The credit in favour of Tinus was opened on 27 August, and this appears to have allowed a reasonable time before the shipment date (*Sinason-Teicher Inter-American Grain Corp v Oilcakes and Oilseeds Trading Co Ltd* (1954)).

However, the contract stipulated that the credit to be opened is to be irrevocable credit, whereas the credit that was actually made available is a revocable one, that is, one where the bank is free to revoke its undertaking to pay the beneficiary at any time before payment is due. In these circumstances, Tinus is entitled to claim damages for a breach of the terms of the contract, such a breach qualifying as a condition.[4] As with Ricok, Tinus appears to have either waived the breach or agreed to a variation to the contract, because he does ship the goods and presents the documents to the bank for payment.

We are told that the contracts are governed by English law. It is also assumed that, as is usual, the documentary credits expressly incorporated the **Uniform Customs and Practice for Documentary Credits (UCP)** published by the International Chamber of Commerce. It appears from the question that Ricok has already been paid on presentation of the shipping documents and nothing turns on the fact that some of the goods are faulty.[5] However, it seems that the bank has paid against a received for shipment bill of lading. Such a bill of lading is not good tender under a cif contract because the buyer cannot confirm that the goods have been loaded within the shipment period. The bank's duty is to examine all documents with reasonable care to ascertain that they appear on their face to be in accordance with the terms of the credit. Gingko Bank does not seem to have scrutinised the documents carefully. Therefore, VisualImpact is not bound to take the shipping documents from the bank.[6] However, we are told that VisualImpact has taken physical delivery of the goods. This in turn means that VisualImpact must have ratified the bank's actions (otherwise the bank would not release the shipping documents to VisualImpact), and such ratification prevents VisualImpact from treating the shipping documents as anything but regular as against the bank.

Precision returns the 2,000 standard model video recorders. Faulty electrical wiring renders the goods unsatisfactory and will give VisualImpact a remedy for breach of s 14 of the **Sale of Goods Act 1979** against Ricok. Furthermore, the use of video recorders is well known, so that faulty electrical wiring would render Ricok in breach of

---

4   See note 2, above.
5   Even if the bank knew that the goods were faulty at the time Ricok presented the shipping documents, it is well established that the courts will not allow revocation at all where the credit is irrevocable.
6   The bank is also prevented from returning the documents to the seller.

the implied term under **s 14(3)** whereby goods should be reasonably fit for that use. The often sought remedy for breach of **s 14(2)** and **(3)** is rejection of the goods and damages. However, this is subject, of course, to **s 15A**, which provides that where the buyer is not a consumer and the breach is so slight that it would be unreasonable for him to reject the goods, the breach may be treated as a breach of warranty.

Faulty electrical wiring, even if easily put right, would hardly appear to be a slight breach. However, rejection will not be available for those goods which have been accepted. **Section 35** of the **Sale of Goods Act 1979** provides that the buyer may be deemed to have accepted the goods, thus losing the right to reject, where *inter alia* he does some act 'inconsistent with the seller's ownership' or where after a reasonable period he retains the goods without indicating that he rejects them. It is unclear whether before the delivery to Precision, VisualImpact had an opportunity to examine the standard model video recorders for the purpose of seeing whether they conformed to the contract. If VisualImpact resells the goods, having inspected them, and Precision then rejects them, it might be argued that VisualImpact has lost the right to reject the goods, it being argued that it had retained them for more than a reasonable length of time (three weeks) before rejecting them (*Bernstein v Pamson Motors* (1987)). On the other hand, it has been held (*Truk (UK) Ltd v Tokmakidis* (2000)) that where goods are bought for resale, the reasonable period of time before the right to reject the goods is lost will normally last for the time it takes to resell the goods, plus a further period of time for the ultimate purchaser to test the goods.

Thus, in determining whether VisualImpact has accepted the goods, the important factor becomes one of whether Precision has accepted the goods *vis-à-vis* VisualImpact. This in turn depends upon whether the three weeks which it took Precision to reject the goods amounts to more than a reasonable period of time and, since **s 35** was amended by the **Sale and Supply of Goods Act 1994**, one of the relevant factors is whether that period allowed Precision a reasonable opportunity to examine the goods for the purpose of ascertaining whether they complied with the contract. Whereas, prior to the 1994 amendment, a three-week period was held to amount to more than a reasonable period of time (*Bernstein v Pamson Motors*), it seems likely that the court would now find that it does not. Thus, Precision, it is submitted, is not restricted to a claim for damages but was entitled to reject the goods, and VisualImpact was similarly entitled. If, as soon as Precision intimated to VisualImpact its rejection of the goods, VisualImpact immediately informed Ricok that it was rejecting the goods, then VisualImpact will not have lost its right to reject the goods. If, on the other hand, VisualImpact failed for some time to inform Ricok that it was rejecting the goods, that delay will have increased the chances of VisualImpact being held to have accepted the goods.

Assuming that Precision validly rejected the goods, Precision will also have a claim for damages against VisualImpact. The *prima facie* measure of those damages will be the difference between the contract price of the goods and (if it is higher) the market price (of goods that comply with the contract) on the day of delivery. If VisualImpact has also validly rejected the goods, that will also be the *prima facie* measure of damages that VisualImpact can claim against Ricok. If VisualImpact has not validly rejected the goods, then it is entitled only to damages. Those damages will, however, include any consequent losses which VisualImpact has incurred in relation to the sub-sale to Precision. In the case of a breach of term as to quality in a contract where goods are bought for resale, the courts are prepared to take into account the effect of a sub-sale upon the losses incurred by the buyer (*Bence Graphics v Fasson UK* (1997)).

As discussed above, the opening of the credit on 27 August was not too late. However, VisualImpact is in breach of the contract in that the credit was not an irrevocable one, but Tinus ships the goods and is paid by the bank on presentation of the shipping documents.

Gingko Bank is only entitled to be reimbursed sums it pays out if it pays on receipt of documents which strictly comply with VisualImpact's instructions. Gingko Bank has paid against the bill of lading which is dated 31 October (and thus appears to fall within the shipment period) but also a certificate of quality dated 1 November. On the face of the documents, read together, the goods could not have been shipped on 31 October. The bank is thus liable to VisualImpact, since the documents do not comply with the terms of the credit which stipulate for a September/October shipment (*Soproma v Marine & Animal By-Products* (1966)). Because VisualImpact appears to have ratified the bank's wrongful act, does VisualImpact have a second right to reject, that is, to reject the goods themselves on the ground that they are not of contract description? The general rule is that where a buyer who accepts documents in ignorance of a defect in them and later discovers the defect and takes delivery of the goods, he will be taken to have waived his right to reject not only the documents, but also the goods on account of that defect (see *Kwei Tek Chao v British Traders and Shippers* (1954), where the facts were almost identical). Thus, since the certificate of quality is dated 1 November, even though the bank and VisualImpact do not read the documents carefully, VisualImpact may not now reject the dolls' houses on the ground that they are not of contract description.

May VisualImpact nevertheless reject the goods since they did not arrive in time to catch the Christmas trade? In *Frebold and Sturznickel (Trading as Panda OGH) v Circle Products Ltd* (1970), German sellers sold toys to English buyers under an fob contract on terms that the goods were to be delivered in time for the Christmas trade. The goods arrived at the destination on 13 November. Due to an oversight (for which the sellers were not responsible), the buyers were not notified of the arrival of the goods until 17 January. The court held that the sellers were not in breach, since they had delivered the goods in such a way that would normally have resulted in the goods arriving in time for the Christmas trade. Applying this case to the question, the dolls' houses did in fact arrive in London on 28 November and therefore in time for the Christmas trade but, because of a shortage of staff at the docks, which could not have been the fault of Tinus, VisualImpact did not know of the arrival until some time after. It seems, therefore, that VisualImpact will have no remedy against Tinus, since Tinus had delivered the goods in accordance with the requirements of the contract. VisualImpact's remedies may be in suing the port authorities, the carriers or their agents or other parties responsible.

QUESTION 41

Gandalf enters into three separate contracts for the sale of 4,000 tons of strawberries to Strauss, 5,000 tons of horsebeans to Horace and 1,500 tons of canola oil to James. Each contract calls for shipment in May, fob Manchester, and contains a clause permitting the buyer, on giving reasonable notice, to call for delivery at any time within the shipment period.

On 5 May, Strauss informs Gandalf that he has nominated *The Winser* to take delivery of the consignment, ready to load on 11 May. Gandalf protests at the length of notice, and since she is not able to have the consignment packed in time, she purchases 4,000 tons of already-packed strawberries from a third party at 5% above the normal market price. Gandalf is able to send the strawberries to the docks at Manchester on 11 May. *The Winser* is not ready to load and Strauss nominates *The Winslet* to take the consignment on 28 May. By this time, the strawberries have deteriorated due to rain seeping through the packaging. Strauss refuses to load the consignment.

On 8 May, Horace nominates *The Dilly* and asks Gandalf to have the consignment ready to load on 20 May. The general market price of horsebeans has unexpectedly dropped by half since the contract was made. Owing to a strike at the farm, Gandalf is not able to send the horsebeans to the docks at Manchester until 23 May, and Horace uses this as a reason for refusing to load the consignment.

On 25 May, James informs Gandalf that *The Forseasons* will be ready to load on 30 May. When Gandalf tries to load the goods, she is informed that recent regulations require an export licence for the supply of canola oil in excess of 1,000 tons. James refuses to accept a smaller quantity when asked by Gandalf.

The contracts are governed by English law.

▶ **Advise Gandalf.**

Answer Plan

This question requires a review of the duties of both parties to an fob contract. In particular, the part of the question regarding the strawberries involves the buyer's duty to nominate an effective ship and the seller's duty to ensure compliance with the implied terms as to quality under the **Sale of Goods Act 1979**. The situation with the horsebeans concerns a seller's failure to load within time.

The part of the question dealing with the canola oil is a little unusual, since it involves a partial prohibition on the export of goods imposed *after* the contract of sale was concluded. The issue is whether the contract is brought to an end because of frustration or whether the contract subsists for that part of the contract where performance was possible. Please note that frustration and prohibition of export have separate origins and consequences.

Since there are three parts to the question, the amount of detail required will be restricted to the time available for answering all the parts.

ANSWER

In the absence of further information regarding express terms in the contract, the basic duties of the parties depend on commercial practice as recognised by English law. Under a 'classic' fob contract, the primary duties of the buyer are to nominate an effective ship to carry the goods, to notify the seller of such nomination in time for him to load the goods and to pay the agreed price (*Pyrene & Co v Scindia Navigation Co Ltd* (1954); *The El Amria and El Minia* (1982)). Once the buyer has nominated a ship, the buyer is required to deliver goods which comply with the terms of the contract to the port in time for loading to take place during the contract period.

STRAWBERRIES

Strauss informs Gandalf on 5 May that *The Winser* has been nominated to take delivery of the consignment on 11 May. Although Gandalf protests at the short notice, this is normally irrelevant since the buyer in an fob contract has the option of when to ship during the contract period. More particularly, there is an express term in the contract allowing the buyer to call for delivery at any time. It is clear, however, that if the buyer nominates a ship in such a way that the seller is not given reasonable time to have the goods ready for loading, the seller is entitled to claim damages[7] for the failure of the buyer to nominate a suitable ship. The question of whether Strauss has given Gandalf adequate notice is one of fact.

In an fob contract, the timing of the nomination of an effective ship is normally of the essence, that is, it is a condition of the contract. If Strauss's notice of nomination is unreasonable, Gandalf is entitled to treat the contract as repudiated and will be entitled to damages (*Bunge & Co Ltd v Tradax England Ltd* (1975)).[8] However, by delivering to the docks on 11 May, Gandalf has probably waived her right to treat the contract as repudiated.

Gandalf has had to purchase the strawberries at 5% above the normal market price. This additional cost cannot be recovered from Strauss since, under a 'classic' fob contract, the seller is responsible for all the expenses of getting the goods over the ship's rail (*AG v Leopold Walford (London) Ltd* (1923)).

Strauss subsequently nominates *The Winslet*. A buyer is entitled to substitute a fresh nomination provided there is time to do so in accordance with the contract. Strauss's first nomination is not irrevocable (*Agricultores Federados Argentinos v Ampro SA* (1965)). Thus, Strauss is entitled to nominate a second ship.

The strawberries deteriorate before loading and Strauss refuses to load the consignment on this basis. The implied terms as to satisfactory quality and as to fitness for a particular purpose under ss 14(2) and (3) of the **Sale of Goods Act 1979** apply to an fob contract, and breach of either term may entitle the buyer to reject the goods and claim damages, provided the buyer is not a consumer and the breach is not so slight that it would be unreasonable for him to reject the goods (**s 15A** of the **Sale of Goods Act 1979**).[9] Since the seller is responsible for the goods prior to loading, it appears that Strauss is *prima facie* entitled to refuse to accept delivery of the defective strawberries on 28 May.

If the strawberries deteriorate due to unsuitable packaging, this would amount to a breach of **s 14(3)**. Where the seller knows that goods are to be shipped, he is under an obligation to ensure that the goods are packaged in such a way that they can endure the sea transit (*Wills v Brown* (1922)). It seems, therefore, that Strauss may be able to

---

7   The seller cannot claim the purchase price if the goods have not been shipped, even if non-shipment is the result of the buyer's failure to give effective shipment instruction: *Colley v Overseas Exporters* (1921).

8   The measure of damages will be that set out under s 50(3) of the Sale of Goods Act 1979 for non-acceptance.

9   Damages will be for non-delivery of goods under s 51(3) of the Sale of Goods Act 1979.

reject the strawberries and will be entitled to recover damages for non-delivery from Gandalf.[10]

HORSEBEANS

Gandalf is not able to send the consignment of horsebeans to the docks until three days after *The Dilly* is ready to load. In a 'classic' fob contract, it is the buyer who has the option of when to ship within the contract period (*Bowes v Shand* (1877)) and, once shipping instructions have been received, the seller must load within a reasonable time. It seems that 12 days' notice is reasonable in this question, since we are told that the delay in sending the horsebeans to the docks was due to a strike at the farm. A failure to load on 20 May is a breach of a condition of the contract and is a ground for rejection (*The Mihalis Angelos* (1971)), because time is of the essence in commercial contracts.

Horace could have chosen to affirm the contract and claim damages for the loss occasioned by the delay but, due to the drop in the market price of horsebeans, it seems more likely that Horace will wish to reject the goods. He will also have a claim against Gandalf in damages for non-delivery.

CANOLA OIL

As for the consignment of canola oil, we are told that Gandalf is only aware of the recent prohibition on the export of such goods without a licence when she tries to load the goods on 30 May. It appears that the prohibition was imposed after the conclusion of the contract. Such a prohibition does not make the contract illegal *ab initio*, but may discharge it under the doctrine of frustration. Since the contract specifically provides that the canola oil is to be exported from Manchester (and within the country which is imposing the prohibition), the contract between Gandalf and James may be frustrated (*Tsakiroglou v Noblee Thorl* (1962)). However, where the prohibition is qualified, as in this question (making a previously unrestricted export of goods subject to a licensing requirement), the contract is not automatically discharged. The court may decide to impose a duty on one of the parties to make reasonable efforts to obtain the licence. In the absence of an express provision as to licence, there is no general rule putting the burden of obtaining a licence on one party or another, and each case would depend on the facts.[11] *Pagnan SpA v Tradax Ocean*

....

10   If the question had not included a reason for the goods deteriorating, the issue would be whether a seller can recover damages for losses incurred because the buyer substitutes another ship.

11   See *Brandt & Co v Morris & Co* (1917) (where the court held that the buyers were obliged to obtain the export licence on the basis that a ship which could not legally carry goods was not an effective ship) and *Pound & Co Ltd v Hardy & Co Inc* (1956) (where the court found that the sellers were obliged to obtain the export licence since the licence could only be obtained by persons registered in the exporting country and as between the parties it was the sellers who were registered).

Transportation (1986) provided that in such cases, the court will ask itself whether the duty imposed on the seller to obtain a licence is absolute or is only to use due diligence. If the duty is to be imposed on Gandalf, then Gandalf will only be able to rely on the prohibition as a ground of discharge if she can show that reasonable efforts to procure the licence would have failed. Certainly, Gandalf only knew of the prohibition on 30 May, giving her only 24 hours to obtain the licence before the end of the shipment period.

The prohibition, however, is only partial, in that the regulations merely restrict the amount of canola oil a seller is allowed to export without a licence to 1,000 tons. In the circumstances, although in the normal course of events a seller is not obliged to accept a smaller quantity of goods than that contracted for, the contract is not discharged but the prohibition may excuse partial performance. Gandalf must supply 1,000 tons of canola oil but is excused from supplying the remaining 500 tons.[12] If James refuses to accept delivery of 1,000 tons of canola oil, Gandalf will be entitled to recover damages under **s 50(3)** of the **Sale of Goods Act 1979**.

> ### Common Pitfalls ✖
> Where a question involves various issues, do not waste time by writing out the facts of the question.

QUESTION 42

Louise agrees to sell to Barbara in Liverpool 1,000 kilograms of saltfish packed in boxes, 25 kilograms in each box, fob Rotterdam, payment by letter of credit on tender of documents to Suresafe Bank. The contract called for October shipment. On 3 October, Barbara nominates *The Windswept* to take the goods and Louise arranges for the consignment to arrive at the docks shortly afterwards. Barbara had not booked shipping space on *The Windswept* but Louise finally manages to persuade the master to take the goods on 31 October. The following day, a fire breaks out on *The Windswept* and the boxes containing the saltfish are wetted while the fire is being extinguished. The boxes are unloaded and repacked in boxes of 50 kilograms. They are reloaded on 2 November. The master of the ship issues a bill of lading for '20 × 50 kilograms saltfish shipped on 31 October'.

---

12 The effect of the partial prohibition is the same as that of physical impossibility caused by the failure of a specified crop.

When Louise presents the documents to Suresafe Bank, she is refused payment on the ground that the bill of lading shows incorrect packaging. Louise takes the bill of lading back to the master of *The Windswept*, who agrees to have the saltfish repacked on the voyage and issues a fresh bill of 40 boxes of 25 kilograms of saltfish.

When the boxes arrive in Liverpool, Barbara discovers that the saltfish had been infected with fungus, causing the saltfish to deteriorate.

▶ Advise the parties.

Answer Plan

Although Barbara nominates a ship, she has not booked shipping space. This is not a fundamental breach of the contract, since Louise does manage to load the goods on the ship nominated by Barbara. The problem is that the goods are damaged and then unloaded and the question of risk will need to be addressed.

Shipping documents have always played a key role in international sale contracts and the second part of this question requires you to discuss whether the bank may refuse to pay against documents which indicate incorrect packaging. The issue of packaging falls squarely within the implied term as to description under s 13 of the **Sale of Goods Act 1979**. Because the saltfish deteriorate, s 14 of that Act will also need to be discussed.

ANSWER

In the absence of further information about the express terms, the contract between Louise and Barbara is a 'classic' fob contract. The primary duties of the buyer are to nominate an effective ship to carry the goods, to notify the seller of such nomination in time for the seller to load goods and to pay the agreed price. The seller's primary duty is to deliver goods which comply with the terms of the contract once the seller has given his shipping instructions.

Where documentary credit is involved, the rule is that the letter of credit must be opened at the very latest before the first day of the shipment period. This is clear from *Pavia & Co SpA v Thurmann-Nielsen* (1952). In this question, we are not told when Suresafe Bank advised Louise of the opening of the credit and, if this was on or after 1 October, Louise is entitled to refuse to ship the goods and may treat the contract as discharged and claim damages against Barbara. We are told that Louise does in fact ship the goods, thus choosing not to treat the late opening of credit (if indeed it was opened on or after 1 October) as discharging the contract.

Although Barbara nominates *The Windswept*, she has not in fact booked shipping space for the goods. It is the prime duty of an fob buyer to give 'effective' shipping instructions, that is, it must be possible and lawful for the seller to comply with them (*Agricultores Federados Argentinos v Ampro SA* (1965)). The essential point is that the seller must be instructed as to the way in which he can perform his duty to put the goods on board. Louise, nevertheless, manages to persuade the master of *The Windswept* to take the goods. Barbara's nomination of *The Windswept* is therefore adequate since the named ship can in fact take the goods, irrespective of her failure to make advance arrangements with the master. Nothing turns on this point, since if Barbara had not reserved shipping space in advance, she runs the risk that her shipping instructions may be ineffective, but she does not commit any breach of contract as long as Louise is in fact able to ship the goods in accordance with the shipping instructions. Despite the fact that Louise only managed to persuade the master of *The Windswept* to take the goods on the last day stipulated within the contract shipment period, all the boxes were in fact loaded by the end of that day.

A fire breaks out on *The Windswept* the next day, 1 November, and the boxes are unloaded. Once goods have been loaded, risk normally passes to the buyer because the seller has fulfilled his obligation to deliver the goods and nothing remains to be done by him under the contract except to tender the shipping documents for payment. Thus, Louise need not have involved herself with the events that occurred after 31 October, and it would have been Barbara's decision whether or not to claim for any damage against the underwriters if she had taken out an insurance policy.[13] Because the goods are unloaded, a problem has arisen. For whatever reason, the saltfish have now been packed in boxes of 50 kilograms per box whereas the contract had stipulated for 25 kilograms per box. The bill of lading issued by the master states '20 × 50 kilograms saltfish shipped on 31 October'.

The requirement that goods must correspond to their description used to be a strict one, entitling the buyer to reject for quite trivial discrepancies, and to do so even though the failure of the seller to deliver goods of the contract description does not in the least prejudice the buyer (*Arcos Ltd v Ronaasen & Son* (1933)).[14] This is no longer the

---

13   An fob seller is not obliged to take out insurance cover for the goods, but s 32(3) of the Sale of Goods Act 1979 imposes on him an obligation to 'give such notice to the buyer as may enable him to insure [the goods] during their sea transit'. If the seller does not do so, the goods are deemed to be at the seller's risk. However, *Wimble Sons & Co v Rosenberg* (1913) established that in a classic fob contract, that is, where the buyer nominates the vessel and gives the shipping instructions, the buyer will normally have sufficient information to enable him to insure so that the seller need not give further notice under s 32(3).

14   In *Re Moore & Co and Landauer & Co* (1921), it was held that goods did not comply with their description when the contract called for 3,000 tins of fruit to be packed 30 tins to a case and the seller delivered the correct number of tins, but some were packed 24 tins to a case.

case due to **s 15A** of the **Sale of Goods Act 1979**. The buyer who is a non-consumer can no longer reject where the breach is so slight that it would be unreasonable for him to do so.

Suresafe Bank was entitled to refuse to pay against the documents which Louise presented, since the bill of lading does not comply with the terms of the credit because it indicates incorrect packaging. This stems from the principle of strict compliance in documentary financing. As Lord Sumner said in *Equitable Trust Co of New York v Dawson Partners Ltd* (1927): 'There is no room for documents which are almost the same, or which will do just as well.' Suresafe Bank has no discretion, in that it must comply strictly with the buyer's instructions as to payment.[15] The bank's right to reimbursement from Barbara depends on it taking up a faultless set of documents and, since the bill of lading indicates incorrect packaging, Suresafe Bank was entitled to refuse to pay Louise, no matter how minor the discrepancy may appear.

Suresafe Bank's duty is to examine all the documents with reasonable care to ascertain whether they appear on their face to be in accordance with the terms of credit. It is not responsible for the genuineness or accuracy of the documents, merely whether they comply, and Suresafe Bank has rightly refused to pay Louise.

It appears that Suresafe Bank has notified Louise of the reason for rejection and Louise does have an opportunity to put right any defect and present the document again, provided that there is time to do so in accordance with the contract of sale and the credit. Louise therefore takes the bill of lading back to the master of *The Windswept*, who issues a fresh bill now stipulating that the cargo is of 40 boxes each containing 25 kilograms of saltfish as was required under the contract.

We are not then told what the parties' actions were, but it is reasonable to assume that Louise then retenders the documents to Suresafe Bank which then pays against them, since the bill of lading now indicates the correct packaging. As far as the date of shipment is concerned, the bill of lading shows 31 October and thus the documents appear on their face in apparent good order and comply with the terms of the credit. In order for Barbara to have taken possession of the goods on arrival, Barbara will have reimbursed Suresafe Bank because a bank will not release the documents until payment by its principal. Once Suresafe Bank has taken reasonable care in scrutinising the documents, it will not be liable to Barbara if the documents later turn out to be forged.

---

15   Lord Wilberforce in *Reardon Smith Line Ltd v Hansen Tangen* (1976) described some of the older cases as 'excessively technical', but that the need for certainty, particularly in international sales, outweighs the need for flexibility.

Barbara discovers that the saltfish have deteriorated due to fungus infection. Although she has previously accepted documents, Barbara may be entitled to reject the goods. An fob buyer has two distinct rights of rejection. As Devlin J made clear in *Kwei Tek Chao v British Traders and Shippers* (1954), the right to reject documents arises when the documents are tendered, and the right to reject goods arises when they are landed and when, after examination, they are not found to be in conformity with the contract.

This would be the case if the goods suffered from some qualitative defect not apparent on the face of the documents. In *Mash & Murrell v Joseph Emanuel* (1961), Cyprus horsebeans were sold cif Southampton. The horsebeans were sound when shipped but were found to be rotten on arrival. On the facts of the case, it was found that the deterioration was a result of fungus infection before or at the time of shipment. The court held that the seller was liable for the deterioration. As Diplock J said in that case: '. . . when goods are sold under a contract such as a cif contract or fob contract which involves transit before use, there is an implied warranty not merely that they shall be [satisfactory] at the time they are put on the vessel, but that they shall be in such a state that they can endure the normal journey and be in a [satisfactory] condition on arrival . . .'

It therefore seems that because saltfish are normally capable of enduring a sea transit, Louise will be liable for any deterioration apparent on arrival. This implied warranty is distinct from the implied term under **s 14** of the **Sale of Goods Act 1979**, the former relating to an undertaking that the goods can endure sea transit as opposed to **s 14(2)** and **(3)**, which are implied terms relating to satisfactory quality and fitness for purpose.

Barbara may thus be entitled to reject the goods for breach of the implied terms as to satisfactory quality and fitness for purpose under **s 14** of the **Sale of Goods Act 1979**, provided that the breach is not so slight so as to treat it as a breach of warranty (**s 15A** of the **Sale of Goods Act 1979**). If the saltfish no longer have commercial value, as it appears in this case, Barbara is likely to be entitled to reject the goods despite the fact that Louise has already been paid against documents.

Furthermore, according to the House of Lords in *Bowes v Shand* (1877), stipulations as to the time of shipment form part of the description of the goods and breach of such stipulations entitles the buyer to reject. Although *Bowes v Shand* was decided before the **Sale of Goods Act 1893**, subsequent cases have acknowledged that the time of shipment is part of the description of the goods and is within **s 13** of the **Sale of Goods Act** (*Aron & Co v Comptoir Wegimont* (1921)). Since the goods were not in fact shipped within the contract period, Barbara may be able to reject the goods on the ground that they did not constitute an October shipment. However, it is arguable whether Barbara can reject the goods, since **s 15A** of the **Sale of Goods Act 1979** provides that where the breach is so slight that it would be unreasonable for the buyer to reject the goods and the buyer does not deal as a consumer, the breach is to be treated as a breach of warranty and not as a breach of condition. Since time is of the essence in commercial contracts, it is submitted that the breach will not be perceived as so slight for it to be treated as a breach of warranty.

Cif Contracts

INTRODUCTION

Under a cif (cost, insurance and freight) contract, the seller is required to arrange the carriage of the goods and their insurance in transit, and all costs of such arrangements are included in the contract price. The essential duties of a cif seller are to obtain a bill of lading, a policy of insurance and any other document required by the contract, and to forward them to the buyer who pays on the invoice when he receives the shipping documents.

Shipping documents play a central role in cif contracts, particularly where documentary financing is concerned. Because the buyer in international sale contracts has two rights of rejection, he retains his right to reject the goods on arrival if they do not conform with the terms of the contract, even if he has paid against shipping documents.

Cif contracts are often concerned with the sale of unascertained goods, and issues concerning the passing of risk and property are often involved. A particular problem arises where unascertained goods are lost before the cif seller has appropriated the goods to the contract.

QUESTION 43

Pauline agrees to buy 10,000 tons of faba beans from Maria out of the 15,000 tons of faba beans currently in Maria's warehouse in Fishbourne, cif Hong Kong. Shortly afterwards, Maria sells to Terry the remaining 5,000 tons of faba beans, fob Bristol, Maria to make the shipping arrangements to Hong Kong. Payment is to be in cash against shipping documents on both contracts.

Maria ships all 15,000 tons on board *The Sunreight* and the cargo of faba beans is put into two separate holds – 10,000 tons in hold No 1 and 5,000 tons in hold No 2. The master of *The Sunreight* is hesitant in signing clean bills of lading because he knows of the rumour that the faba beans were suspect, having been lying in Maria's warehouse for some time. The gossip is that the faba beans are unlikely to be usable by the time the cargo arrives in Hong Kong. Nevertheless, he is persuaded by Maria and signs two clean bills of lading, one relating to hold No 1 and the other to hold No 2.

Before the ship sails, the faba beans are severely wetted due to an exceptionally heavy storm. Water penetrates into both holds due to inadequate sealing of the hatch covers. The master notes on both bills of lading as follows: 'Cargo wetted by rain after shipment.'

After the ship sails, Maria tenders the bill of lading relating to hold No 1, with the insurance policy and the invoice, to Pauline who, having now heard about the rumours regarding the faba beans, refuses to pay on the ground that the bill of lading is not 'clean'. Maria tenders the bill of lading relating to hold No 2 to Terry, who also refuses to pay on the ground that because he had not been given any information about the shipping arrangements, he had not taken out an insurance policy covering the sea transit.

▶ Advise Pauline and Terry as to their legal position.

Answer Plan

Shipping documents have always played a key role in international sale contracts, and the first part of this question requires you to discuss the time when the bill of lading must be 'clean'. The fact that Pauline has heard of rumours concerning the cargo does not entitle her to reject the documents, but she does have the right to reject the goods on arrival. The cif buyer's two rights of rejection are separate and distinct.

As far as Terry is concerned, this is a straightforward question about the fob seller's statutory duty under s 32(3) of the **Sale of Goods Act 1979**.

ANSWER

Both Pauline and Terry are refusing to pay against shipping documents. If these documents conform to the contract, then Pauline and Terry must accept them, otherwise they will be in breach of contract even if the goods themselves do not comply with the contract when they arrive (*Gill & Duffus SA v Berger & Co Inc* (1984)).

Pauline is refusing to pay on the ground that the bill of lading is not 'clean'. A clean bill of lading is one that does not contain any reservation as to the apparent good order or condition of the goods or the packing (*British Imex Industries Ltd v Midland Bank Ltd*

(1958)). The time to which such a reservation must relate to prevent the bill of lading from being clean is that of shipment. In *The Galatia* (1980), a bill of lading was issued stating that the goods had been shipped in apparent good order and condition, but bore a notation that they had been subsequently damaged. The court held that the notation did not prevent the bill from being clean.

Applying *The Galatia* to this question, Pauline cannot reject the bill of lading on the ground that the bill is not clean. The master of *The Sunreight* is neither bound to take samples of the faba beans nor to have them analysed, nor otherwise investigate the cargo even if he is aware of rumours concerning the quality of the cargo. The master is justified in issuing a clean bill of lading. The note that was added referred to damage that occurred after loading. Thus, the bill of lading is still clean.

If Maria has tendered the shipping documents (which, in a cif contract, will include an insurance policy and an invoice in addition to a bill of lading (*The Julia* (1949)) in accordance with the contract, Pauline must pay against them. It seems that Pauline has wrongfully refused to do so. It should be said, however, that a buyer in international sales contracts has two rights of rejection. For non-compliance with the contractual terms, he may have a right to reject documents, and a right to reject the goods on delivery where the breach is not slight (**ss 13, 14** and **15A** of the **Sale of Goods Act 1979**). These two rights of rejection are quite distinct (*Kwei Tek Chao v British Traders and Shippers* (1954)). A cif buyer to whom documents have been tendered is not entitled to refuse to pay until he has examined the goods for the purpose of determining whether the goods are of the contract quality. Even if Pauline hears of the rumours and suspects that the faba beans are not in accordance with the contract, she is nevertheless bound to pay on tender of documents which are in accordance with the contract.[1]

Pauline is thus advised to pay against the shipping documents because by doing so, she retains her possible right to reject the goods on arrival provided that the breach is not so slight as to be treatable as a breach of warranty (**s 15A** of the **Sale of Goods Act 1979**). Certainly, even if the faba beans are of satisfactory quality on shipment but are in such a state that they cannot endure a normal sea transit, Maria will be in breach of an implied warranty entitling the buyer to claim damages (*Mash & Murrell Ltd v Joseph Emanuel* (1961)). This implied warranty is distinct from the implied term under

---

1   There is a controversial decision of the High Court of Australia (*Henry Dean & Sons (Sydney) Ltd v O'Day Pty Ltd* (1927)) which suggests that a buyer may be entitled to reject documents where the documents are, but the goods themselves are not, in accordance with the contract. The sellers, when refusing to pay against documents, are taking a risk but one that was 'justified by the result'. This problem is yet unresolved in the English courts.

s 14(1) of the **Sale of Goods Act 1979**, the former relating to an undertaking that the goods can endure sea transit, as opposed to **s 14(2)** and **(3)** which are implied terms relating to satisfactory quality and fitness for purpose. If the faba beans at the outset were of satisfactory quality and usable, then no action arises under **s 14**. But, because faba beans are normally capable of enduring a sea transit, Maria will be liable for any deterioration apparent on arrival.

Even if the faba beans were of satisfactory quality at the time of shipment and were in such a state that they could have endured the sea transit, the cargo was damaged due to rain penetrating through improperly sealed hatches. It may be that Pauline will have an action against the carrier (but if, as we are informed, this is due to exceptionally heavy weather, perhaps the carrier might be covered by the excepted perils under the **Hague-Visby Rules**). It must be said, however, that in order to take the benefit of the contract of carriage, Pauline must be the holder of the relevant documents and the only way Pauline will be the holder of the documents is to have paid Maria for them. If Pauline does pay Maria, Pauline will have the right to sue the carrier for breach of his duty to take proper care of the goods, as is required under the contract of carriage.[2] Since Maria is under a duty to make a reasonable contract of carriage (**s 32(2)** of the **Sale of Goods Act**), Pauline will have a good action against the carriers.

Furthermore, once Pauline has paid against the shipping documents, she will have the insurance policy assigned to her and she will be able to claim against the underwriter if she can show that the damage to the faba beans by heavy storm conditions is a peril insured against.[3]

As for Terry, he is refusing to pay against the shipping documents because he did not receive information from Maria as to the shipping arrangements and so he has not insured the cargo. In an fob contract, a seller is not obliged to obtain insurance cover for goods, but **s 32(3)** of the **Sale of Goods Act 1979** provides that the seller must give such notice to the buyer as may enable the buyer to insure the goods during the sea transit. If the seller fails to do so, the goods are at the seller's risk during sea transit. In a 'classic' fob contract, it is the buyer who makes the shipping arrangements and thus

....

2   Under s 2(1) of the Carriage of Goods by Sea Act 1992, the lawful holder of a bill of lading has the right to sue the carrier under the contract of carriage 'as if he had been a party to that contract'.

3   Marine insurance is not usually found in undergraduate commercial law syllabuses and students will not be expected to discuss the implications of whether or not Maria, who arranges the policy, has disclosed the rumours that surround the quality of the faba beans. Remember that contracts of insurance are contracts *uberrimae fidei*, that is, of utmost good faith, so that even if a non-disclosure does not relate to the loss, an insurer may decline to pay against a claim.

a seller need not give notice under **s 32(3)** where the buyer already has enough information to be able to insure (*Wimble Sons & Co v Rosenberg & Sons* (1913)). The contract between Terry and Maria appears to be an fob contract with additional services, obliging Maria to make the necessary shipping arrangements. If Maria has not given Terry notice to enable him to insure, then although the cargo will be at Maria's risk during the sea transit, Terry is not entitled to refuse to pay against the shipping documents. **Section 32(3)** imposes a statutory duty and not a contractual duty. Thus, if the goods arrive safely, Terry has no cause of action because of the lack of insurance cover. As was discussed above, however, if the goods are not of satisfactory quality or unfit for their purpose, Terry may have a second right of rejection, that is, against the goods on arrival, provided he is a non-consumer and the breach is not so slight that it would be unreasonable to treat it as a breach of condition (s 15A of the **Sale of Goods Act 1979**).

In order to have an action against the carrier for breach of the contract of carriage, Terry must, like Pauline, have paid against the shipping documents. If Terry does not accept the documents but wishes to claim damages against the carrier in tort, the position following *Leigh and Sillivan v Aliakmon Shipping, The Aliakmon* (1986) is that he must show that at the time of the damage, he had legal ownership of the goods.[4] Because he will not be able to do so (having refused to pay against the documents), Terry does not have a claim in tort and must pursue his claim in contract against Maria. Terry is thus advised to pay against the documents and reserve the possibility of rejecting the goods on arrival. If the cargo is damaged during the sea transit, Terry will then have a claim against either the carrier for breach of the contract of carriage or Maria for breach of s 32(3).

QUESTION 44

Discuss the rights of the parties in all of the following situations:

(a) Dennings bought a quantity of silk from Bagel, a Belgian silk manufacturer, 'cif Southampton'. The contract did not stipulate the type of vessel to be used. Bagel was unable to find a cargo ship, but knew that Dennings needed the silk urgently, and so sent it on a canal barge, which was not designed for sea journeys. As a result, the silk was damaged by sea water.

(b) A quantity of wool was bought by Dennings from Machette 'cif Bristol'. Machette bought the wool from Hertz, who claimed to have shipped it. Machette tendered to Dennings a bill of lading which recorded that the wool

....

4   It is not clear what the position is now following the **Carriage of Goods by Sea Act 1992**, which seems to have done away with this requirement.

was on a ship called *Starwings*. When this ship arrived there was no wool on board, and it was discovered that no wool had ever been carried on the ship.

(c) Dennings bought cotton from Yangon Ltd, 'cif London'. Shortly afterwards, Dennings found a cheaper supplier and so rejected the documents tendered by Yangon. When Yangon threatened to bring a claim, Dennings responded by correctly stating that when the cotton arrived it was not of satisfactory quality.

Answer Plan

Part (a) requires a clear grasp of the fundamental principles of cif contracts and that contracts are subject to the express terms agreed between the parties.

Part (b) raises the time-honoured argument that a cif contract is more akin to a sale of documents than a sale of goods. The consensus, however, is that a cif contract is a genuine sale of goods contract which the seller performs using documents.

Part (c) raises the issue of whether a buyer who wrongfully rejects the documents may rely on a subsequent right to repudiate on the grounds that the goods are defective to justify his initial wrongful repudiation. The general rule set out in *Gill & Duffus v Berger* needs to be discussed.

ANSWER

(A) BAGEL

According to the House of Lords in *Johnson v Taylor Bros* (1920), the duties of the cif seller are to ship the goods, to procure proper shipping documents and to tender the documents to the buyer. Thus, Bagel fulfils its part of the bargain by tendering to Dennings proper shipping documents. Although the goods have been damaged by sea water, in cif contracts this is irrelevant. A buyer must still pay against the proper documents. Unless the contract stipulates otherwise, Bagel must tender three documents: the bill of lading, the insurance policy and the commercial invoice. We are not told whether or not Bagel has tendered these documents to Dennings.

We know that Bagel was unable to find a suitable cargo ship, hence a barge was used instead. Unless the contract between Dennings and Bagel specified what type of vessel was to be used, as long as Bagel makes a reasonable contract of carriage, Bagel is not in beach of its cif duties and Dennings must pay against the documents (**s 28** of the **Sale of Goods Act 1979**). However, Bagel is the seller of silk, and ought to have been aware of the nature of the goods being shipped. It is therefore questionable whether shipping silk using a barge is a reasonable method of carriage. Certainly, Bagel needs to tender a bill of lading. If the terms of the contract of carriage for barges are approximate to those for cargo ships, it may be that Bagel has fulfilled its duties.

Dennings needs to be assured of its rights against the carrier (under the contract of carriage) and the insurer (under the insurance policy). Therefore, if Bagel makes a reasonable contract of carriage with the barge owners and the endorsement to Dennings of the bill of lading provides Dennings with rights under **s 2(1) Carriage of Goods by Sea Act** (that is, a lawful holder of the bill of lading can sue the carrier as if he were a party to the original contract of carriage) and satisfies all other requirements of the bill of lading (such as providing continuous documentary cover (*Hansson v Hamel and Horley* (1922)), and the insurance policy satisfies the terms of the cif contract, then Dennings needs to pay Bagel against the documents. Dennings' claim will be against the carrier and/or the insurer.

On the other hand, if the contract of carriage is not a reasonable one, Dennings can reject the documents at the time they are tendered to him for payment. The goods in that situation remain at Bagel's risk and Bagel bears the loss of the silk being damaged by sea water.

(B) MACHETTE

The cif seller has a choice. He either ships goods in accordance with the contract, or he buys goods afloat. We are told that, as between Dennings and Machette, Machette has bought goods afloat, that is, the original shipper was Hertz. If the cloth was lost in transit, Machette is entitled to tender the proper shipping documents to Dennings, and Dennings must pay even though both parties know that the goods have been lost (*Manbre Saccharine v Corn Products* (1919)). If this was the case, Dennings' remedy is against the carrier under contract of carriage or against the insurer under the insurance policy.

However, it seems that no cloth had ever been shipped. Because a cif seller can demand payment against shipping documents, some argue that the cif contract is more akin to a sale of documents than a sale of goods. The consensus, however, is that a cif contract is a genuine sale of goods contract which the seller performs using documents. A seller who tenders a bill of lading showing goods have been shipped when this is not true has not performed his contractual duties. It makes no difference that Machette is not the shipper but an intermediate seller in a chain of contracts. Professor Goode argues that a buyer can reject tender of documents in these circumstances. This is because even a cif buyer is contracting primarily to buy goods, not claims. So, if goods are lost or damaged before the contract of sale is made, a cif buyer cannot be made to accept the tender of documents, because there were no goods conforming to contract at the time the contract was made. Thus, Dennings can reject the documents against Machette.

However, it sounds as though Dennings has already paid against the documents. Although Dennings cannot now reject the documents, he does have a second right of rejection. According to Lord Devlin in *Kwei Tek Chao v British Traders* (1954), the buyer's right to reject goods arises when they are landed and when after examination are found to be not in conformity with the contract. Assuming the fact that no cloth was ever shipped was not apparent on the face of the shipping documents, Dennings may rely on his second right to reject. There has been a total failure of consideration, and Dennings will be entitled to the return of the purchase price he has paid and damages for non-delivery, which is assessed by reference to the difference between the market price and contract price at the due date for delivery (s 51). Alternatively, since, as against the indorsee, the bill of lading is conclusive evidence of the facts contained, Dennings may wish to claim against the shipowner of *Starwings*, who is estopped from denying that the cloth was shipped. Similarly, Machette can make his claim against Hertz.

(C) YANGON

As discussed above, the cif buyer has two distinct rights of rejection (*Kwei Tek Chao v British Traders*). We are told that Dennings has rejected the shipping documents because it found a cheaper supplier. The courts do not question a party's motive for rejection. If Dennings had the right to reject, then Dennings had that right irrespective of market price movements. However, nothing in the question suggests that the documents were defective, so Dennings should have accepted the documents and paid against them. Dennings' wrongful rejection of conforming documents amounts to a repudiatory breach, entitling Yangon to s 50 damages for non-acceptance (since the bill of lading represents goods).

Dennings, however, claims that the goods were defective. The question is whether Dennings' wrongful rejection of the documents is justified on the ground that the goods are subsequently found to be defective. The general rule is set out in *Gill & Duffus v Berger* (1984). The House of Lords in that case made it clear that a buyer's rejection of conforming documents is a wrongful repudiation. This is true even if the buyer subsequently discovers that the goods themselves are not in accordance with the contract. As Lord Diplock said, the duties to ship goods and to present documents are separate and independent duties. Thus, Dennings' wrongful rejection amounts to a repudiatory breach.

QUESTION 45

Caesar agreed to buy the following goods under separate contracts:

(a) 1,000 tons of oats cif Antwerp from Cicero;

(b) 2,000 potatoes fob Yarmouth from Brutus;

(c) 3,000 staves of Latvian timber cif Mumbai from Portia.

Each contract stipulated for payment by irrevocable letter of credit at Allied Bank on presentation of the shipping documents, and called for shipment in August/September.

The following events have occurred and you are asked to advise Caesar:

(i) Cicero has the oats ready to load by 10 September, but discovers that no credit has been opened and hence refuses to load. The credit was in fact opened on 28 September, and although Cicero begins to load the oats, loading was not completed until 1 October. The bank refused to pay against the shipping documents, which included the bill of lading showing a shipment of 1 October.

(ii) Allied Bank informed Brutus that the credit was opened on 30 July. Caesar contacted Brutus to say that he wanted his local representative to inspect the potatoes before shipment, but Brutus refused to allow the representative to do so. The bank paid on presentation of the shipping documents. On arrival of the vessel, the potatoes were found to have been damaged due to severe storms during the voyage. The shipment date was 10 August, but Caesar knew nothing of this.

(iii) On 7 August, the Latvian authorities announced that the exportation of timber was prohibited as from 1 September. Since the market price for timber was rising, Portia used the prohibition announcement as an excuse for not being able to ship the contract goods.

Answer Plan

Part (a) concerns the opening of credit, which comes too late to enable Cicero to load the goods within the contract shipment period.

Part (b) involves a discussion as to an fob buyer's right to examine the goods. In relation to this, a comparison to domestic sale contracts must be made since in that situation, the point of delivery is the normal place of inspection, whereas in international sale contracts, there is no such rule. Was Caesar entitled to insist on an inspection at the point of shipment (which in international sale contracts is the point of delivery)? What are the effects of Brutus' refusal to allow Caesar's representative to inspect?

The answer should also deal with the fob seller's statutory duty under s 32(3) of the **Sale of Goods Act 1979**.

Part (c) asks you to discuss whether Portia is entitled to rely on the prohibition of timber as justifying her refusal to deliver (for instance because the contract has been frustrated).

ANSWER -

(A) CICERO

The general rule is that documentary credit must be opened in accordance with the terms of the contract of sale. The contract between Caesar and Cicero does not provide a date for the opening credit but it does, however, stipulate a period for the shipment of goods. It is clear from *Pavia & Co SpA v Thurmann-Nielsen* (1952) that in these circumstances, the documentary credit must be opened at the very latest on the first day on which shipment may take place. In a cif contract, the seller is not bound to tell the buyer the precise date on which he is going to ship, because it is the seller who has the option as to the time of shipment. Whenever the seller does ship, he must nevertheless be able to draw on the credit. Thus, Cicero is entitled to refuse to load the goods if the credit has not been opened, and is entitled to treat the contract as discharged because of Caesar's breach. Furthermore, Cicero will be entitled to claim damages.[5]

---

[5]   The measure of damages in these circumstances is not limited by the market price rule in s 50(3) of the Sale of Goods Act 1979, but may extend to the seller's loss of profits, provided that they are not too remote under the rule in *Hadley v Baxendale* (1854); *Trans Trust SPRL v Danubian Trading Co Ltd* (1952).

The credit is opened on 28 September and Cicero begins to load. However, there is insufficient time before the end of the shipment period to complete the loading. *Bunge & Co Ltd v Tradax England Ltd* (1975) involved an fob contract where the buyer nominated a ship which was not ready to load until two hours before the end of the last working day of the shipment period; it was held that the seller could have rejected the nomination. Although Cicero is a cif seller, and thus has the option of when to load, his option was restricted to that part of the shipment period when the letter of credit was open. By loading part of the goods within the available period, he has not waived his right to treat the contract as repudiated because of Caesar's failure to comply with the contractual stipulations as to payment.

When Cicero tenders the shipping documents to Allied Bank, the documents are rejected. Since the bill of lading gives the shipment as 1 October, as far as the bank is concerned, it is not obliged to pay the seller because the documents do not comply with the terms of credit (*Equitable Trust Company of New York v Dawson Partners Ltd* (1927)). Allied Bank's right of reimbursement depends on it taking up a faultless set of documents and since the bill of lading indicates a shipment date outside that permitted under the terms of credit, Allied Bank is entitled to refuse to pay Cicero. Cicero's remedy is against Caesar for failure to have the documentary credit opened in his favour in time for him to load the goods before the end of the shipment period.

(B) BRUTUS

Brutus refuses Caesar's request for an inspection of the potatoes to be carried out before shipment. Under **s 35(2)** of the **Sale of Goods Act 1979**, there is no 'right' to inspect the goods before shipment, but if the buyer had not done so, there is no legal acceptance when the goods are shipped until the buyer has had a reasonable opportunity to inspect them upon delivery.

The fact that the buyer here was not afforded an opportunity to inspect the goods before shipment does not deprive him of his right to inspect at the contractual place of examination. This means that although Caesar was not given an opportunity to look at the goods when he asks to do so, he is nevertheless entitled to ask to inspect (and be allowed to do so) at the contractual place of examination.

Where is this contractual place of examination in Caesar's case? **Section 35(2)** refers to the place of delivery and this reflects the rule at common law, where it was held in *Perkins v Bell* (1893) that there is a presumption that the place of examination is the contractual delivery point.

'Delivery' in this instance is to be construed according to the terms of the fob contract. Where it is a classic or a strict fob case, namely, where the buyer acts as shipper of the goods, then the buyer is entitled to inspect the goods or have the local representative look at the goods before the ship sails. Where it is an fob contract with extended services, then the seller acts as the buyer's agent in shipping and hence the contractual (note: not necessarily coinciding with the statutory!) point of delivery for the purposes of **s 35(2)** would be at the point of arrival. So, unless the contract provides otherwise, the assumption is that inspection and examination of the potatoes is postponed until the consignment arrives at the destination, and that is the place for examination. Even then, if Brutus knows that the potatoes are being resold to Caesar's sub-buyer, then the opportunity to examine goods is postponed until his sub-buyer has had an opportunity to examine.

We will need to inquire as to whether the buyer had waived the right to inspect. If Caesar was requesting inspection at a non-contractual time, Brutus was acting within his rights not to let Caesar inspect the goods. If, however, Caesar did not purport to exercise his right to inspect at the contractual time, it is possible that such an omission might be construed as a waiver (especially in the case of a non-consumer transaction). In *B&P Wholesale Distributors v Marko* (1953), when the goods arrived, the buyer was given an opportunity to inspect the goods at the docks, but the buyer did not avail himself of the opportunity. Instead, the buyer transported the goods to his depot and then examined the goods. The court held that the buyer had not lost his right to reject. He would only be deemed to have waived his right to examine the goods if he had been given a genuine and practical opportunity to make a proper examination of the goods at the docks.

If Caesar had been offered a real and practical opportunity to inspect the goods, then he may not be able to quibble with any defects or deficiencies which that inspection could have revealed. However, where the goods deteriorated as in the present case and it is possible that an inspection could not have revealed the inherent vice in the goods, then the buyer retains his statutory and contractual right to damages for unfit goods as long as the deterioration was caused by the state of the goods as they were at shipment: *Mash & Murrell Ltd v Joseph Emanuel* (1961). Deterioration caused by the sea passage shall naturally be borne by the buyer (as he is the shipper) and any claim (if any) would have to be brought against the carrier under the contract of carriage.

It is also possible that Caesar wished to inspect the potatoes in order to discover matters necessary for him to take out effective insurance. There is no information in the question leading to the suggestion that Brutus must have made the shipping arrangements. Unless the fob contract stipulated otherwise, Brutus is not obliged to obtain insurance cover for the goods. It is Caesar's responsibility to ensure that insurance cover was in place if he required it. We are told that the goods are damaged during the voyage, but we are not told whether or not Caesar had insured the potatoes. Since Caesar only knew of the date of shipment after the damage occurred, it may be that under the contract, Brutus had the responsibility to make the shipping arrangements. Thus, if Caesar had not taken out effective insurance cover because he did not have sufficient information to insure, then **s 32(3)** of the **Sale of Goods Act 1979** places the risk of damage after shipment on the seller, Brutus. Although in a 'classic' fob contract, it is the buyer who makes all shipping arrangements (*Pyrene Co Ltd v Scindia Navigation Co Ltd* (1954)), it seems in this question that Brutus might have made them, otherwise Caesar would have had sufficient information on which to insure the goods.

Thus, if Brutus is in breach of **s 32(3)** by failing to give notice to Caesar and Caesar has not insured the goods, although the risk in goods normally passes on shipment, Brutus bears the damage to the potatoes during the voyage.

(C) PORTIA

Once the contract has been concluded, a contract may be frustrated because of supervening governmental prohibition rendering the contract illegal. However, the prohibition operates as a frustrating event only if it is final and extends to the whole time still available for the performance of the contract. Portia will not be able to rely on the prohibition of export to excuse performance, since the Latvian authorities had indicated in advance that the export of timber would only be prohibited from a future date within the shipment period.

In *Ross T Smyth & Co Ltd (Liverpool) v WN Lindsay Ltd* (1953), the contract provided for the shipment of horsebeans from a Sicilian port, cif Glasgow during October/November. On 20 October, the Italian authorities announced that the exportation of horsebeans was prohibited as from 1 November except under special licence. The sellers failed to ship. The court held that the buyers were entitled to claim damages, since the prohibition did not operate as a frustrating event.[6] Applying this case to the question, although Portia has the option of when to ship, she is not entitled to refuse to ship the goods before 1 September. The prohibition merely limited her option of when to ship from two months to one month and, when the announcement was made, Portia should have shipped the goods between the date of the announcement and 31 August. Caesar is thus entitled to claim damages from Portia.

---

6   If the prohibition of export had been instantaneous, it would have operated as a frustrating event. If, on the other hand, the Latvian authorities indicated that an export embargo might be imposed, then Portia would probably not be in breach if she did not ship between the time of that announcement and the subsequent date of the embargo: *Tradax Export v André & Cie* (1976).

QUESTION 46

Zorro ships 10,000 tons of peanut oil from Southampton to Hamburg via Antwerp on board *Garcia*. While the goods are afloat, Zorro enters into the following three separate contracts:

(a) to sell 5,000 tons of peanut oil to Diego cif Antwerp, payment to be made by letter of credit to be issued by Diego's bank;

(b) to sell 3,000 tons of peanut oil to Montero cif Hamburg, payment by cash against documents;

(c) to sell 2,000 tons of peanut oil to Elena *ex Garcia*, payment in full in advance.

The voyage between Antwerp and Hamburg is beset with difficulties and the master of *Garcia* informs Zorro that 1,000 tons of peanut oil have been lost. Diego's bank accepts a bill of exchange on tender of documents which include a delivery order for 5,000 tons of peanut oil, but Diego refuses to take delivery of the goods, claiming that the peanut oil is of inferior quality. Zorro couriers the shipping documents to Montero, who rejects them because they included a delivery order indicating that 500 tons of peanut oil have been lost. Elena refuses to pay Zorro because only 1,500 tons of peanut oil had been discharged at Hamburg.

▶ **Advise Zorro.**

Answer Plan

Shipping documents have always played a key role in international sale contracts and normally shipping documents include the bill of lading. In all three parts to this question, however, a delivery order is tendered. In the absence of an express term in the contract, is the seller entitled to tender such a document where the sale involves a part of a bulk quantity?

Part (a) also involves **s 13** of the **Sale of Goods Act 1979**. Part (b) requires you to discuss whether goods must be appropriated to the contract before loss. Part (c) involves a straightforward discussion of **s 30** of the **Sale of Goods Act 1979**. Note, however, that the contract with Elena is *ex ship*.

ANSWER

Neither the contract with Diego nor the contract with Montero requires Zorro to supply goods from those on board *Garcia*. The contract with Elena, however, does so require. When did the loss of the 500 tons occur? Was it before risk passed to the buyer? Risk will, however, have passed under the first two contracts (with Diego and

Montero) when the goods passed over the rail of the ship on their way into the ship. Thus, assuming (as seems to be implied by the question) that the loss occurred during the voyage, the risk falls upon the buyer under a cif contract. Of course, that is so provided that the buyer has taken up, or has no legitimate reason for not taking up, the documents.

(A) DIEGO

As far as Diego is concerned, his bank has taken up the documents and, it being his bank, Diego is presumably bound by what his bank has done. Thus, Diego – although he may have been entitled to reject the documents – cannot now resile from the acceptance of the documents by his bank. To put it another way, he is estopped from rejecting the goods on any ground which would have entitled him to reject the documents (*Panchaud Frères v Etablissements General Grain* (1970)). Thus, he is not entitled to reject the documents or the goods on the ground that he should not have been tendered a delivery order, but a bill of lading. In any case, it may be that the cif contract in this case expressly or impliedly provided for the tendering of a delivery order instead of the more normal bill of lading. This may be so especially if both buyer and seller (Zorro and Diego) contemplated that the contract would be performed by delivery of documents relating to goods consisting of an undivided part of a cargo.[7] As already indicated, however, even if Zorro was not entitled to tender a delivery order, the documents tendered were accepted and Diego is estopped from relying on that non-compliance. On the other hand, a buyer under a cif contract has two rights of rejection: (i) to reject non-complying documents; and (ii) to reject goods which on arrival prove to be in breach of condition (except on any ground which would have entitled him to reject the documents) (*Kwei Tek Chao v British Traders and Shippers* (1954)). Thus, if the goods when tendered are in breach of condition, Diego is entitled to reject them. It is possible that the peanut oil being 'of inferior quality' means that: (i) there is a breach of an express term of the contract; and/or (ii) there is a breach of one of the conditions implied by **s 14** of the **Sale of Goods Act 1979** (as to satisfactory quality or fitness for purpose).[8] In the case of (i), it is only if either: (a) the express term amounts to a condition; or (b) the breach is such as to deprive Diego of substantially the whole of the benefit of the contract, that the buyer will have a right of rejection. From the facts given, it is impossible to determine whether the goods being of inferior quality amounts to a breach of condition, express or implied.

---

7   Even if this were the case, the delivery order must be one issued by the ship so that the document should give the buyer some contractual rights against the ship. (Under the **Carriage of Goods by Sea Act 1992**, this has the same effect as a bill of lading in transferring property.)

8   It is unlikely to amount to breach of the condition implied by s 13, since the matter of quality is not normally regarded as part of the contract description (*Ashington Piggeries v Christopher Hill* (1972)).

If, in fact, Diego's bank has accepted documents which it was entitled to reject and which it ought to have rejected, then although Diego is estopped as indicated above, he will have a remedy against his bank if the bank has acted contrary to his instructions in accepting the documents.

(B) MONTERO

Unlike Diego, Montero has rejected the documents. The reason that motivated him to reject the documents is irrelevant. What is relevant is whether he had a valid reason to reject the documents. He can rely on a valid reason, even if at the time of his rejection he relied upon an invalid reason, and he was unaware of the existence of the valid reason (*Glencore Grain Rotterdam BV v Lebanese Organisation for International Commerce* (1997)). There are two possibly valid reasons: firstly, that he was tendered a delivery order rather than a bill of lading – though, as seen above, it may be that the contract expressly or impliedly allowed tender of a delivery order; secondly, that the delivery order showed less than the contract quantity. It is unclear whether Zorro had appropriated[9] the lost 500 tons of peanut oil to Montero's contract before the goods were in fact lost. Cases such as *Re Olympia Oil and Cake Co and Produce Brokers Ltd* (1915) indicate that a seller *can* appropriate lost cargo since, in a cif contract, the buyer has the benefit of a contract of carriage and a policy of insurance so that, in the event of loss, the buyer has a claim against either the carrier or the insurer, even though the loss or damage to the goods occurred before those documents were tendered (*Manbre Saccharine Co Ltd v Sugar Beet Products Co Ltd* (1919)). There is academic opinion, however, that the seller *cannot* make a valid tender of documents after the loss of the goods unless, before the loss occurred, they had become fully identified as the contract goods. In this case, they appear not to have been fully identified. Indeed, the problem does not even state that the goods supplied to Montero must come from the cargo on *Garcia*. It would appear that Zorro could have complied with the terms of his contract with Montero by buying a cargo of peanut oil afloat (cif Hamburg) and using that cargo to fulfil his contract with Montero. Thus, although the matter is not free from doubt, Zorro is advised that his tender of documents to Montero was not valid and that accordingly Montero was entitled to reject them.

(C) ELENA

The difference between *ex* ship and cif contracts is that in the former, documents do not stand in the place of goods so that actual delivery of the goods must be made (*The Julia* (1949)). So far as Elena is concerned, the risk in an *ex* ship contract, unless the

---

9   'Appropriation' here is used in the sense that the seller has contractually bound himself to deliver certain goods. There can be appropriation in this sense even though the goods remain 'unascertained' because they form part of a larger bulk.

contract specifically provides otherwise, passes upon delivery from the ship against payment. According to **s 30(1)** of the **Sale of Goods Act 1979**, where the seller delivers a quantity less than he has contracted to sell, the buyer has the option of either rejecting them or to accept the part-delivery and pay for them at the contract rate. However, according to **s 30(2A)**, the buyer who does not deal as a consumer will not be able to reject the goods under **s 30(1)** if the shortfall is so slight that it would be unreasonable for him to do so. A shortfall of 500 tons, in the present instance, is not slight. There is no question of Elena getting her money back, since she has not yet paid the price. She has refused to pay. It seems, therefore, that Elena is entitled to reject the goods and to refuse to pay (**s 30(1)** of the **Sale of Goods Act**).

Common Pitfalls ✘

Be careful not to spend too long on the first or the first two answers and run out of time for the last answer.

QUESTION 47

Maradona agrees to sell to Tevez 1,500 computers, cif Buenos Aires, shipment by 31 January, payment by Messi Bank's letter of credit, the bank to accept Tevez's bill of exchange. Tevez arranges for the opening of the letter of credit and Messi Bank informs Maradona of this on 25 January. Maradona arranges for *The Achilles* to ship the goods and loading began on 30 January and finished on 1 February. During loading, 10 computers are dropped into the sea and five more are later damaged. The master signs three bills of lading, the first being dated 30 January, the second 31 January and the third 1 February. The total quantity shipped referred to in the bills of lading was 1,490 computers and a notation was made referring to 'five computers damaged after loading'. Maradona tenders the documents including an insurance policy covering the goods 'from warehouse to warehouse' to Messi Bank, which rejects them. Maradona then tenders the documents to Tevez who, hearing that *The Achilles* has been involved in a collision, also refuses to pay.

❱ Advise Maradona.

Answer Plan

Much of the question is concerned with the passing of risk in cif contracts. Normally, risk will pass to the buyer on shipment (that is, when the goods are delivered over the ship's rail), but here the seller has obtained warehouse to warehouse insurance cover for the benefit of the buyer. Does this fact alter the time at which risk normally passes to the buyer?

When the buyer rejects documents, all rights of property (if transferred) and liabilities of risk re-vest in the seller, and we will need to discuss whether Tevez was entitled to reject the documents and/or the goods. If he was, the damage to the computers which has occurred will be at Maradona's risk.

Two further points need to be discussed: firstly, the effect of one of the three bills of lading being dated outside the contractual date of shipment (are the goods therefore of contract description?); secondly, the fact that a smaller quantity of goods was shipped (is a buyer entitled to reject the smaller quantity of goods tendered?).

ANSWER

Maradona's primary duties as a cif seller are to ship goods of the description contained in the contract, to procure the shipping documents and to tender those documents in the manner agreed (*The Julia* (1949)). Tevez's main obligation is to be ready and willing to pay the price.

The contract between Maradona and Tevez does not provide a date for the opening of the credit. It does, however, stipulate a date by which shipment must take place: 31 January. Following *Pavia & Co SpA v Thurmann-Nielsen* (1952), Tevez must open the credit within a reasonable time to allow Maradona to arrange and make shipment by 31 January. We are told that Messi Bank informs Maradona on 25 January that the letter of credit was opened. If this does not allow Maradona sufficient time to make the necessary shipping arrangements and load the goods, Maradona is not obliged to ship the goods and is entitled to treat the contract as repudiated by Tevez and claim damages. However, Maradona has chosen not to accept Tevez's breach as discharging the contract because he ships the goods. The contract therefore remains open to the benefit of both parties.

We are told that during the loading operation, 10 computers are dropped into the sea. Normally, risk under a cif contract does not pass before shipment (*Law and Bonar Ltd v British American Tobacco Ltd* (1916)). This is based on the assumption that goods are at the buyer's risk only once insurance cover begins. In a 'classic' cif contract, the seller takes out an insurance policy to cover the goods as from shipment. In this question, however, we are told that Maradona has effected 'from warehouse to warehouse' insurance cover.[10] It may be that since cover is available as from Maradona's

---

10   Institute Cargo Clauses (on which most cif contracts are now covered) cover loss or damage from warehouse to warehouse plus 60 days after landing, and during loading and unloading.

warehouse, this excludes the general rule that risk in the goods does not pass before shipment. It is possible, therefore, that the goods are at Tevez's risk from the beginning of the insurance cover. It should be said, however, that such a variation of the general rule should be by express agreement, and there is nothing in the facts to indicate either that Tevez agreed to warehouse cover or that, if he did agree to such cover, that was indicative of the intention to place risk on him before shipment. If the general rule applies, then any damage prior to shipment is at the seller's risk and Maradona must bear the loss of the 10 computers.

Once goods have been loaded, risk passes to the buyer. This presupposes that the buyer does accept property in the goods, that is, by accepting the documents and/or the goods. If Tevez has the right to reject the documents and/or the goods and he does so, then even if property has passed to him (and therefore risk as well), all rights re-vest in the seller (*Kwei Tek Chao v British Traders and Shippers* (1954)). The only significance of the passing of risk on shipment, therefore, is that it prevents Tevez from claiming from Maradona for loss which occurs after shipment. If the whole contract is discharged, then property re-vests in Maradona and Tevez will not bear the risk during any part of the transit.

As far as the five computers are concerned, the damage appears to have occurred after loading. Thus, if Tevez does accept the contract, he must bear the loss, although he may have a claim against the underwriters of the insurance policy and/or against the carrier for breach of duty under the contract of carriage.

The master of the ship issues three bills of lading, indicating that 1,490 computers were shipped in total. According to **s 30(1)** of the **Sale of Goods Act 1979**, where the seller delivers a quantity less than he has contracted to sell, the buyer has the option of either rejecting them or to accept the part-delivery and pay for them at the contract rate. However, by **s 30(2A)**, the buyer who does not deal as a consumer will not be able to reject the goods under **s 30(1)** if the shortfall is so slight that it would be unreasonable for him to do so. A shortfall of 10 computers, in the present instance, may be considered slight. Even if it was, Tevez is not deprived of his right to the full quantity sold merely because he accepts the smaller quantity shipped.

It seems, therefore, that Messi Bank has rightly rejected the documents tendered by Maradona, since the bills of lading do not disclose shipment of the correct quantity of goods. Furthermore, one of the bills of lading indicates a late shipment: 1 February. This is not merely a breach by Maradona of the duty to ship the goods by 31 January, but also means that the goods tendered did not match the description by which they were sold. The requirement that goods correspond to their description, until recently, entitled the buyer to reject for quite trivial discrepancies and to do so even though the failure of the seller to deliver goods of the contract description does not in the least prejudice the buyer (*Arcos Ltd v Ronaasen & Son* (1933)). *Bowes v Shand* (1877) established that the time of shipment is part of the description of goods. In that case, a contract for the sale of rice provided for shipment in March/April. Most of the rice[11] was loaded in February and the balance in March. Four bills of lading were issued, three bearing February dates and one a March date. The court held that this was a February shipment. Applying this case to the question, since one-third of the goods was shipped too late, it is submitted that Maradona is in breach of **s 13** of the **Sale of Goods Act 1979** in not shipping goods complying with the contract description. However, it is arguable whether Tevez can reject the goods, since **s 15A** of the **Sale of Goods Act 1979** provides that, where the breach is so slight that it would be unreasonable for the buyer to reject the goods and the buyer does not deal as a consumer, the breach is to be treated as a breach of warranty and not as a breach of condition. Since time is of the essence in commercial contracts, it is submitted that the breach will not be perceived as so slight for it to be treated as a breach of warranty.

It seems that Messi Bank has rightly rejected the shipping documents. Maradona then tenders the documents directly to Tevez for payment. Tevez is entitled to refuse to accept the documents, since the contract has provided for payment by letter of credit and that the only acceptable method of tender was to Messi Bank (*Soproma SpA v Marine & Animal By-Products Corp* (1966)). The principle of short-circuiting credits prohibits direct presentation to the buyer where the documents have been rejected by the bank. This does not mean that Tevez must reject the documents, since he is always entitled to accept defective tender, but clearly he does not wish to do so. Tevez rejects the documents on the ground that the goods may have been damaged afloat due to a collision. This of itself is not a good reason for rejecting, because the seller is not in breach by tendering documents relating to goods damaged afloat, provided that the documents themselves are in order. The giving of an improper reason for rejecting documents does not prevent Tevez from justifying his rejection, provided that there was good reason available at the time of rejection.

Maradona is therefore advised that Messi Bank was entitled to reject the documents because they revealed that an incorrect quantity of goods was shipped and that the shipment was late. In addition to these reasons, Tevez was entitled to refuse the documents, since the contract had provided for payment by Messi Bank. Maradona is liable in damages to Tevez for non-delivery.[12]

....

11   8,150 bags of rice out of 8,200.
12   The measure of damages will be calculated in accordance with s 51(3) of the Sale of Goods Act 1979, that is, the difference between the contract price and the market value the goods would have had, had the documents and goods both been properly delivered.

QUESTION 48

Describe the stages for the opening of a documentary credit and its operation. Why do commercial parties use documentary credits?

Answer Plan

This question requires you to demonstrate knowledge of how letters of credit operate in international commerce and an appreciation of the commercial reasons for their use.

You should approach the first part of the question as follows:

❖ explain the stages for the opening of a commercial credit pursuant to a term to that effect in an international sale contract;

❖ identify the main parties to the transaction (applicant, issuing bank, advising/confirming bank and beneficiary) and mention the different contracts between these parties;

❖ identify the two main principles underlying the system, namely the principle of autonomy and the principle of strict compliance.

For the second part of the question, you should discuss the main problems of dealing with foreign contracting parties and that the goods will be in transit for some time, with one or the other party being out of pocket during that time unless financing can be obtained from the banking system. Explain how these are addressed by the letter of credit system.

ANSWER

If the contract of sale provides for payment by documentary credit, the credit opened in favour of the seller must comply in all respects with what was agreed in the contract of sale. The buyer must ensure that the letter of credit issued to the seller complies with what was agreed under the contract. For example, if the contract requires a confirmed credit, then the setting up of an unconfirmed credit is not sufficient. The buyer must open the credit as a condition precedent to the seller's duty to delivery: *Garcia v Page* (1936). The buyer's duty to furnish the documentary credit is absolute. If the credit is not in accordance with the contract, the seller can refuse to ship the goods.

If the seller has the right to reject the letter of credit as non-conforming, the buyer may cure the defect if there is sufficient time. If the buyer does not cure or has no time to cure, he commits a repudiatory breach and the seller can treat the contract as discharged and claim damages.[13]

The letter of credit is considered as conditional payment so, whilst the credit is alive, the seller's right to sue for the price is suspended. If the credit is honoured, this constitutes payment under the contract of sale. If it is dishonoured (for example, if the Issuing Bank (IB) or Advising Bank (AB) does not pay on the presentation of conforming documents), the seller's right to sue the buyer for price or damages revives.

The seller is entitled to a letter of credit within a reasonable time. The date when the seller is actually ready to ship is irrelevant because the seller usually has the option of when to ship within the full shipment period under the contract. The seller is not required to notify the buyer in advance of the date of shipment as a pre-condition of obtaining the letter of credit. Unless the contract says otherwise, this means that the letter of credit is to be made available to the seller no later than the earliest shipment date under contract (*Pavia v Thurmann-Nielsen* (1952)).

STAGES FOR THE OPENING OF THE CREDIT

The stages for the opening of the credit are as follows:

(a) The buyer applies to his bank, known as the Issuing Bank (IB), to open a credit in favour of the seller, undertaking the payment of the contract price against presentation of specified documents. The buyer must ensure his instructions are clear and conform to the contract of sale. The IB is not concerned with the contract of sale, so the IB is unlikely to see the contract of sale document. The IB will act on the buyer's instructions only.
It will be most unusual for a bank these days not to include in its terms and conditions a clause incorporating the **Uniform Customs and Practice for Documentary Credits (UCP 600)**.[14] The **UCP 600** covers only irrevocable credits.[15]

(b) The IB can issue the letter of credit directly to the seller but almost always arranges for notification by another bank, called the Advising Bank (AB) (sometimes also called the Correspondent Bank) in the seller's country.

---

13 The seller can of course waive the breach and accept a non-conforming letter of credit. If he waives, then he loses the right to complain of the breach later: *Alan v El Nasr Export* (1972).

14 The UCP 600 is effective from 1 July 2007.

15 If parties want to use revocable credits, they will have to issue the credit subject to the UCP 500 instead or incorporate their own terms of revocability.

Notification by the AB *is* the letter of credit. The IB is bound to the seller as soon as the seller receives the notification.[16]

(c) Unless the letter of credit says the credit is available only with IB, it must nominate a Nominated Bank which is authorised to pay. Unless the Nominated Bank is a confirming bank, it is not under an obligation to the seller to pay. However if, which is usual, the contract of sale calls for a confirmed credit, the IB will ask the AB to add its own undertaking to honour the credit on presentation of the documents. This undertaking is known as 'confirmation', that is, IB's promise to pay is reinforced by a separate promise to pay by the Confirming Bank (which is usually the AB). **Article 8** of the **UCP 600** clearly states that confirmation by a confirming bank constitutes an undertaking to pay *in addition to* that of the IB.

The advantages for the seller to have the credit confirmed by the AB are obvious. The seller does not have to rely exclusively on a foreign bank (the seller may not know how reliable the foreign bank is and need not sue the bank in a foreign country should it have cause to). If the AB does not add its confirmation, the credit is known as 'unconfirmed' credit.

(d) After the goods have been dispatched, the seller must present the transport documents in accordance with the terms of the letter of credit. Usually the letter of credit will provide for the seller to present them to the AB (rather than the IB) because it is more convenient for the seller to present to a bank in his own country. Presentation is usually made by the seller's bank, not by the seller himself. The seller's bank acts as a collecting bank (in a similar way as if it were collecting a cheque). When the seller's bank presents the documents to the AB, it does so not in its own right but as the seller's agent.

If the documents are in order, then the AB pays in accordance with the letter of credit. AB then passes the documents to IB. The IB then releases them to the buyer.

CONTRACTUAL RIGHTS AND OBLIGATIONS

Once the credit is opened, each party's contractual relationship with each other has its own rules.

(I) RELATIONSHIP BETWEEN THE BUYER AND THE IB

The relationship between the buyer and the IB is that of banker and customer. The terms of the contract are usually set out in the IB's standard form of application which

---

16 Note that there is no consideration moving from the seller to Issuing Bank. It is generally accepted that a letter of credit is treated as a promise binding through mercantile usage, so that it is enforceable without consideration. Documentary credit therefore is an exception to the doctrine of consideration.

invariably incorporates the **UCP**. The IB is responsible for ensuring that the letter of credit issued to the seller complies strictly with the instructions contained in the application for credit and that payment is made only on presentation of documents that fully comply with the terms of the credit (**Art 14(b)** of the **UCP 600**). This is one of the fundamental principles of documentary credit – the doctrine of strict compliance. The **International Standard Banking Practice for the Examination of Documents under Documentary Credits** (**ISBP**), which is a practical complement to the **UCP**, contains paragraphs of best banking practice, explaining in detail how the rules in the **UCP** are to be applied by banks on a day-to-day basis, particularly in relation to **Art 14** of the **UCP** ('Standard for Examination of Documents').

When the IB issues the letter of credit to the seller, the IB acts as principal and not as agent of the buyer. This means that the buyer cannot give instructions to the IB to withhold payment or to change the terms of the letter of credit (where the credit is irrevocable). The IB is entitled and obliged to ignore such instructions as long as the documents are presented within the shipment period and conform. This is known as the principle of the autonomy of credit. **Article 4** of the **UCP 600** makes it clear that the credit is separate from and independent of the underlying contract of sale. Banks deal with documents and not with goods.

(II) RELATIONSHIP BETWEEN THE IB AND THE AB

The relationship between the IB and the AB is that of principal and agent. The AB must strictly comply with the instructions in the letter of credit.

(III) RELATIONSHIP BETWEEN THE IB AND THE SELLER

The IB undertakes to pay the seller on presentation of the documents. The undertaking will be honoured even if there is a breach of the underlying contract of sale. The IB's undertaking is given by it as principal and not as the buyer's agent. The doctrine of strict compliance applies. Each document presented by the seller needs to be consistent with each other and all the documents must appear on their face to relate to the same transaction. Each bank involved in the credit has a maximum of five banking days following receipt of the documents in which to examine the documents and decide whether to accept or reject, and inform the seller (**Art 14(b)** of the **UCP 600**).

(IV) RELATIONSHIP BETWEEN THE AB AND THE SELLER

By adding its confirmation, the AB is giving its undertaking that the credit will be honoured on presentation. This is given by the AB as principal, not as agent of the IB. This undertaking is completely distinct from that given by the IB. It is not a matter of the IB and the AB being jointly and severally liable. The IB's undertaking and the AB's undertaking are separate and self-contained.

The AB as a confirming bank must honour the credit if the documents presented by the seller appear on their face to conform, and the AB is not concerned with the underlying contract of sale. Thus the doctrines of strict compliance and the autonomy of credit apply to the AB where it has confirmed the credit.

(V) THE RELATIONSHIP BETWEEN THE AB's AND THE BUYER

Because of privity of contract, English law does not recognise any relationship between the AB and the buyer as far as the credit is concerned. If the AB pays against non-conforming documents, the B's remedy is against the IB.

PURPOSE OF DOCUMENTARY CREDITS

Because international sales often involve a long interval of time between the despatch of goods and their arrival, during this period the parties are exposed to financial risks. The seller invariably wants to be assured of payment and to be paid without delay while retaining an interest in the goods until he is paid. On the other hand, the buyer will not want to pay for goods until he has received them, or least something that represents the goods. The documentary credit system is designed to alleviate the financial risks involved for the parties to an international sales contract.

Documentary credit provides the seller with security (if irrevocable) but it also costs money. Banks involved with issuing, advising and confirming charge for services. The cost is passed to the buyer. It may be that a buyer is reluctant to agree to payment via letter of credit. It depends on whether the seller is in a position to insist on letter of credit as the payment method without having to cover the cost, which in turn depends on the relative bargaining power of the parties. In practice, the seller usually only requires a letter of credit where he has not yet developed a sufficient relationship with the buyer to enable him to adopt a cheaper payment method. Documentary credit remains, however, the most common method of payment in international sales.

The advantages of payment using documentary credit to the seller clearly include an assurance of payment irrespective of the solvency of the buyer; an assurance of payment irrespective of any disputes with the buyer concerning the underlying goods (under the principle of autonomy of credit); if the credit is transferable, the seller can use it to finance his own acquisition of goods; and not have to pursue the buyer in a different country, with all the risks and cost that this carries.

The system has fewer obvious advantages for the buyer. However, without the credit system, the transaction would possibly never come about at all, as the seller might not be willing to trade with a foreign buyer unless he was assured of payment. Moreover, the doctrine of strict compliance benefits the buyer considerably in that he can insist on a perfect tender of documents if payment is to be made. In the light of a very high percentage of non-compliant/defective tenders,[17] the buyer effectively has a right to call off the transaction should the market have moved against it.

> **Common Pitfalls** ✗
>
> Students must not merely give a general description of the parties to letters of credit and how letters of credit worked without relating these descriptions to the question asked.

QUESTION 49

(a) Discuss the implications of the rule that risk passes on or as from shipment in cif contracts.

(b) In the case of unascertained goods, is the cif seller entitled to appropriate lost goods to the contract?

Answer Plan

Not an easy two-part question. In particular, part (a) involves the concept of risk passing 'as from' shipment and the retrospective effect of this rule gives rise to a number of difficulties.

As far as part (b) is concerned, the cases and academic opinion are divided. The general rule in domestic sales is clear – goods may not be appropriated once lost. But, what is the rule in international sale contracts?

ANSWER

(A)

The general rule is that **s 20** of the **Sale of Goods Act 1979**, which links the passing of risk to the passing of property, is ousted in international sale contracts. In *The Julia* (1949),

---

17   In *Bankers Trust v State Bank of India* (1991), there was expert evidence that discrepancies are found in nearly 50% of cases which may justify rejection of the documents presented by the seller.

Lord Porter said that risk generally passes 'on shipment or as from shipment' in cif contracts, whereas property passes at the time the buyer pays and takes up the documents. Lord Porter's statement contains two rules: where the seller ships goods for the buyer, risk passes at the time of shipment, that is, *on* shipment; where the contract is made after shipment, risk passes at the time of the contract but retrospectively, that is, *as from* shipment.

The implications of the rule might appear harsh on the buyer because, for instance, risk, unlike property, may pass to the buyer although the goods are unascertained goods which have not been appropriated by the contract. Furthermore, a buyer to whom risk, but not property, is transferred by the seller is not entitled to sue the carrier in the tort of negligence (*Leigh and Sillivan v Aliakmon Shipping Co* (1986)).[18]

If goods are shipped and lost during the sea transit, the seller is still entitled to tender shipping documents to the buyer and to claim the purchase price. The buyer's remedy is normally a claim against the carrier or the insurer because, on taking up the documents, the buyer takes the benefit of the contract of carriage and policy of insurance and is, therefore, able to claim in respect of loss from the time of shipment. Thus, although the rule that risk passes on or as from shipment does at first seem harsh, the buyer is not without a remedy where goods are lost, as long as the buyer is not exposed to risks not covered by the contract of insurance or carriage (*Groom v Barber* (1915)).

There are situations where the buyer has to pay for the goods whilst receiving nothing. In *Manbre Saccharine v Corn Products* (1919), goods were lost when the ship was sunk during World War I. The insurance policy did not cover war risks but, because the terms of the policy were usual at the time the contract was made, the buyer had to bear the loss.[19] On the other hand, where the seller fails to make a proper contract of carriage as he is contractually bound to do under a cif contract, he will be in breach of the contract of sale and the buyer will be entitled to reject and no question of risk arises.

. . . .

18   There is now apparent contradiction between the **Carriage of Goods by Sea Act 1992** (which allows for the transfer of property irrespective of whether the goods are in bulk and unascertained goods) and which implemented *The Elafi* (1982) and s 16 of the **Sale of Goods Act 1979** (which does not allow for the transfer of property in unascertained goods until the goods have become ascertained). The position is unclear. Note, however, under s 20A and s 20B of the **Sale of Goods Act 1979**, a pre-paying buyer of some or all of its goods of an identified bulk becomes an owner in common of the bulk (see Question 14).

19   In fact, the buyer escaped liability in this case because the seller did not tender the proper shipping documents.

A particular difficulty arises with the concept of risk passing to the buyer *as from* shipment. Where goods are first shipped, then deteriorate and are subsequently sold, it is clear that the rule that risk passes with retrospective effect means that the buyer has to bear the risk of deterioration which had already occurred when the contract of sale was made. It should be noted, however, that although the cif seller's obligations as to quality relate to the time of shipment, the seller impliedly undertakes that the goods are in such a state as to be able to withstand a normal sea transit (*Mash and Murrell v Joseph Emanuel* (1961)), so that the seller remains liable for deterioration if the goods suffer from some defect before risk in them has passed to the buyer *as from* shipment.

It can be seen, therefore, that there are cases where goods are lost in transit in circumstances where the buyer has no claim against the carrier or insurer, and that this sometimes involves hardship for the buyer, because the buyer has to pay the purchase price to the seller on tender of the shipping documents or, if he has already paid, he cannot recover the price on the ground that there was a total failure of consideration.

(B)

Cif contracts are often concerned with sale of unascertained goods, and problems arise where such goods are lost before the seller has appropriated the goods to the contract. The general rule in domestic sales is that a seller who has not actually appropriated any goods to the contract is not entitled to rely on the fact that he had *intended* to do so before the goods were lost. However, Aitkin J in *Groom v Barber* (1915) said that:

> 'The seller must be in a position to pass property by the bill of lading if the goods are in existence, but he need not have appropriated the particular goods in the particular bill of lading until the moment of tender.'

Although the question of appropriation was not discussed, *Manbre Saccharine v Corn Products* (1919) suggests that a cif seller is entitled to tender documents relating to a cargo which he knows to be lost. 'Appropriation' in the sense that the seller is bound contractually to deliver the goods in question in order to pass property will hardly ever take place under a cif contract before tender of documents.

The decided cases and academic opinion do not provide a clear answer to the question. Certainly, *Re Olympia Oil and Cake Co and Produce Brokers* (1915) suggests that a cif seller can appropriate lost cargo to the contract (and the buyer's remedy is, therefore, against the carrier or the insurer). Rowlatt J in that case pointed out, however, that to allow appropriation after loss might lead to unjust results: if the market price of the goods rose (or the insurance policy did not cover the loss), the seller would tender the documents relating to the lost cargo; whereas, if the market price fell, the seller could buy an alternative cargo to fulfil the contract and claim on the insurance policy in respect of the lost goods. Of course, if the seller is not entitled to appropriate lost goods, he may suffer hardship, for example where he is liable to his supplier for goods appropriated *before* loss without being able to pass on that appropriation to the buyer *after* loss.

In the absence of clear authority to the contrary, academic opinion suggests that a cif seller of unascertained goods cannot appropriate a lost cargo, that is, he is not entitled to tender documents relating to the goods which have been lost unless at the time of loss he had appropriated the particular goods to the contract by binding himself contractually to deliver those goods that have been lost.

Index